The Filmology Movement and
Film Study in France

Studies in Cinema, No. 33

Diane M. Kirkpatrick, Series Editor

Professor, History of Art
The University of Michigan

Other Titles in This Series

The Filmology Movement and Film Study in France

by
Edward Lowry

Assistant Professor
Center for Communication Arts
Southern Methodist University
Dallas, Texas

UMI RESEARCH PRESS
Ann Arbor, Michigan

Produced and distributed by
UMI Research Press
an imprint of
University Microfilms International
A Xerox Information Resources Company
Ann Arbor, Michigan 48106

Library of Congress Cataloging in Publication Data

Lowry, Edward, 1952-
  The filmology movement and film study in France.

  (Studies in cinema ; no. 33)
  "A revison of the author's dissertation, University
of Texas at Austin, 1982"—T.p. verso.
  Bibliography: p.
  Includes index.
  1. Moving-pictures—Study and teaching—France—
History. 2. Moving-pictures—Aesthetics. I. Title.
II. Series.

PN1993.8.F7L68 1985   791.43'07'044   84-24099
ISBN 0-8357-1630-9 (alk. paper)

Contents

Preface

Filmology remains all but unknown in America at the present time. This is partly because no previous study has attempted a comprehensive survey of its project, its work and its contributions. More significant in this respect, however, is the fact that most of the primary sources pertinent to the subject remain untranslated. As a result, the majority of the translations from French which appear in this text are my own. In the rare cases where reliable translations are already available to the English reader, I have made use of them. To maintain some consistency, I have translated the titles of all the articles cited, since they are often quite descriptive. Titles of books, periodicals and films remain in their original language.

I could never have completed this project without the assistance and encouragement of Christian Metz and Raymond Bellour, with whom I had the opportunity to study at the Centre Universitaire Américain du Cinéma et de la Critique in Paris. Nor would I ever have undertaken this subject had not Jacques Aumont and Michel Marie introduced me to the work of the filmlogists. I owe a special debt of gratitude to George Wead, my long-time advocate and friend at the University of Texas who steered me through two graduate degrees, and to Thomas Schatz, for critiquing my work and convincing me of its significance. Finally, I wish to thank all of those who have read this manuscript in its various stages and have taken the time to offer their comments, their criticisms and their support. I cannot name them all, but neither can I fail to mention Dana Polan, George Lellis, David Rodowick, Dudley Andrew, Robert Davis, Paul Gray, Robert Hill and the Graduate Colloquium in Film Theory at the University of Iowa, Fall 1982.

Part I

A History of Filmology

1

A Science of Film

The concerns encompassed by film theory are broad and eclectic, running a gamut from questions about the effects of film on viewers to analyses of the filmic text as signifying discourse, from charting the mythologies of genres and stars to defining an aesthetics of the cinema. It is the medium of film which focuses these concerns and which has been taken as an object for examination by sociology, psychology, linguistics, psychoanalysis, philosophy, anthropology and aesthetics. Yet the application of these fields to the study of film has occurred in a sporadic and piecemeal fashion. There is little sense that things could be otherwise, given the fact that the conventional study of film theory has evolved as an amalgam of writings by "great thinkers" on the cinema, each representing a different cultural, historical and intellectual context, each adopting a methodology drawn from his/her own field of expertise. The result is a view of film theory which is more biographical than intellectual, more concerned with personal differences than with theoretical coherence.

Writing in 1971 on the development of film theory prior to his own relatively recent application of semiology to the cinema, Christian Metz situates the work of the traditional canon of film theorists within a historical context which he labels "the first era of general reflection on film."

> During this first phase, what was called the theory of film . . . consisted of a global, on occasion sustained and precise, focusing of attention on the filmic or cinematic fact: an eclectic and syncretic, and in some cases very enlightening study which made use of several methods without applying any of them in a consistent manner, and sometimes without being aware of doing so. In a *third phase*, which we can look forward to entering some day, these diverse methods should be profoundly reconciled (which may imply the mutual disappearance of their present forms), and the theory of film will then be a true, not syncretic, synthesis capable of precisely determining the domain of validity of the different approaches and the articulation of different levels. It would appear that we are today entering the second phase, in which a tentative but necessary methodological pluralism may be defined.[1]

Clearly, Metz sees the development of the "third phase"—an era in which film theory would be synthetic and systematized—only as the result of a rigorous, pluralist, but organized examination of film theory during the "second phase" of reflection, of which he considers himself a part.

Yet we may trace the beginnings of this "second phase" to a theoretical enterprise which began almost two decades before the first major work of Metz; to an organized attempt by the French intellectual community to arrive at a comprehensive, methodical approach to film within the context of the university and its established fields of study. Under the banner of the neologism "filmology,"[2] an academically based movement devoted to the construction of "a science of film" emerged in the wake of the 1946 publication of Gilbert Cohen-Séat's influential *Essai sur les principes d'une philosophie du cinéma*. A philosophical tract which raised a variety of questions about the cinema, and which addressed them directly to the intellectuals and scholars of the day, Cohen-Séat's *Essai* involved a twofold project. First, he sought to draw attention to what he considered to be the necessity of serious film study and to the significance of film to the concerns of existing academic disciplines. Second, he proposed the outline of a methodology intended to provide a framework for the comprehensive analysis of the subject, beginning with a basic division of phenomena into "filmic facts," which included the phenomena of the film itself (as stimulus, as artwork, as discourse), and "cinematic facts," which involved those phenomena of the cinema as institution (economic, cultural, socio-historical, anthropological).[3]

With nearly unprecedented impact, Cohen-Séat's *Essai* served as a rallying point for the cinematic concerns of the French academic community, leading very quickly to the legitimation of film study within that most traditional bastion of the French academy, the Sorbonne. By September of 1946, the Association pour la Recherche Filmologique had been created; and by July 1947 it had begun publishing an official journal, *La Revue Internationale de Filmologie*, providing a forum for some of the leading scholars of France and other European nations to discuss film from the viewpoints of their various fields of study. Among those who associated themselves with filmology during its first decade were Etienne Souriau, holder of the Sorbonne's chair of Aesthetics and the Science of Art since 1945, and co-founder of the *Revue d'Esthétique* in 1948; Henri Wallon, Professor of the Collège de France and one of the country's most influential child psychologists, who had headed his own laboratory in experimental psychology since 1922; Edgar Morin, a Marxist sociologist who would play a key role in the serious study of popular culture in postwar France, and who would eventually coin the term *cinéma vérité* in reference to his collaboration with filmmaker Jean Rouch on the 1960 documentary, *Chronique d'une été*; Léon Moussinac, Director of the Ecole Nationale des Arts Décoratifs, and a significant figure in the film culture of the 1920s, largely responsible for bringing the Soviet cinema to the attention of French intellectuals; as well as numerous other professors of the Université de Paris and academic institutions throughout Europe. The First International Congress of Filmology, held at the Sorbonne in September 1947, established filmology as an international movement centered in Paris; and the creation of the Institut de Filmologie within the Université de Paris one year later, in September 1948, marked the official acceptance and institutionalization of film in France as a legitimate course of study leading to an academic degree.

Curiously, filmology remains virtually unknown in America and largely unexamined as a movement even in France, despite references to certain of its key figures in current French film studies and the specific influence of their writings on the early work of Christian Metz. Mostly regarded now (if at all) as a somewhat arcane, if not completely obscure tangent of film theory, filmology deserves reexamination in terms of the crucial historical and theoretical position it occupies. Historically, filmology marked the moment of film's legitimation as a serious subject of study and the beginning of film study as an institutional practice. Further, it played an important role in focusing the attention of French intellectuals on the cinema in the late 1940s and early 1950s, representing an approach historically parallel to, yet theoretically at odds with the better known tradition of André Bazin and *Cahiers du Cinéma*. It is significant also to note that, in contrast to the affinity of the French intelligentsia for the cinema during the period of the active avant-gardes of the 1920s, the postwar intellectual appeal of filmology was not aesthetic so much as it was sociological, arising from a humanistic concern for the power, influence and even the utopian possibilities of film as a mass medium, and that it was couched in terms of urgency and crisis.

Theoretically, filmology situated film as the object of a science—that term being understood in a broad sense which included among other things the psycho-physiological testing of viewers, the tenets of a scientific sociology in the tradition of Emile Durkheim, and the "proto-structuralist" aesthetics of Etienne Souriau. Most significantly, filmology sought to organize the "sciences" represented by the various academic disciplines in pursuit of a comprehensive theory of film. It is in terms of this problematic (a term which Louis Althusser defines as "the particular unit of theoretical formation"[4]) that filmology asserts its importance for current film theory.

The study of filmology which follows is intended to be something more than a mere archeological undertaking, rescuing a lost theory from obscurity. It is grounded in a belief that the way in which a question is posed determines the sorts of answers one is likely to receive. To the extent that filmology represents the first major attempt to delineate, structure and institutionalize intellectual concerns regarding the cinema, its problematic has played a significant role in the formulation of questions which still affect the practice of film scholars and of film pedagogy within the Western university. Despite the shifts in methods and concerns which have taken place since the inception of filmology, the problematic which it established for film study has changed relatively little.

The decade following World War II in France is renowned as a very rich one for film culture, less for the films produced than for the critical activities which flourished around the cinema during this period. The end of the Nazi Occupation and its censorship permitted the rebirth of an active ciné-club movement in 1945 and the importation of five years of forbidden films, primarily the Hollywood product of 1940-44. What followed was an intensification of interest in the cinema and an outpouring of film publications eclipsing even the very active period of the 1920s. The years between the Liberation and the mid-1950s provided the setting for Bazin's articulation of a realist film theory and his championing of Italian Neorealism, for the publication of the first volumes of Georges Sadoul's massive film history, for the coining of the term *film noir*, for the founding of *Cahiers du Cinéma* and *Positif*, and for their polemical insistence upon the *politique des auteurs*.

Given this context, it is certainly not surprising that postwar France provided the setting for the institutionalization of film study within the university. Yet to understand the way in which filmology represents a new problematic for film theory, it is necessary to examine some of the social, intellectual and institutional factors which surrounded its inception.

Film study *could* be legitimated in France, for example, partly because of a tradition, stretching back to the avant-garde of the 1920s, which linked cinema and the French intelligentsia. In addition, the commercial film industry in France had demonstrated enough stability and influence not only to survive the German Occupation, but to be regarded during the Liberation as an important national institution and cultural heritage. Further, the tumultuous postwar period provided conditions ideal for the success of Cohen-Séat's project. Not only was there a new burst of intellectual activity, represented most clearly by Jean-Paul Sartre and the existential phenomenologists, but there was also a sense of moral and intellectual crisis, a recognition in the wake of the war's devastation of the ineffectuality of intellectual pursuits in confronting the world's practical, political realities. It is within this context that Cohen-Séat posed the question of film in terms of crisis.

A former journalist and film producer with an abiding interest in philosophy, Cohen-Séat was not himself an academic, though he had influential friends within the scholarly community; therefore, the critique he launched from the fringes of the intellectual establishment bore a certain ring of truth for those within its circle. The philosophic tone of his *Essai*, its frequent citations of great thinkers and social philosophers and the very eloquence of its complicated prose are aimed squarely at the core of French intelligentsia; and he delivers his argument in terms of a challenge to academics to face up to the crisis posed by the cinema. Chiding intellectuals for their disinterest in film, he writes

> What will astonish the historian is that so enormous a discovery [the cinema], in a period so full of methodical disciplines, has been allowed to develop by chance, at the whim and under the pressures of commerce, and in back rooms, ultimately drawing less serious examination than that which accompanies the sale and use of a common linament.[5]

Cohen-Séat's astonishment at the disinterest of scholars in the cinema arises from a strongly positivist belief in the ability of scientific inquiry to organize phenomena in such a way as to provide mankind the means of improving its condition and of directing the course of history. In this sense, Cohen-Séat's call to arms is spurred by a strong sense of social mission, reflecting the resurgence of humanism during the immediate postwar period.

In outlining this social mission, Cohen-Séat situates the cinema within a schema accounting for both its humanistic, universal aspects, which he refers to as its "quality of humanity," and its democratic, mass tendencies, or its "quantity of humanity."[6] In these terms, he views the cinema as "the mechanism for a conciliation of humanist and collective values."[7] For the cinema to achieve this potential, he proclaims, men and women of ethics and wisdom must be willing to apply their best efforts to its accomplishment.

Yet Cohen-Séat demands more than attention for the cinema. He demands the rigor of method which the established disciplines could contribute to its study. Therefore, his *Essai* individually addresses those disciplines which he argues have the most to contribute and the most to gain from an organized study of film: sociology, anthropology, linguistics, aesthetics, philosophy, psychology, psychoanalysis and physiology.

Cohen-Séat's call for a science of film was intended to appeal to the intellectuals of the day. It was certainly in accord with the logical positivism which seemed to inform nearly every academic discipline during this period. At least within the French university, the social sciences took their nomenclature quite seriously, to the extent that psychology, sociology and even aesthetics attempted to apply the same "scientific" rigor to their fields of study that biologists and physicists did to theirs. By posing the cinema neither as art nor as industry, but as the object of a science, Cohen-Séat was able to assert its significance to those in charge of the French academy.

In the dynamic process of establishing a problematic for film theory, filmology followed a pattern which Thomas S. Kuhn has observed is characteristic of the early stages of a science's development.

> No natural history can be interpreted in the absence of at least some implicit body of intertwined theoretical and methodological belief that permits selection, evaluation, and criticism. If that body of belief is not already implicit in the collection of facts... it must be externally supplied, perhaps by a current metaphysic, by another science, or by personal and historical accident.[8]

The traditional theory of film presents itself as a series of observations from a variety of authors and contexts, separate and enclosed, sometimes systematized within themselves, but without an overall "body of intertwined theoretical and methodological belief" which would allow for their evaluation. The eclecticism of filmology, however, found an organizing "body of belief" in its sense of social mission and its goal of constructing a positive science of the cinema. Scientific positivism provided filmology with what Cohen-Séat referred to as its "directive ideas"[9]—that impulse toward systematization so crucial to the evaluation of any body of knowledge and to the development of any field of study. Its system was drawn from the methods of other disciplines, related and intertwined as they were in the academic institution of postwar France.

As late as 1971, Christian Metz writes,

> the sole division of labor within the study of film that can be envisaged, for the time being, is one of those divisions said to be "based on methods," but which is based, in fact, on the insufficiencies of these methods.[10]

Filmology marks the beginning of that division of labor to which Metz refers. But that division alone does not result in the kind of synthetic theory Metz hopes someday to see. In historical terms, however, the insufficiency of filmology, the fact that it did not produce a unified and synthetic theory of film, is less important than the degree to which it posed the questions of film and cinema from a very specific perspective, and molded them to fit the concerns of established fields of study, providing a means by which film could be studied psychologically, sociologically, anthropologically, linguistically, aesthetically.

The following chapters provide a history of filmology as a movement and of the context in which it emerged, beginning with a discussion of the French film community from the 1920s, through the periods of the Occupation and the Liberation, up to the point of the publication of Cohen-Séat's *Essai*. I then examine Cohen-Séat's *Essai* in terms of its theoretical foundations and its rhetorical project, emphasizing both its positivist assumptions and its sense of social mission. The historical overview of filmology which follows primarily takes the form of a survey of *La Revue Internationale de Filmologie*, of the various organizations and university courses which arose in support of the movement, and of the criticisms leveled at filmology from outside its circle. Such an overview provides an indication of the development of the movement from the eclecticism of its early years to its increasing polarization and ultimate narrowing of interests in the direction of empirical studies.

The second part of this book is devoted to an examination of the specific work done under the aegis of filmology. I have grouped the movement's aesthetic and linguistic concerns under the heading of the "filmic fact," and its socio-anthropological concerns under the "cinematic fact," preserving Cohen-Séat's division of phenomena where possible. The key psychological studies of filmology are not as easy to classify, since they are concerned with both the psychological effects of the *filmic fact* on the viewer as well as the broader questions regarding the *cinematic* situation itself. For the most part, the psychological considerations of filmology seem to be divided more logically according to method. Therefore, writings on phenomenological psychology and psychoanalysis are treated in a separate chapter from the empirical and experimental studies conducted by filmologists.

Throughout this study I have attempted to emphasize three basic themes which seem to define the filmological problematic: (1) the notion of positive science which underlies nearly all of its work; (2) the sense of social mission which surfaces again and again; and (3) its definition in terms of the institutional structure of the university. In the concluding chapter I will argue that each of these themes provides a link between the problematic of filmology and the state of contemporary film theory.

Wherever opportune, I have drawn comparisons between the specific work of the filmologists and more recent developments in film theory, emphasizing the extent to which both attempt to answer similar questions. The final chapter makes this link more explicit through a specific examination of the influence of filmology on the work of Christian Metz.

2

A Context: The French Film Community

Filmology emerged in the tumultuous period immediately following the Liberation of France after four years of German occupation. The popular elation associated with General Charles DeGaulle's triumphant return to Paris in August 1944 was severely undercut by the political and social turmoil which ensued. A wide variety of political parties and Resistance groups vied for a say in the reshaping of the French government. Widespread poverty, along with acute shortages of food, shelter and power, hit Paris and the larger French cities very hard, contributing to the growth of a rampant and very lucrative black market.[1] The return of some two million French prisoners from Germany following V-E Day not only compounded the shortages, but wrought a devastating effect on morale by bringing the horrors of the concentration camps home to France.[2] The years 1944 and 1945 also saw the trial and execution of a number of traitors and collaborators from the Occupation period, including certain prominent members of the Vichy government.[3] By virtue of personal charisma and his popularity as the figurehead of the Resistance, DeGaulle was able to organize a volatile coalition of the Communist and Socialist parties with the newly formed Catholic party (Mouvement Républicain Populaire) which brought him to power in the election of October 1945.[4] By January 1946, however, he had tendered his resignation over what he considered to be the attempts of the National Assembly to usurp his authority.[5] By that time the Cold War had begun in earnest, and the 1946 accords between France and the United States, making France eligible for aid under the Marshall Plan, placed it somewhat reluctantly in the American camp against the Soviet Union.[6]

By the time Cohen-Séat's *Essai sur les principes d'une philosophie du cinéma* was published in 1946, the turbulence of the Liberation had yielded a new and rather tentative stability. It would be some time, however, before the concerns and questions raised during the previous five years would be laid to rest. Cohen-Séat's *Essai* and other writings on the cinema from the same time bear the marks of this period of moral and intellectual crisis, demonstrating a strong sense of the cinema's social mission. This context is of importance since it helped to formulate the call for a science of film.

The year in which Cohen-Séat's *Essai* appeared was in many ways a landmark year for the French film community. It was the year in which new institutions replaced those which had controlled the film industry during the Occupation. It was also the year of the first Cannes Film Festival, originally scheduled for September 1939, but postponed by the mobilization and the war.[7] The end of the strict political censorship imposed by the German military command opened the way for a flood of films unreleased in France during the war, and the public response was enthusiastic. The ciné-club movement, brought together under a centralized organization the year before, numbered almost seven times as many clubs in June 1946 as it had in 1945.[8] Amidst the postwar publication boom, a large number of film books appeared in 1946 and such defunct journals as *La Revue du Cinéma* began publication once again. The establishment that year of such organizations as the Comité français du Cinéma pour la Jeunesse, headed by the influential child psychologist and Professor of the Collège de France Henri Wallon, suggested a new seriousness of concern for the cinema's social power and potential.[9] It was also in September of 1946 that Gilbert Cohen-Séat set up the Association pour la Recherche Filmologique.

The Tradition of the Film Community

December 28, 1945 marked the fiftieth anniversary of the first public projection of films by the Lumières' *cinématographe*, an event commemorated early in 1946 by the publication of Marcel L'Herbier's *Intelligence du cinématographe*, in which he argued that the very popularity for which the cinema was condemned was, in fact, its greatest strength. "Ennobled by an ecumenical quality, called by the richness of its means to serve a global function," he wrote, "the *cinématographe* figures precisely as the agent for the linking of humanity."[10] Heralding the new sense of social mission for the cinema, L'Herbier was himself a linking figure between the first flourishing of serious interest in film in France during the 1920s and early 1930s, and the renewal of this interest in the postwar period.

During the years of 1919-24, L'Herbier played an important part in the circle of filmmaker critics led by Louis Delluc—a circle which included Germaine Dulac, Jean Epstein and Abel Gance. The main forums for their writings were Delluc's two film magazines, *Ciné-Club*, first published in 1920, and *Cinéa*, which appeared the following year.[11] It was Delluc who coined the term "ciné-club" in reference to a group of film devotees who assembled to watch and discuss films; and between 1921 and 1939, a large number of these clubs began to appear throughout France.[12] The first important ciné-club, Le Club des Amis du Septième Art, was established in 1921 by Ricotto Canudo, who had done much to popularize a serious interest in the cinema through his columns in *Les Nouvelles Littéraires.*[13] Of equal importance was Le Club Français du Cinéma, founded by Léon Moussinac, a close friend and collaborator of Delluc's. Due to their status as private, non-profit associations, the ciné-clubs were both tax-free and outside state censorship. It therefore became their function to present to their members those films previously unreleased or prohibited by the government; and as a result, the ciné-clubs played a key role in establishing the status of film art in France. It was Delluc who first brought *The Cabinet of Dr. Caligari* to Paris in 1921, and Moussinac who screened *Battleship Potemkin* in 1926, despite the French ban on Soviet films. By 1928 the ciné-clubs were federated under the direction of Germaine Dulac herself.[14]

Canudo died in 1923 and Louis Delluc in 1924, but the movement they had begun continued to flourish. In 1924, the first full-time avant-garde cinema was established at the Théâtre au Vieux Colombier in Paris; in 1926, it was joined by Les Ursulines, and in 1928, by the first Right Bank art film house, Studio 28.[15] In these theatres the films of the burgeoning avant-garde found an audience.[16] The cinematic experiments of the mid- to late-1920s by such members of the avant-garde art community as Fernand Léger, Marcel Duchamp, Jean Cocteau and Man Ray,[17] and the collaborations between filmmakers and artists from other media (e.g. L'Herbier and Léger on *L'Inhumaine*, 1923; Dulac and Antonin Artaud on *La Coquille et le clergyman*, 1928; Luis Buñuel and Salvador Dali on *Un Chien andalou*, 1928), provided important links between film and the more traditionally accepted arts. The climate of experimentation also spawned some of the earliest work of such innovative filmmakers as René Clair and Abel Gance.

Despite the flourishing ciné-clubs, the French filmgoing public of the 1920s was quite limited. In 1928, L'Herbier declared, "It cannot be denied that currently, for 75% of the French population, the cinema does not exist."[18] Surveys made in 1928 and 1929 show that the percentage of the French public attending the movies was somewhere between 7 and 15 percent, a figure probably divided between the most popular kind of filmgoer and the intellectual crowd. In 1929, the film press was also extremely limited; and the popular press provided weekly reviews at best, with an emphasis on "artistic" films.[19] In a period of what Noël Burch refers to as the "embourgeoisement" of the cinema, the concerns of a broader public began to show themselves in the establishment of a board of censorship (the Commission de Contrôle) and of a governmental office concerning the cinema, both of which occurred in 1928.[20]

Despite the fact that the 1930s were to produce some of the most outstanding films ever to emerge from the French commercial cinema, works by directors such as Jean Renoir and Marcel Carné, the French avant-garde had virtually disappeared by the early thirties. René Clair, Marcel L'Herbier and Abel Gance had begun to establish themselves among the ranks of commercial filmmakers, while the key artist-filmmakers of the late 1920s had turned their interests elsewhere. André Bazin has suggested that the advent of sound played an important role in the growing disinterest of the avant-garde, once this elite group "saw the cinema over which it had had so direct an influence escape it in the technical, economic and human revolution provoked by sound."[21]

In 1935, Henry Langlois and Georges Franju founded a ciné-club called the Cercle du Cinéma, devoted to the projection of a classic repertoire of films without the traditional ciné-club discussions. Their efforts led directly to the creation of the Cinémathèque Française in 1936. Enjoying the same tax- and censorship-free status as the ciné-clubs, the Cinémathèque began to acquire, through the careful purchases of Langlois, an impressive number of presumably lost works by pioneer French filmmakers such as Georges Méliès, Fernand Zecca, Emile Cohl and Louis Feuillade.[22]

The auspicious attention enjoyed by the cinema in France between the world wars had succeeded in legitimating the young medium to an extent which had occurred almost nowhere else. The activity of the avant-garde during the 1920s left little question as to the cinema's artistic potential. These films had been canonized in a number of active film magazines, while the ciné-clubs and art houses developed for them a small, but enthusiastic public. With the creation of the Cinémathèque Française, the cinema began to acknowledge its legacy and to examine its own history. The renewal of serious attention to the cinema after the Second World War had this base upon which to build. It remained only for Cohen-Séat to initiate the task of legitimating this art as an object of study with implications reaching far beyond merely aesthetic parameters.

The Film Community Under the Occupation (1940-44)

With the partial occupation of France by Germany in 1940 and the establishment of the Vichy government, much of the activity within the French film community was curtailed or redirected. New and strictly enforced political censorship proclamations ended the free-programming privileges of the ciné-clubs, and the early 1940s saw a drastic reduction in their number.[23] A new centralization of the film industry, based on a number of institutions established in the final days of the Third Republic, took effect under the control of the occupying power. In July 1939 a Service du Cinéma had been created with the goal of centralizing subsequent policy decisions regarding the industry, especially in matters relating to regulations and professional licensing. The new office was charged with monitoring rental percentages and box office receipts, as well as with acting as intermediary for bank loans to the industry. In the same month a Comité d'Organisation de l'Industrie

Cinématographique (COIC) was established by law as a centralized professional organization for the industry. Under the Vichy government, with its emphasis on a corporatism dependent on the strict cooperation between state and industry, the Service du Cinéma and the COIC served as means for the Germans to exert constant pressure on the film industry. Nevertheless, under the direction of producer Raoul Ploquin, the COIC was able to guarantee the survival of the French cinema, which seemed faced by the imminent cessation of all production in the early days of the Occupation.[24]

The Occupation of Paris by the Germans on June 14, 1940 closed the city's cinemas. Five days later only 20 of them had reopened. But by August, some 225 programs of films were circulating in the Occupied Zone, most of them German films; and in October, 500 Parisian cinemas were operating under the new regulations of the occupying power.[25]

The first German order affecting the cinema in France was issued in September 1940, and submitted all exhibited films to the censorship of the military administration. One month later, a second order called for the seizure of all negatives produced after January 1939, and prohibited the further manufacture of negatives.[26] A December 1941 order put into effect a new series of regulations placing the power of "preventive control" of films under the Secretary-General of Information and Propaganda and a consulting committee charged with "the defense of good morals and the respect of national traditions."[27]

American newsreels were banned, one French newsreel company was closed for being "Jewish," and the remaining two French newsreel producers combined with the support of German capital to form a monopoly of the market.[28] The Vichy government also began to issue a series of anti-Jewish measures which, by November 1941, effectively prevented Jews from working in the production, distribution and exhibition of films in France.[29] A French subsidiary of the German production company U.F.A. was created under the name of Continental, and was responsible for producing 30 of the 220 films made in France during the Occupation.[30]

Despite the loss, during the years immediately prior to the war, of five of France's greatest directors—Jean Renoir, René Clair, Max Ophüls, Julien Duvivier and Jacques Feyder (the last to Switzerland, the rest to Hollywood)—and of a number of popular actors and actresses, the French film industry enjoyed a surprisingly productive period during the early 1940s. Some 25 new directors, mostly from the ranks of the industry hierarchy, emerged to fill the gap; they included such names as Jacques Becker, Henri-Georges Clouzot and Robert Bresson.[31] In a review of Carné's *Les Visiteurs du soir* and Bresson's *Les Anges du péché* in 1943, Bazin declared: "Perhaps I will scandalize some readers in asserting that, of all the French artistic activities since the war, the cinema is the only one which has progressed."[32]

By mid-1942, the COIC had accomplished its mission of reorganizing, regulating and "purifying" the French cinema; and in May its director was replaced by a directorial committe. At the same time the government's Service du Cinéma was converted into a Direction Générale du Cinéma, maintaining at its head Louis-Emile Galey, who was now made directly responsible to the new Vichy head of state, Pierre Laval.[33] It was under this reorganized institution that a number of steps were taken to stimulate the French film industry and to restore it to health.

The most significant of these steps in institutional terms was the creation in October 1943 of the Institut des Hautes Etudes Cinématographiques (IDHEC), the first official film school to be established in France. IDHEC was the realization of the dream of Marcel L'Herbier, who became the school's first president. In answer to the need which he felt existed for the training of new filmmakers, L'Herbier had formed his own production house Cinégraphique in 1922. Modeled on the painters' *ateliers*, Cinégraphique provided technical training and advice for young filmmakers, who were encouraged to pursue their own projects freely. L'Herbier had been unable to interest the government in his idea of an official film school until 1943, when he found the sympathetic ear of Galey.[34]

The stated goals of IDHEC were threefold: (1) the training of technicians and assistant directors for the film profession, (2) the expansion of cinematic culture, and (3) the creation of an archival center at the disposal of film professionals. IDHEC was conceived not only as a technical school, but as a center of theoretical study as well, drawing its teaching staff both from the ranks of trained professionals and from the professors within the French university and the Ecole des Beaux Arts.[35]

During the final days of the Occupation, Bazin touted IDHEC as one of the most important manifestations of the French cinema's "will to live":

> IDHEC represents for the first time in the world, in the country of Lumière and Méliès, an attempt at the methodical creation of film directors.... The cinema will not only gain new men, recruited from a social and intellectual milieu where it has had little appeal; but in addition, the necessity of teaching will help it to become conscious of itself. No art reaches fulfillment except in relation to this consciousness necessary to its transmission.[36]

Under the aegis of Director-General Galey, the presidency of L'Herbier and the directorship of Pierre Gerin, classes at IDHEC began in January 1944, less than eight months before DeGaulle's return to Paris.[37] In October 1947, Gerin would be replaced by Léon Moussinac, united with L'Herbier to give the first official French institution of film study two of the most influential names from the French film community of the 1920s.[38]

The Film Community and the Liberation (1944-46)

The period of Liberation was a difficult one for the French cinema, as it was throughout the political and institutional life of France. It was a period of confused alliances, of accusations and purges, of reassessment and reorganization. Early in 1944, six Resistance groups within the French cinema, led by members of the trade union (Confédération Générale de Travail), created a Comité de Libération du Cinéma Français. With actor Paul Blanchar as its president and such influential men as Jean Painlevé, Louis Daquin, Jean Grémillon and Jacques Becker among its members, the committee drew up a plan of action for the end of the Occupation, with top priority given to a purge of the film industry and a curtailment of the powers of the COIC. On August 19, 1944, during the Paris Insurrection, the Comité de Libération occupied and replaced the COIC. The proposals which they made to the new provisional government were quickly accepted, and Jean Painlevé was appointed the new Director-General of Cinema.[39] At the first meeting of film professionals called by the Comité de Libération on September 16, 1944, Louis Daquin expressed the committee's intentions to "defend the national legacy of French cinema, while assuring its quality through the services of non-commercial, technical control and a professionally-based council to pass judgement on the competence and professional honor of members of the industry."[40]

As Director-General, Painlevé supported the continuation of the organizational institutions of the French cinema established during the Occupation, with the hope of giving them a new democratic slant. The Direction Générale du Cinéma, he proclaimed, "in no case wishes to be the dictatorial organ known during the Occupation."[41] Still there awaited an extremely difficult and sensitive transitional period. "The task is arduous," wrote Bazin, "for it is not limited to the purging of the film industry; it requires the reorganization of the French cinema upon new bases; and the human, economic and political problems which that entails, it seems, are even more complex."[42]

Making judgments on matters of "professional honor" seemed the most complex issue of all. Perhaps the best-known case involved the film *Le Corbeau*, directed by Henri-Georges Clouzot for Continental in 1943. A mystery-thriller set in a small French town, the film had enjoyed great popularity in Germany. During the Liberation, however, it was banned as anti-French, Nazi propaganda. A debate ensued as L'Herbier, Carné and Claude Autant-Lara rallied to Clouzot's defense, while Georges Sadoul argued on the contrary that the film would have been acceptable had it been made before or after the Occupation, but not during it. The ban on the film was finally lifted in 1946.[43]

The ethical question remained that of what constituted "honorable" action during a period of foreign occupation. The Vichyites had continually justified their stance as the lesser of two evils, given the threat of total defeat at the hands of a superior German military force in 1940. Marshall Pétain himself pled in his own defense before the High Court of Justice on July 23, 1945:

> When I asked for the armistice, in agreement with the military chiefs, I performed an act of salvation. The Armistice saved France, and by leaving the Mediterranean free and by saving the integrity of our Empire, it contributed to the victory of the Allies. My government was legally formed, and was recognized by all the Powers of the World . . . I used this power as a shield to protect the French people . . . Will you try to understand the difficulty of governing under such conditions? Every day, with the enemy's knife to my throat, I had to struggle against his demands. History will tell you all I have spared you, even though today my opponents think only of reproaching me with what was inevitable.[44]

Pétain's justifications were ill-appreciated in the period of the Liberation, but they raise the complexity of the issues involved. With regard to the film industry, Paul Leglisse states the dilemma as follows:

> It remains to be seen if it was opportune during this period to undertake an activity which would benefit the cinema, but which risked favoring the intentions of the enemy power. On the other hand, one could argue that the occupying power would have then applied its own directives without regard for professional interests, and that this would have been more disastrous for the French cinema.[45]

If the "purification" of the industry undertaken by the Comité de Libération provided the simplest solution to a complex problem, it did not do so without angering a number of those close to the industry. The 1954 expanded edition of Maurice Bardèche's and Robert Brasillach's prewar *Histoire du cinéma* mounts a savage attack on the Comité de Libération, which had "emerged from the woodwork" and "taken upon itself the functions of the COIC, to which it quickly added the power of denunciation and an office charged with arrests, pursuits and cooperation with examining magistrates." The passage continues by pointing out that Painlevé himself had been employed by the COIC during the Occupation, and that Louis Daquin had supported the screening of the Franco-German newsreels and had been an employee of Continental as well.

> It is true that all these gentlemen have excuses. M. Jean Painlevé resigned at an opportune time. M. Louis Daquin did indeed work for Continental, but it was to spy on the movement of the enemy in the cinematic sector.[46]

It is important to note here, however, that Bardèche and Brasillach were both outspokenly pro-Nazi during the Occupation, and that Brasillach was executed for treason during the Liberation. It is Bardèche, his brother-in-law, who is the author of the preceding passage.[47]

On the eve of the Liberation, Bazin proclaimed, "The French cinema is not dead, it is not even sleeping; its silence is that of an armed vigil."[48] Thirty years later Truffaut would assert,

> For those who today reproach the French cinema for taking too small a part in political issues in comparison, for example, to the Italian cinema of opposition, it must be recalled, without abusively prolonging the comparison, that the Italian cinema from 1940 to 1944 was almost entirely Mussolinian and Fascist, while the French cinema of the Occupation succeeded 98% in not being Pétainist.[49]

Clearly, the questions raised regarding cinema's responsibility and the ethics of those working within the industry during the Occupation were not quickly laid to rest. Though discussion of the industry purge was generally considered too sensitive for discussion in the postwar literature on film, the moral mission of the cinema became a predominant topic. No discussion of the way in which this mission was conceived is complete without an understanding of the turbulent period from which it emerged.

The Moral and Social Mission of the Cinema

At the end of the Occupation, the French film industry was in a state of disrepair: equipment was old and outmoded, production costs were high and the financial structure weak.[50] The administrative framework of the cinema, split as it was between the government's Direction Générale du Cinéma and the professional organization of the COIC, resulted in enormous bureaucratic redundancy, and bore the marks of an institution developed under foreign occupation. Its reorganization was undertaken in 1946. In October of that year, a law went into effect which grouped the powers of the two branches under a single, financially autonomous administration responsible to the Ministry of Information: the Centre National de la Cinématographie Française (CNCF).[51]

The most pressing problem of the postwar French cinema was economic. By the end of 1946, French production seemed on the way to resuming its former output: 97 films produced in that year, as compared to a prewar average of 120. By January 1948, however, production had dropped drastically (74 films in 1947), and it was estimated that unemployment was as high as 75 percent in some branches of the industry.[52] The cause of this collapse was undoubtedly the Franco-American financial agreements of May 1946. The Blum-Byrnes Accords, as they were called,[53] annulled debts owed to the U.S. by France and opened up more American credit for the French government. But these accords also included provisions highly favorable to American films in the French market. Prior to the war there existed a quota system on the number of foreign films which could be released in France each year. This was intended to protect the French film industry; and in 1937 the box office share of French productions amounted to between 60 and 70 percent of the total French market, with American productions representing 25 percent. The Blum-Byrnes Accords abolished, for all practical purposes, the French quota on American films, with the result of placing the French film industry, already in a state of poor repair, in disastrous competition for its own market with Hollywood, which was not only functioning at its peak during this period, but had a five-year backlog of films to release in France. In the first quarter of 1946, American films accounted for 51 percent of box office receipts in France, while the home product could claim only 39 percent.[54] Though the reaction of the industry was heated, French Président du Conseil Léon Blum could answer only that the interests of the film industry were secondary to the "indispensable compensations on a national scale" gained by the accords.[55]

The French filmgoing public was torn between an allegiance to the national cinema and an enthusiasm for viewing the Hollywood films denied them during the Occupation. Writing in the first issue of Jean-Paul Sartre's journal *Les Temps Modernes* in October 1945, Roger Leenhardt, an influential film critic who would soon become a major director, lamented the fact that, since the Liberation, the Americans had seen fit to send to France only their second-rate films; yet he also expressed the acute loss of Hollywood films felt by the French film community during the war:

> For the film-lover...the American cinema was not an exotic product, a sort of chocolate whose disappearance, no matter how unfortunate, caused no real pain. Hollywood represented a true cinematic value. The consumer of celluloid sought his staple, his essential nourishment in the consistency and savor of the Californian product.[56]

Yet there was also a clearly recognized need for the French cinema to develop along its own lines if it were to return to its former stature. Louis Daquin noted that the isolation of the French film industry during the Occupation had had certain benefits, enabling French directors, "now deprived of all American films, and who, until that time, had been unable to break away from American technique, which was undeniably perfect but devoid of style, to rediscover a source of authentic, truly national inspiration."[57] During the first days of the Liberation, Bazin expressed his hopes for this authentically French cinema:

> For four years our cinema, despite its excellent qualities, has been marked by social exile, which has sapped its strength. Its incontestable artistic value, the flexibility and exactitude it has accomplished in its style must, if it is to survive new contingencies, adapt itself to a new climate. In the flood of grandeur, violence, hatred, tenderness and hope which will wash across us from the American cinema, we will not be able to hold on unless we too plant our roots more deeply into the spirit of our times, in its angers and its anxieties, as well as its dreams. The French cinema will not survive unless it can become greater by rediscovering an authentic expression of French society.[58]

Following the Franco-American agreements of 1946, an open resentment against the American cinema emerged. After five years of German domination during the Occupation, it looked as though the French film industry was to be dominated once again—this time by Hollywood. In his 1948 book on the social mission of the cinema, André Lang condemned the Blum-Byrnes Accords for "making us consent to favored treatment of American productions, obliging us to worry about their quality and their influence on the French public."[59] Thus the problems facing the postwar film industry were seen not only as economic, but as philosophical and sociological issues with national and moral implications.

By 1946, the French reaction to the newly released American films was decidedly mixed. In that year Georges Charensol, former president of the Association of French Film Critics, wrote with a certain irony: "While waiting for the American cinema to find its Fountain of Youth in the use of color, we must recognize that, with the exception of *Citizen Kane*, it has given us nothing of real importance since the Liberation."[60] Many seemed to agree with Fernand Grenier, Communist member of the National Assembly, who declared that the Blum-Byrnes agreements on the cinema merely provided a means for Hollywood to get rid of "wagonloads of 'turkeys' " on the French market.[61] Reporting on the films at the first Cannes Film Festival in 1946, Bazin decidedly preferred the postwar realism of the French and Italian films, which he distinguished markedly from the American films he saw there. "There is not a single American film presented at Cannes," he wrote, "in which the spectator can feel himself the least bit 'concerned,' engaged by the subject or its characters (except perhaps *The Lost Weekend*)."[62]

Denied the economic measures necessary to protect the French cinema in its sociological mission of restoring French culture, the administration of the cinema placed a new emphasis on aesthetic quality. Whether or not the government should exercise control and censorship of the industry was not the question. The new mission of control was conceived as apolitical and aesthetic. Georges Huismann, President of the Commission de Contrôle des Films, which had been reestablished on July 4, 1945, stated the necessity of such control in the following terms:

> In the current state of our country's institutions, state control represents the protection of cinematic distribution itself. To control no longer means to direct, and it is in no way a question of the state casting cinematic production within a standard mold, based on the lamentable model of the former totalitarian states....
>
> Nothing is important but the technical, artistic and intellectual quality of the films shown, for only films of quality can restore public opinion and assure the French cinema its properly shining place around the world....
>
> If state control of films is limited to a strict appreciation of quality, it will be the barrier which halts the producers of "turkeys" and unequivocally prohibits bad films from carrying to foreign countries false images of French creativity....

> Since everyone agrees that the cinema constitutes one of our key industries, why treat the production and sale of films with less sympathetic vigilance than that of cognacs, champagnes, automobiles or the latest creations of Parisian high fashion? All these have maintained their place in foreign markets only by virtue of their exceptional quality.[63]

Thus, in marked contrast to the overtly political censorship of the Occupation, the state's regulatory duties were now seen in terms of quality control. The idealism of this mission made it more difficult to implement than to express, and politics proved difficult to avoid. In 1948, André Lang called on the French government to take the role of the cinema more seriously, in his book *Le tableau blanc*, for which he proposed the subtitle: "On the importance of the democratic state to understand in time the interest and the import of great scientific discoveries and to utilize the *cinématographe* for the good of man."[64] Lang takes to task the organizational structure of the CNCF, which required submission "to the exigencies of different ministries which bend the cinema to suit their purposes, profiting from old decrees which they will not allow to be repealed." He further decries the inability of the new Centre to "get rid of obstacles instead of multiplying them." "The C.N.C.F.," he writes, "must become an independent organism, separate from politics, free from its movements and initiatives, charged with the noble mission of elaborating and fixing the general policy of the cinema in all domains, and of assuring, without weakness or complacency, its indispensable continuity." In Lang's view, the CNCF had two major duties: (1) preventative, i.e., "to prevent the cinema from corrupting and injuring," and (2) educative, in the sense of rendering a service to society.[65]

The new concern for the sociological and moral role of cinema was nowhere better expressed than in an inquiry initiated by IDHEC in the summer of 1946. In a survey on the future of the cinema in France, the following questions were posed.

1. Is the current cinema favorable to artistic culture in general? to the molding of social and moral character?

2. What will the filmgoing public be seeking from the cinema?

3. Does the education of the public seem useful and possible?

4. Should it be addressed to the masses or to a specific public?[66]

In the publication results in their *Cahiers*, IDHEC chose to answer in detail one response from a Dr. Robert of Chambéry which especially intrigued them. Robert was adamant in his opposition to the questions themselves:

> What is required is not furnishing an educated public with any kind of cinema whatsoever, but furnishing an educated cinema to any kind of public whatsoever.... To present this problem otherwise is to lead opinion astray, and we protest with all our powers the error which has been committed.

His argument strongly supports a strict moral control of the cinema. "What is contrary to the molding of moral character," he writes, "cannot be favorable to any culture at all."[67]

IDHEC found itself in substantial agreement with a number of Robert's premises. Indeed, they admit that, during its first 50 years, "the cinema has only rarely been an art" and for practical purposes remained "nothing but a business" which too often "speculated on the passions and instincts of an undiscerning public." For that very reason, IDHEC argues, a "censorship of quality" has been instituted to protect a public which, "despite already considerable efforts of sociology and education, remains in an elementary state of thought and judgment."[68] Thus, the quality control of the cinema is asserted in primarily moral terms.

Nevertheless, the IDHEC reply is careful to defend the "total freedom" of artistic expression, except in the cases of pornography and the "apology for vice and crime."[69] A dilemma arises, therefore, between the ideal of artistic freedom and the moral well-being of the public, a dilemma stated in terms of the cinema's sociological uniqueness among the arts:

> We are also aware that the cinema differs considerably, by its nature and power, from other existing arts. It is a collective art, which is thus distinguished from the individual arts practiced over the centuries. These arts could valuably claim total freedom of expression, since their effect on the public was slow and progressive, while the cinema addresses itself to the masses. In addition, the means of expression utilized by the individual arts were infinitely less dangerous in their power and dissemination than that of the cinematic image, whose power of impregnation and mental suggestion on the conscious and unconscious faculties of the spectator is well known.
>
> There is consequently no doubt that the cinema poses a social and moral problem singularly more grave than that of literature and painting...and that, as imperfectly cultivated as it is, the public of the darkened movie house finds itself assaulted without defense, without intellectual or moral protection against the spell of artists enamoured of conceptions which are too advanced for them....
>
> ...we can understand the terror inspired in moralists and educators by certain films, like those of Buñuel or Stroheim which, like uranium, can provoke across a vast surface of the human consciousness a psychological conflagration and an extremely dangerous moral disintegration.[70]

The sociological questions raised by the cinema are stated here in terms almost identical to those employed by Cohen-Séat in his *Essai*, which appeared at virtually the same moment.

The IDHEC reply agrees in principle with the response of Dr. Robert, going even further to delineate a crisis of great novelty: "We are thus the first to recognize that a completely new problem is raised with regard to film, and that is why we have begun our inquiry on 'The Cinema and Morality.' "[71] IDHEC refuses, however, to relinquish the ideal of freedom of expression, adopting a nationalist stance in its defense:

> Without wishing to prejudice the outcome of our inquiry, we can still suppose that nothing will emerge from it which is not eminently liberal. It would seem inconceivable that a majority of our correspondents would opt for a regime which would direct the cinema in a country where the psychological and cultural maturity of the average spectator, though far from satisfactory, is still by far the most advanced in the world.[72]

The only proposal IDHEC makes is the education of the film industry and of the public regarding the crisis.

At the same time, Cohen-Séat was drawing the attention of the intellectual and academic communities to this very problem. The cinema could no longer be regarded as just an industry, or even as an object which might be viewed aesthetically. It was now seen as the object of a social crisis.

The Postwar Resurgence of the Film Community

The postwar years saw a new enthusiam in the filmgoing public in France. Not only were there five years of American films to catch up on; the relaxation of censorship made available a number of French films previously forbidden. Jean Vigo's *Zéro de conduite*, prohibited since 1933, finally received a *visa de censure* in 1945, and opened in November at the Panthéon Theatre in Paris on a bill with André Malraux's previously unreleased *L'Espoir*, a film based on his well-known novel about the Spanish Civil War and actually shot amidst the fighting in Spain in 1938-39.[73]

The restoration of freedom in programming to the ciné-clubs resulted in the immediate proliferation of these groups during the postwar years. In November 1944, just after the Liberation, only one ciné-club is known to have existed, and its membership numbered only 400. By June 1946 there were some 83 clubs, with a membership of close to 50,000.[74] In March 1945 these clubs were brought together in the Fédération Française des Ciné-Clubs, under the official presidency of Jean Painlevé, the Director General of Cinema, and with Georges Sadoul as secretary.[75] The Fédération was also granted certain institutional powers, with its representatives sitting on the official board of censorship (which approved film projects for production) and on an advisory board to the Ministry of Education. In October 1947, the Fédération began publishing its first official journal, *Ciné-Club*; and the month before, at the second Cannes Festival, a Fédération Internationale des Ciné-Clubs was formed, with headquarters in Paris and member clubs in Italy, Switzerland, England, Ireland, Belgium, the Netherlands, Portugal, Poland, Hungary, Egypt and Argentina.[76]

With the Liberation, the Cinémathèque returned to full activity, in better shape than it had begun the Occupation. Langlois had managed to convince Parisian representatives of the German Reichsfilmarchiv, who were themselves film devotees, to allow him to conserve a number of films, especially American, which were considered "questionable." Thus in 1943, with the creation of the Direction-Générale du Cinéma, the Cinémathèque Française was permitted to pay personnel to continue the work of conserving films and to begin the task of cataloguing its already formidable collection.[77] In August 1946 Jean Grémillon, the new president of the Cinémathèque, estimated that its holdings included approximately 100,000 films.[78]

The legitimation of film as an object of study had been given a big boost by the activities of IDHEC. From its inception IDHEC had provided public screenings of films with filmmakers in attendance, as well as general lectures on film technique, aesthetics and history. In February and March of 1944, IDHEC presented, in cooperation with the Service des Etudiants of the Université de Paris, screenings of Louis Daquin's *Premier de cordée* and Jean Gremillon's *Le Ciel est à vous*, a program by which, in Bazin's words, "the very young university of cinema made overtures to the very old Université de Paris."[79]

In fulfillment of its stated mission of bringing cinematic culture to the public, IDHEC established a cultural service in 1945, with Bazin as one of its first directors. This service published a *Bulletin de l'I.D.H.E.C.*, and during 1946, sponsored film festivals in Lille, Lyon and Strasbourg.[80]

In the first months of the Liberation, IDHEC also sponsored a number of lectures of primary public and intellectual interest. In February 1945, Jean Mitry spoke on the American films which had yet to be released in France;[81] and on March 13 of that year, IDHEC sponsored a lecture by the renowned phenomenological psychologist Maurice Merleau-Ponty on "The Film and the New Psychology," which was published in the *Bulletin* and reprinted in Merleau-Ponty's *Sense and Non-Sense*.[82]

In December 1943, Bazin wrote that the study of the cinema had at last come of age:

> The time is past when Paul Souday[83] could respond to the interviewer of *Les Nouvelles Littéraires* that no serious critic could be interested in the cinema. We already have a history of the cinema by a professor of the Sorbonne, and surely we will have one day an 800-page thesis on the comic in the American cinema between 1905 and 1917 or something of that sort. And who will dare contend that this is not serious?[84]

In his 1944 book *Cinéma total*, René Barjavel argues the necessity of teaching film in the high school, less for its aesthetic value than for its sociological impact:

The cinema is consumed weekly by each citizen in large or small doses. Laborers who have never encountered chimeras and who barely know how to sign their names come seeking in the darkened movie houses the only spiritual food available to them. They are almost always served an abominable cuisine. Thus the sensibility and intelligence of a people is corrupted. Some day it will become necessary to consider this problem seriously. To give the public a high quality cuisine will require educating the diners.[85]

The sociological concern for the well-being of the filmgoing public placed a special emphasis on the young, viewed as the most impressionable part of the film audience, as well as France's hope for the future. André Bazin founded Les Jeunesses Cinématographiques, a ciné-club aimed at introducing the young audience to the classics of the cinema and developing in them an appreciation of cinematic art. The club sponsored screenings as well as lectures by critics and technicians, hosting such guests as director René Clément and screenwriter Charles Spaak.[86]

Le Comité Français du Cinéma pour la Jeunesse, founded in 1946 by Henri Wallon, one of the key figures in filmology, took a more analytic approach to the problem of youth and the cinema, its stated goal being "to delineate the different areas of the cinema by categories of age and mentality, and to show that each stage of human development corresponds to appropriate themes as well as appropriate art forms and presentation." On a practical plane, the committee pledged its support and cooperation in the production of films aimed at youth.[87]

M. Lebrun, Director of the Museé Pédagogique and Vice-president of the Comité Français du Cinéma pour la Jeunesse, led the move to establish an International Committee for Educational Films, with the coordination of the newly formed UNESCO. The goal was to establish a service of educational films in every participant country, each providing a national catalogue to be compiled by UNESCO in an international listing. Educational films then could be exchanged among participants on the basis of international accords established in 1933.[88]

As early as 1926, G. Michael Coissac's *Le cinématographe et l'enseignement* had posed the importance of film in teaching.[89] The subject was raised again in 1944 by M. Prudhommeau in the booklet *Le cinéma éducatif et l'avenir*, which traces the activities of the Commission du Cinématographe d'Enseignement, d'Education et de Recherches, which had been created by the Front National Universitaire.[90] That same year, Jean Benoit-Lévy, a documentary filmmaker and former secretary-general of the French committee of the International Institute of Educational Cinema, published a book entitled *Les grandes missions du cinéma*. Having spent the Occupation in Canada, Benoit-Lévy writes of the National Film Board of Canada, formed in 1939, as an exemplary model of a government-supported endeavor aimed at fulfilling the important educational mission of the cinema.[91]

Partly due to the easing of the paper shortage of the year before, 1946 was also a very busy year in publishing,[92] and the postwar enthusiasm for film manifested itself in the publication of the greatest number of books on the cinema since the 1920s and early 1930s. The earlier period had produced a number of books by such important writers as Moussinac[93] and Epstein,[94] as well as film histories by G. Michel Coissac,[95] Georges Charensol,[96] and Bardèche and Brasillach.[97] In 1946 Georges Sadoul published the first volume of his *Histoire générale du cinéma*[98], and Alexandre Arnoux his film history *Du muet au parlant.*[99] The following year Sadoul's second volume appeared,[100] as did the first volume of R. Jeanne and Charles Ford's *Histoire encyclopédique du cinéma.*[101]

The year 1946 also saw new books by Marcel L'Herbier[102] and Jean Epstein;[103] and the major works of Léon Moussinac were compiled and reprinted in *L'âge ingrat du cinéma.*[104] Collections of articles by filmmakers also appeared, such as Marcel Lapierre's *Anthologie du cinéma*[105] and Denis Marion's *Le cinéma par ceux qui le font.*[106] In addition, two significant technical books on the cinema were published in 1946: H. Piraux's *Lexique technique anglais-français du cinéma*[107] and *Essai de grammaire cinématographique,*[108] written by A. Berthomieu, a founding partner with Gilbert Cohen-Séat of the company Bertho-Films.[109]

Serious articles on film found their way into a number of prestigious journals of the period, the most notable of which was probably *Les Temps Modernes*, which published a series of analytical treatments of film form by Albert Laffay in 1946 and 1947.[110] But the most prestigious work on the cinema to appear in 1946 was undoubtedly André Malraux's *Esquisse d'une psychologie du cinéma*, a treatise written in 1939 from notes Malraux had made during the preparation of his film *L'Espoir*. This article first appeared in the periodical *Verve* in 1939, but was reprinted in 1946 in a limited hardback edition and then with another of Malraux's essays in *Scènes choisis.*[111] At this time Malraux was a highly respected author and something of a cultural hero in France. During the Spanish Civil War he had been active on the Loyalist side against the fascists; then, in 1940, he had joined the French Army to fight the Germans, was taken prisoner, and escaped. During the Occupation, he had taken an active part in the Resistance, was imprisoned once again and, toward the end of the war, commanded the brigade in Alsace-Lorraine. At the time of the reprinting of his *Esquisse d'une psychologie du cinéma*, Malraux was serving as the French Minister of Information, a post to which he had been appointed by DeGaulle in 1945.[112] "Although Malraux presents this text as 'reflections born from the experience of shooting parts of *L'Espoir*,' " Gilles Roignant comments, "nothing is further from production notes than this 'sketch.' Indeed it is a matter of an interrogation of the cinema and of a meditation on its intellectual and moral values."[113] Bazin proclaimed that

"Malraux is the contemporary writer who has talked the best about the cinema."[114]

It is important to note that during this period certain key theoretical works on the cinema were not readily available in France. Sergei Eisenstein's writings had appeared in French only in excerpted form,[115] although they would soon be available to readers of English.[116] The work of Rudolf Arnheim[117] and Béla Balázs[118] was available only in German. It was for Bazin to begin a French tradition of theoretical writing on the cinema in such articles as "Ontology of the Photographic Image" (1945)[119] and "The Myth of Total Cinema" (1946).[120] With much of his major theoretical work appearing during the formative period of filmology, Bazin remained curiously apart from the movement, unlike such film devotees as Georges Sadoul and Henri Agel. It was Bazin who in fact represented an alternative path in French film writing, which would finally be crystallized in the influential *Cahiers du Cinéma*.

The origins of *Cahiers du Cinéma*, which began publication in 1951, can be traced directly to Jean Georges Auriol's *La Revue du Cinéma,* a film magazine which had appeared between 1929 and 1931, and which began publication again in 1946. This second series of *La Revue du Cinéma* lasted only until 1949, but during its four years it published a number of notable articles, including pieces on the early cinema by Georges Sadoul[121] and a very careful, three-part analysis of the "non-visual" elements of film, written by Pierre Schaeffer.[122] In the first issue, Auriol wrote a lengthy discussion of the relationship between *mise-en-scène* in the cinema and that of classical painting.[123] The last issue of the magazine was devoted entirely to the role of costume in the cinema.[124] *La Revue du Cinéma* had its share of film reviews as well, but it also paid careful and consistent attention to issues of film history and aesthetics.

Auriol was instrumental in the creation of a ciné-club called Objectif 49, which was committed to the *cinéma des auteurs* and served to focus the interests of a number of future writers for *Cahiers du Cinéma*. As Jacques Doniol-Valcroze has written, "For *Cahiers* it was never a matter of anything more than continuing the work of Jean George Auriol."[125] Bazin's resumption of Auriol's task in *Cahiers du Cinéma* represents the tradition of film study from the perspective of the film devotee, a tradition which would develop simultaneously, but separately from filmology, with its academic base.

It was within this climate of a revitalized film community that Cohen-Séat's *Essai* pointed a new direction. After nearly five years of censorship and isolation during the Occupation, and a turbulent period of purging and restoring the cinema, the French film community seemed anxious to embark on a new and significant mission. But in the context of postwar France, the cinema was no longer perceived simply as an art or as a popular entertainment. Its aesthetics were linked to morality and its popularity to social action. Only within this context can the impact of Cohen-Séat's *Essai* be understood.

3

Cohen-Séat's Philosophy of Cinema

Born in Algeria in 1907, Gilbert Cohen-Séat completed his schooling in Bordeaux and Paris, and in 1929 embarked on a career as a journalist. The founder of at least two film production companies, Orsay-Films and Bertho-Films (with A. Berthomieu), he became the chairman of the Inter-Ministerial Committee of Cinema in 1936, and in 1938 served as the president of the master craftsman program for the French film industry. In 1946, the same year in which his *Essai sur les principes d'une philosophie du cinéma* appeared, he worked as editor-in-chief of the *Appel de la Haute-Loire*, published by the Departmental Committee of Liberation. A filmmaker in his own right, he demonstrated a concern for the social role of the cinema by directing such educational shorts as *Classe enfantine*.[1] As a filmmaker, scholar, statesman, author and businessman, Cohen-Séat was a figure respected by those in French academia, politics and the film industry at the time his *Essai* first appeared. His varied background provided a basis and a validity for the breadth of concerns treated in his volume on the cinema, enabling his followers to designate him "truly a man of the cinema."[2]

The text published by Cohen-Séat in 1946 was originally conceived as only the first volume of a much longer *Essai*. This volume, subtitled "The Cinema in Contemporary Civilization," was to be followed by three others: volume II, "Aesthetics and Individual Psychology"; volume III, "Cinematic Values and Collective Mentality"; and volume IV, "Methodology." The subsequent volumes never appeared. The exact reason for this is unclear, although the quick appearance of the *Revue Internationale de Filmologie,* less than a year after the publication of volume I of the *Essai,* provided a forum for the general discussion of those topics proposed by Cohen-Séat for his later volumes.

As the title clearly states, Cohen-Séat's *Essai* is a philosophic tract. To this extent, his goal is the posing of certain questions, which is to say, the establishment of a problematic with regard to the cinema. This problematic reflects a number of philosophical concerns which are not themselves examined by Cohen-Séat; that is, his philosophy of cinema is based upon a variety of assumptions which are not themselves the subject of his inquiry. The crisis which he elaborates in his *Essai* is not a philosophical crisis *per se*; it arises instead from the absence of an application of philosophical principles to a socio-cultural force which Cohen-Séat feels has been ignored by scholars for too long.

For Cohen-Séat the cinema is a great deal more than a new invention. It is a medium which works on society in a completely new way, whose power presents a profound challenge to humanity. The title of chapter 1 of his *Essai*, "Intervention of the Cinema," indicates his vision of the cinema as an intrusive force with uncertain effects. The scope of this intervention is suggested by a range of concerns running from aesthetics to sociology, a polarity established in the first sentence of Cohen-Séat's text.[3] He likens this polarity to the foci of an ellipse:

> We can relate all that applies to human quality to one of these foci which is precisely humanism; while the other, which we might call "democracy," constitutes the pole of numbers, of the quantity of humankind.[4]

This model represents for Cohen-Séat "the duality of the permanent and progressive work produced by a social body."[5] It is a model which defines human work in terms of specific, idealized goals, with aesthetics leading toward humanism and sociology toward democracy. This is the idealism which points the direction of Cohen-Séat's analysis of the cinema and which informs the type of questions he formulates.

Cohen-Séat's basic philosophical assumptions are grounded in empiric positivism; and the epistemological basis for his philosophy of cinema is closely linked to the tradition represented by Auguste Comte, who defined positivism in terms of a search for scientific answers to questions formerly answered by theology and metaphysics. Cohen-Séat views the scientific method as the progressive means by which man can understand and finally control the phenomenon of the cinema; the danger of the cinema lies in the fact that it has arisen without the direction of reason. This is the basis of his appeal to intellectuals involved in rigorously methodical pursuits in other fields.

Cohen-Séat quotes liberally from such French positivists as Emile Durkheim, Theodule Ribot, Paul Lacombe, and Hippolyte Taine.[6] It is the sociological method of Durkheim, however, which provides the clearest basis for his approach to the cinema. For Durkheim,

> Positive philosophy ... asserts that the eternal ambition of the human mind has not lost all legitimacy, that the advance of the special sciences is not its negation, but that a new means must be employed to satisfy it. Philosophy, instead of seeking to go beyond the sciences, must assume the task of organizing them and must organize them in accordance with their own method—by making itself positive.[7]

It is this positivist impulse which allowed Durkheim to formulate a science from the study of society; and it is Durkheim's sociology which shapes Cohen-Séat's formulation of filmology, the science of film. The philosophy of the cinema forwarded by Cohen-Séat therefore entails the organization of a number of scientific concerns in a positive study of film. In addition, Cohen-Séat's filmic and cinematic facts originate in Durkheim's identification of phenomena which he calls "social facts" and which can be treated as the objects of scientific study. Further, Cohen-Séat's conception of the cinematic institution as a "system of representations" is closely modeled on the "collective representations" which Durkheim saw as the social substance uniting individuals in a society.

The thrust of Cohen-Séat's positivism is quite clear in his idealized conception of human works and the polarities of humanism and democracy. His enterprise is based on a teleological assumption of the purposive evolution of civilization and the supposition "that man is capable of creating the conditions of a superior life."[8] Thus, the crisis of the cinema is attached to its role in achieving civilization's *goal,* which "assumes that, in the march of civilization toward whatever end, the blossoming *(épanouissement)* of human life constitutes, according to our logic, a primordial condition."[9] In this sense, then, the works of humankind are divided by their direction toward two major goals: "to arrange nature for the comfort of individuals" and "to help individuals achieve humanity."[10] Embodying both of these functions, the cinema is for Cohen-Séat "the engine of the conciliation of humanist values and collective values," the conciliation of human quality and the quantity of humankind.[11]

Thus, Cohen-Séat's positive organization of scientific pursuits in the discipline of filmology aspires not only to create an understanding of the cinema but to direct the cinema toward specific goals. As put forward in the *Essai,* his argument may be traced in three stages: (1) the power and potential of the cinema; (2) the crisis posed by the cinema; and (3) the bases for a positive science of the cinema.

The Power and Potential of the Cinema

Cohen-Séat's understanding of the cinema as a conciliation of the values of human quality and quantity is based on two considerations. First, as a mass medium, the cinema reaches an audience of unprecedented size. Second, as a "system of representations,"

> this fact of civilization [the cinema] seems triumphant, from its very beginnings, over the main obstacle where all cultural forms—even those of the religious fact itself—have previously fallen: the demand for a homogenous unity and a direct universal efficiency. This too is without precedence.[12]

Cohen-Séat's point of reference here is Durkheim's conception of the *conscience collective,* which he defines in *The Division of Labor in Society:*

> The totality of beliefs and sentiments common to average citizens of the same society forms a determinate system which has its own life; one may call it the *collective* or *common conscience.* . . . It is, thus, an entirely different thing from particular consciences, although it can be realized only through them. It is the psychic type of society, a type which has its properties, its conditions of existence, its mode of development, just as individual types, but in a different way.[13]

For Durkheim, collective representations reflect aspects of the *conscience collective;* they create systems of values, ideas and symbols which define a society and legitimate its institutions. Cohen-Séat, however, views the cinema as a collective representation whose effects go beyond a single society even more effectively than religion. His conception of the cinema's universality is closely linked to Durkheim's understanding of humanism—"the idea of a common human nature and universal values as the ultimate basis of dignity— as the highest cultural ideal of modern society. . . . Humanism was the universalistic *conscience collective* of modern societies."[14]

Dismissing what he calls the "miniscule" film (the documentary, the educational film) in his pursuit of the universal cinema, Cohen-Séat is concerned with film as leisure activity and as game. It is the commercial cinema of spectacle and entertainment which is "the language spoken and the sign understood everywhere."[15] Its power and importance arises from its universality:

> For the first time in the history of mankind, all the crowds around the entire world play the same game. And understand that it is exactly the same: not with different traditions, as in music and dance; nor with different techniques, as in puppetry . . . nor to a greater or lesser degree of perfection, but the very same to the last degree.[16]

Cohen-Séat sees the universality of the cinematic sign as the basis of its unique humanist potential. As regards democracy, this universality is a means of bringing together disparate groups and of uniting individuals separated by "biological, intellectual or social privilege" in "a single public of a singular ubiquity, the very institution of the public."[17]

The humanist thrust of Cohen-Séat's vision of the cinema's potential glorifies the effacement of national and cultural differences, while in fact working to deny traditions and techniques alternative or parallel to the dominant commercial cinemas of France or the United States. He tempers his argument with only the slightest cultural relativism when he states that the desirable "homogenizing" power of the cinema need not destroy "the *personality* of a human group or its sincerity."[18] Nevertheless, his vision of the cinema's potential is rooted in the observation that, under its power, the "notion of aesthetic and moral community" has been so altered that it "ceases to respond to the psychological differentiation of a restricted group," offering instead a "common idea" which is shared by millions of people around the world.[19]

Like Durkheim's *conscience collective,* this "common idea" is grounded in the notion of the individual within society. On this point, Cohen-Séat cites a passage from Gaston Richard, a disciple and later a critic of Durkheim:

> The common knowledge and symbols, the beliefs and rules of common action enter into the contents of the individual consciousness and alter it.... Not everything individual succeeds in becoming general, but everything general has begun to be individual.[20]

From a humanist perspective, this effect of the general on the individual is extremely hopeful, since it provides a basis for a shared system of values.

The cinema's potential to unite diverse individuals and societies in a "common idea" is derived from what Cohen-Séat sees as a universal quality of humankind, "the initial identity of the representative life of all human beings."[21] This seems to imply not only that certain practices are shared by all human beings, but that the mechanisms of perception are shared as well. Cohen-Séat argues that it is this similarity among individuals and groups which the cinema employs to create a super-reality *(surréalité),* "anterior to concept and indifferent to language,"[22] a reality stripped of the barriers that separate human beings, and which actually becomes a part of the collective representation of the life of humankind.

Therefore, for Cohen-Séat, the mission of the cinema is clear. It provides the form for the representation of collective ideals, which Durkheim writes "cannot be constituted or become conscious of themselves unless they are fixed upon things which can be seen by all, understood by all, and represented in all minds."[23] Cohen-Séat cites a passage where Durkheim describes the way in which collective thought transforms society:

> in a word, [collective thought] substitutes for the world it reveals to us the sense of a completely different world, which is nothing but the shadow projected by the ideals it constructs.[24]

Clearly, Durkheim's description of collective thought could be applied almost *verbatim* to the cinema.

The collective representation of the cinema is for Cohen-Séat both the product of a universal humanist impulse and the single means by which humankind may be united under the value of humanism.

All this is placed in the hands of man by means of his invention, and he is reflected by it because it is there that he commands, dictates, composes, expresses and finally is expressed; and it is first around the human—ordered, individual and universal—that a progressive concentration of populations ideally occurs by means of the cinema, and on a level and a scale previously unknown.[25]

Thus the cinema places an immense power and responsibility in the hands of humanity, offering the opportunity "to create a useful instrument in the service of what we venerate the most: good sense, culture, the dissemination of spiritual forces."[26] The spectacle is the means by which people may be changed most comfortably and efficiently for their own good and the good of society, Cohen-Séat argues, for "once people are gathered together, one can direct them elsewhere and, as the words indicate, distract them and educate them."[27]

In deciding upon the proper course for the cinematic spectacle, Cohen-Séat stresses the importance of the age-old dreams of humanity.

The originality of the cinema carries the mark of all true originality: it will not be a manner of turning aside tradition, but a way of restoring and transmitting it.[28]

To this extent, the cinema may be seen as the fulfillment of the philosophers' prophecies. It accomplishes the dream of a truly public theatre, presented in the eighteenth century by Diderot when he wrote:

To change the face of the dramatic genre, I ask nothing but a vastly expanded theatre where a play may be shown in which its subject requires different locales distributed in such a way that the spectator lives all of the action. . . . We await the genius who will be able to combine pantomine with discourse, to intermingle a spoken scene with a silent one, to make use of the meeting of two scenes and, even more, of the link, whether terrible or comic, to be made between these scenes.[29]

It seems to be what Michelet had in mind when he proclaimed, "give [the people] the sovereign teaching which was the entire education of the glorious cities of antiquity: a theatre truly of the people."[30] It recalls Nietzsche's evocation of the Dionysiac in its accomplishment of "universal signs" common to all.[31]

To the extent that the cinema enables the realization of such "old dreams," Cohen-Séat proclaims with enthusiasm that "civilization is engaged with the cinema in one of those limitless adventures where destiny's detours are found."[32] That this potential has yet to be achieved is central to the crisis which he sees posed by the cinema for the attention of filmology.

The Crisis Posed by the Cinema

For Cohen-Séat, the appearance of the cinema signals a "critical moment" in the evolution of mankind, one of history's "periods of effervescence" during which "the great ideals upon which civilization rests are constituted." Cohen-Séat quotes Durkheim to the effect that these "periods of creativity and novelty" are those in which "men are brought together more intimately, where meetings and assemblies are more frequent, relations closer, and the exchange of ideas more active."[33] As both the product and the agent of such a period, the cinema poses a number of the critical questions facing modern man.

The novelty of the cinema and its central role in the development of human communication is virtually without precedence. The comparison of its invention to that of the printing press is tempting, Cohen-Séat observes, but ultimately misleading. As with the cinema, the printing press contributed to "the accelerated communication of man with his neighbors," and its effects were profound:

> for four centuries, all the significant movements, be they intellectual or social, political or economic, those of knowledge, of calculation, of ways of reasoning, have obtained their penetrating force and their effectiveness, regarding both the elite and the masses, from the diffusion of printing.[34]

Certainly, a large part of Cohen-Séat's hope for the cinema is based on the assumption that this new medium might have similar effects on the course of human history.

Nevertheless, Cohen-Séat notes, there is a significant difference between the development of printing and that of the cinema: "the works which in the final analysis gave rise to the birth of printing already existed before its diffusion."[35] Printing "perfected" the written work by enabling it to be copied; but its basis, its *logos*—verbal thought—preexisted its invention. Therefore, printing remained enclosed within "languages, their 'discourses' and their usages."[36]

Here Cohen-Séat makes a distinction between the invention of film *(filmographie)*, a phenomenon of "mechanism and technique, of material power and convenient processes" (and thus with certain similarities to printing) and the invention of the cinema, whose works and "the vision of the world they represent overwhelm in vertiginous fashion the mechanical effects and all the supports of film."[37] While the invention of film was essentially technological, the invention of cinema involved the creation of a new reality,

> at once outside of our time and yet submitted to time, submitted to a space and a truth outside our space and truth, surpassing our intellect upon which it depends, obeying the mechanical even as it thwarts it; and which, submitting to these restraints without relinquishing its sovereignty, ends by creating a universe which is added to our universe.[38]

This new realm created by the cinema becomes a part of the *conscience collective* and exercises an unknown effect on the minds of individuals, where it may be detected in terms of

> unconscious judgments, unconscious inductions, new and secret syllogisms, as well as commentaries and interpolations; or, on the other hand, critical suppressions of sensations interpolated into the real by who-knows-what kind of imperfection or purpose of our faculties, a whole world of generic perceptions or basic impressions which unleash a mysterious assault on our usages, our "normality," our experience, and even our feelings.[39]

Thus, for Cohen-Séat, the cinema represents an autonomous logic whose effects go beyond the rational mind, working at the level of a gestalt involving the interrelationship of the viewer's mind and body.

From this standpoint, he poses the question of the relationship between the film and the viewer. Regarding the effects of this new collective representation on the individual, he observes:

> We cannot say to what extent this new morphology of the world (which is already offered to us in terms of the passions and of actions which concern us) tends to satisfy our minds, or if it actually, in a sense, constructs them.[40]

This curious link between the spectacle and the public arises from the fact that, in the cinema, "the consumer is excluded from the game of creation."[41] Traditionally in the arts, Cohen-Séat notes, an intimate dependence existed between expression and understanding, between the individual creative consciousness and a well-defined, receptive audience. With the cinema, however, "popular need" is cut off from the creative act, existing only "as an invisible and poorly represented void whose mysterious mold the work must seek to fit by chance."[42] Cohen-Séat sees the arbitrariness of this relationship as a result of "a crisis of civilization," arising from the replacement of the artisan by the "soulless" mechanism.[43] Only as an individual within the society for which the cinema acts as a collective representation does the viewer participate in any meaningful exchange with the film. Isolated from the creative activity, s/he is unable to affect the spectacle which directly affects him/her.

Given the "subtly suggestive action of filmic images and the confused suggestibility of the viewer under the sway of the cinematic emotion,"[44] the effects of the cinema on the spectator assume a primary importance for Cohen-Séat:

> From the most elementary *receptions* to the most complex *ideo-motor* mechanisms, all the elements of the "natural function" of the mind are individually susceptible, according to their nature, under the influence of this new excitation.[45]

In addition to his assertion of film's psycho-sensory effects, Cohen-Séat poses the question of its possible physiological effects on the viewer. Certainly, the film's provocation of affective reactions suggests some effect on the motor elements which accompany these reactions.[46] Further, each individual may undergo different reactions under the same circumstances:

> Tied to the simultaneous intervention of visual, audial, verbal and musical excitations, this singular agitation is exercised unequally on highly different subjects and, above all, on unequally disposed partial egos, but always in the same very powerful specific conditions.[47]

Finally, Cohen-Séat compares the unique psychological state created by these specific conditions to the state of hypnosis, suggesting the cinema's power to weaken the ego and the individual's powers of control.[48]

Once again, Cohen-Séat provides a sociological and humanist focus for the questions regarding the affective life of the individual in a new context provided by the cinema:

> certain physiological influences which nature has until now limited to the individual consciousness will find in film a virulent instrument and will leave traces of their passage in the collective life. And this collective life affects not only one group, nor even one people, but masses of groups and peoples. And would this not be, on the simplest terrain which could be produced (or at least prepared or oriented) the first "understanding" between apparently disparate individualities and collectivities?[49]

For Cohen-Séat, the cinema occupies a key historical position in the purposive evolution of mankind because it provides the instrument by which mankind may be united in a single *conscience collective*. Therefore the critical nature of the questions he raises lies in the fact that they remain unanswered. As he acknowledges regarding the possible physiological effect of film, "it would undoubtedly be as imprudent to affirm it as to deny it."[50]

Given an instrument of such vast potential, Cohen-Séat asserts, man has yet to accumulate the data which would help direct it toward its best end. In fact, the crisis of unanswered questions is compounded by the lack of any serious attempt to pose questions at all. Nothing guarantees that the cinema will fulfill its potential, he adds, or that it will even maintain that potential for very long. Here he poses the "final problem" of the cinema as he sees it:

> either the cinema will be able to conserve of its unity nothing but a material appearance, and the *presence of the public* signifies nothing but a passing curiosity regarding the novelty of the game; or civilization should expect an important intervention from the cinematic emotion. Nothing suggests, in either case, that what occurs must do so without the will of man.[51]

In these terms, Cohen-Séat views the greatest potential for cinema's failure in its loss of this unity, its division "by borders and by languages" to the extent that "each production would carry more and more the marks of its local origin." In that case, he asserts, the cinema would lose sight of its mission, becoming nothing more than "a sort of enlarged transposition of previous means of expression," if not simply a functionary of economic interests.

> But if, on the other hand, the technique and aesthetic of film, evolving in a universally homogenous manner—as is possible and even probable—begins to institute the substance and form of a game which is indifferent to ethnic and cultural subtleties, then spiritual life— after all, the human form of life—will perhaps have found an incomparable instrument, and art a new path.[52]

Cohen-Séat's argument that the cinema's proper course is to become even more universal is based on a conception of film as a means of communication with the potential to transcend differences of culture and language.

This goal provides the context for his comparison of language and cinema. In terms of its social function, he observes, the cinema bears certain similarities to language *(langage)*, yet it is not itself *a language (langue)*.[53] Whether or not it can become a language is still uncertain, although it is clear that Cohen-Séat's conception of the cinema as a system of "universal signs"[54] aspires to something like a universal cinematic language, the basis of which goes much deeper than the creation of a system of signs. "It is less a matter of this 'writing' awaiting its calligraphy (whose art has already appeared)," he writes, "than it is of this logic awaiting its laws, this liberty its form."[55] Clearly, Cohen-Séat believes that this form can be one in which a universal collective representation is possible; and it is the appropriate development of such a form which presents the most critical question in humanist terms:

> The question is whether the cinematic message, insofar as it is constant and common, can overtake, retain, develop or create elements of spiritual life—which can escape the *character* of each individual spectator, and which, before being of man, of his sentiments and of their imitation, belongs to the substance of the human being, so to speak, to the very essence of humanity.[56]

The idealism of universal humanist values provides an excuse for the ethnocentrism implicit in Cohen-Séat's rejection of the cinema's capacity to reflect cultural and ethnic differences. At the same time it denies a correlation between the direction of the cinematic institution and its economic domination by Western nations. For if it is "possible and even probable" that film might evolve in a "universally homogenous manner," it is certainly a matter of those industries which economically dominate world cinema working toward that end. In fact, Cohen-Séat suggests that the status quo of the cinematic institution provides a basis for the universality of filmic art when he refers to "the economic demands which tend to make film an international merchandise."[57]

Nevertheless, Cohen-Séat opposes the purely economic considerations which have guided the development of the cinema. The dictates of economic exploitation and its relationship to the ideal of humanism provide the main topic for his second chapter, "Natural Evolution and Tendencies." Here he poses the crisis presented by the cinema's undirected evolution. Seen as the outgrowth of the medium's anarchic development, the power of the cinema itself poses a threat:

> Isolated from life, plunged in darkness, bathed in music, lulled by dreams, brought to the most perfect state of receptiveness, seized by the eyes and ears, by passivity and even by unconsciousness, the public is placed for a long while at the mercy of a strange mechanical power.[58]

The mass nature of the cinematic audience, which provides an important basis for Cohen-Séat's vision of universality, is presented here as a factor leading away from the ideal. It is the mass which has made the cinema lucrative and which has submitted its direction to the dictates of merchants.

From the beginning, Cohen-Séat argues, the cinema has developed "unreasonably," "like a force of nature," and its rules were established as if by "a toss of the dice."[59] No time was devoted to understanding the medium before exploiting it for profit. The quickness of its dissemination and its almost instant popularity made the cinema a gold mine for "businessmen and those of imagination," but "a rocky ground for scholars."[60] And though the question has arisen as to whether the cinema was to be "an art or a commerce," it has been the single rule of economic exploitation which has directed its development.[61] As Cohen-Séat characterizes it, the cinema "was a consumable product which the crowd of consumers gladly consumed."[62] The directive force of the cinematic institution became simply the supply of this consumable product.

> Entrenched behind the aphorism that "the public is the only power which has no need of reason to validate its actions,"[the cinema] in its redoutable popular favor, validated the fact that man in his boredom could very well sell his soul to the devil for a little supernatural power.[63]

Employing a strictly traditional Christian metaphor for posing the dilemma of the cinema, Cohen-Séat situates the question in specifically moral terms. And, only a year after the end of World War II, his condemnation of the cinema as "the most singular tyranny of the crowd and its most astonishing submission"[64] certainly intends to bring to mind the fascist manipulation of the masses and the scars of the Nazi Occupation.

Cohen-Séat thus poses the crisis of the cinema in terms of its lack of any strong moral and humanist direction, which bodes ill for humanity.

> It was inevitable that such a game of chance and cash, on the enormous scale of the cinema, would eventually result in a very grave crisis of spirit and feeling.[65]

Thus he believes that the actual historical development of the cinema has in many ways run counter to the realization of its potential.

This is the kernel of the crisis he addresses to the scholars of his day, whom he chides for complacency.

> For a long time we have assisted at the birth of film, by negligence or by some other form of routine. We have maintained our indifference and contempt for a long time. It would be strange indeed if cinematic art regulated itself one fine day to conform to our desires.[66]

The "we" of this passage clearly refers to the scholars and intellectuals who have chosen to ignore the cinema, and to the academic institution itself. But if the cinema is to be changed for the better, Cohen-Séat argues, it must be done by those who understand its potential.

> Film remains in a primitive state, despite the breadth and speed of its evolution. We take comfort in thinking that certain things are there by nature and never change because we have never seen them change.[67]

Such an attitude is directly opposed to the notion of positive science and the goal of mankind's progress. In this respect, he presents the negligence of intellectuals regarding the cinema as the most basic kind of logical contradiction. For the sake of the future, he argues, scholars, researchers and intellectuals in every field of study must be willing to apply their methodical disciplines to the cinema. It is from this notion of crisis that the problematic of filmology is born.

The Bases for a Positive Science of the Cinema

When Cohen-Séat refers to film as a "logic awaiting its laws," he refers to the positivist goals of his proposed study of the cinema. For the positivist, as characterized by Comte, "our real studies are rigidly confined to the analysis of phenomena with a view to the discovery of their actual laws, i.e., their constant relations of sequence or similarity."[68] If Cohen-Séat's notion of the laws of film is neither quite so strict nor constant, it is clear that he ascribes to a belief in a "true meaning of film," which is the goal of both the filmic creation and its study.[69]

In its state of "anarchy" and "primitive carelessness,"[70] the cinema created for itself a set of "laws without real foundation" which became its "unformulated dogma."[71] To a large extent, these are the laws of exploitation, of the marketplace, which do explain a certain aspect of the cinema, but which do not represent its potential, its proper form, or its "true meaning."

> The cinema has taken no road which would lead it beyond this original confusion, to put itself in order or to order within itself that which already exists.[72]

Cohen-Séat sees the goal of filmology as the introduction of this kind of order to its subject in order to create a "true" understanding of film.

To this effect, he quotes the dictum: "to understand is to systematize."[73] This is not to say that any order adopted will lead toward the desired goal. Rejecting the arbitrary dogmas of "upstart aesthetes," Cohen-Séat observes that it is quite simple "to confuse results and causes, to prefer the right of legitimating rules to the duty of studying facts."[74] Even with proper "seriousness" and "method," he admits, "it is still possible to arrive at only approximate results and uncertain principles."[75]

The order sought by Cohen-Séat can be provided only by positive science, which provides "directive ideas" that enable the study of an object to remain on the course of a specific goal. Therefore, the project of the filmologist is "to compose with this chaos" which is the cinema.[76]

> For, should it all be reduced in the final analysis for us to distinguish, to classify, to conceive methodically, to organize systematically the principal obligations [of the cinema], to discern those which are in fact nothing but the power of disorder and those which do indeed belong to the nature of things, and thus to determine an ensemble of sufficiently defined processes, there would remain no less a certain number of directive ideas, destined to be modified constantly by contact with technical developments but also capable of continuation, of pushing forward technical development and of orienting it.[77]

These directive ideas, which for Cohen-Séat are grounded in humanism, provide an orientation for the positive science of film.

As with Comte and the empiric positivists, the scientific method provides the organizing principle which Cohen-Séat seeks. He sees empirical objectivity as the only hope of ordering the numerous issues raised by the study of film. Chaos arises from the lack of such objectivity, which is demonstrated by the special interests that have guided the cinema. "Is it so surprising," Cohen-Séat asks,

> that those who are by chance involved in defining or measuring the cinema do so according to their own needs and the particularity of their purpose? Once we stop to consider it, the person who makes films is situated on an entirely different plane from the one who comments on them, and if both employ the same terms, it is in an altogether different sense.[78]

In other words, the multiplicity of existing approaches to the cinema represents a variety of subjective perspectives and a division of purpose.

Nevertheless, Cohen-Séat himself proposes a plurality of approaches to the study of film. The difference is that he appeals to the established fields of study on the common ground of their unity of method and purpose. Each of these "methodical disciplines" is linked to the others by an analytic/scientific methodology. As positive sciences, they also share a common goal. With these facts in mind, Cohen-Séat proposes that "they determine together the point of departure of a common research."[79]

Cohen-Séat nevertheless sees the necessity of a preliminary step which is the establishment of a common vocabulary to fix the meanings of terms previously employed in different ways by a variety of groups. To this end, the second part of his *Essai* is entitled "Fundamental Notions and Vocabulary of Filmology," and is followed by a glossary of basic technical terms applying to the cinema.

By far the most significant definition of terms introduced by Cohen-Séat is that of the dichotomy between cinematic facts and filmic facts. This distinction permits the analysis of film both as an object and as a social force. Cohen-Séat's approach to a cultural institution in terms of "facts" or specific phenomena is again linked quite closely to Durkheim and his "social facts." As defined by Durkheim,

> A social fact is every way of acting, fixed or not, capable of exercising on the individual an external constraint; or again, every way of acting which is general throughout a given society, while at the same time existing in its own right, independent of its individual manifestations.[80]

Harry Alpert adds that, for Durkheim, "social facts are in nature, i.e. have distinctive empirical properties and form real systems," that they are "subject to the same principles of determinism...so fruitfully postulated by all the sciences," and that there exists between them "invariant relations, i.e. laws, which express the necessary bonds between social phenomena."[81] These are the assumptions about social phenomena which allow Durkheim to treat sociology as a natural science.

Isolating similar empirical phenomena manifested by film and the cinema, Cohen-Séat supports the scientific claim of filmology by relating it to the model offered by sociology. What is interesting is his separation of these phenomena according to their relationship to film as a material object and to the social institution of the cinema.

The filmic fact, as defined by Cohen-Séat, "consists in expressing life, the life of the world or of the mind, of the imagination or of beings and things, by a *determined system* of the combination of images.[82] The filmic fact therefore includes those aspects of the film as an object, as a combination of "visual images—natural or conventional—and audial images—sounds or words."[83] Yet it also encompasses the "determined system" by which these images are combined; that is, the filmic fact bears on the question of film signification and film language.

The cinematic fact relates to the cinema as a social phenomenon. Its realm is the "circulation in *human groups* of a resource of documentations, sensations, ideas, feelings, materials offered by life and given form by the film in its fashion."[84] Therefore, the cinematic fact is almost identical to Durkheim's social fact, except that it is specific to the social role of the cinema.

In practice, Cohen-Séat admits, filmic facts and cinematic facts can be conceived only in terms of one another, making it impossible to define either one as the "fundamental aspect" of the cinema.[85] The key to the cinematic/filmic dichotomy may lie in its resumption of the dichotomy established by Cohen-Séat between the approaches of sociology and aesthetics, as well as between the "quantity of humanity" and "human quality." This last dichotomy, reflecting the importance assigned to humanity on both sides of the balance, indicates the sociological bent of Cohen-Séat's goal, a fact confirmed by his dependence on the model provided by Durkheim.

In a revision to this section which appeared in the second edition of the *Essai* in 1958, Cohen-Séat adds further emphasis to the sociological nature of the problematic:

> ...a more exact analysis must take as its object the human significance of these instruments and the consequences which will result from them. In other words, our perspective does not begin with the making of films, but with the consumption of the spectacle. It is indeed within and during the "representation" that we find the object and the new activity instituted by the cinema.[86]

It is the cinematic institution which orients the study of both the cinematic and the filmic fact, since the single commonality shared by the various filmic/cinematic phenomena is that they all belong to "a universal institution."[87] Furthermore, the positivist model adopted by Cohen-Séat privileges the study of the social fact which he dubs "cinematic," since it is within this realm that the laws of cause and effect can best be discerned. Posing the question of how scientific ideas about the cinema are to be developed, he notes that "our idea of an object is nothing but the sum of ideas of its effects."[88]

In this sense, Cohen-Séat refers to the film itself as "an architectural endeavor, an effort to combine and link visual and audial images in an agreeable or effective fashion, proper in any case to some collective design, which suits cinematic expression."[89] To the extent that the filmic fact reflects the "determined system" of a "collective design," it demonstrates a very close attachment to what Cohen-Séat defines as the cinematic fact.

In his critique of Cohen-Séat's dichotomy, Christian Metz acknowledges the importance of isolating the filmic fact as a "manageable, specifiable signifying discourse."[90] For Metz's purposes, the filmic fact focuses the concerns of a semiology of the cinema by specifying the film as a text and as "a linguistic object."[91] Yet Metz finds the institutional fact of the cinema to be clearly inseparable from the filmic fact as defined by Cohen-Séat.

> Thus one can say of a certain configuration of montage that it is *properly cinematic,* or that it *belongs to the language of the cinema.* And it is clear, although paradoxical, that the cinema thus conceived is situated *within* what Cohen-Séat calls the filmic fact.[92]

The difficulty of strictly applying the filmic/cinematic distinction arises again and again in the early attempts of the filmologists to define their respective approaches, despite Cohen-Séat's insistence that

> one would not bring the enormous quantity of social factors attached to the cinema into the realm of aesthetics, nor bring within the bounds of sociology the breadth and minutia of problems regarding filmic art.[93]

Far more than this division of facts, the various university disciplines were what organized the filmological approaches to the cinema. Within the range he envisions as including psychology, psycho-physiology, ethics and philology, it is impossible even for Cohen-Séat to identify which concerns are wholly cinematic or filmic.[94]

No answers can be expected, Cohen-Séat observes, until filmological research provides them; and the next step must be the methical analysis of specific phenomena.

> ...it seems evident that any methodical enterprise remains dependent upon a laborious preliminary investigation, and that we must first cross the period of apparent disorder and real fecundity where every notion is studied separately and thoroughly explored.[95]

He predicts that the first product of such a "laborious preliminary investigation" will be a series of monographs on specific subjects, a function which would soon be fulfilled to a large extent by the *Revue Internationale de Filmologie.*

Turning to the positivist philosophers for support, Cohen-Séat quotes Ribot, who observes that "all this is undoubtedly not a science, but without it there is no science."[96] From Henri Bergson, he forwards the idea that the path of filmology will become manifest in the study "of elements and different groups of facts, each of which, without bringing us to a desired conclusion, points a direction in which it will be found."[97] It is finally the empiric positivism of Taine which assures the correctness of such a procedure, and Cohen-Séat quotes him to the effect that "science neither proscribes nor pardons; it states and explains."[98]

Thus, it was a positivist belief in the scientific method coupled with an understanding of the cinema as an autonomous object which situated the questions posed by filmology. These ideas rapidly assumed a central role in orienting the study of film within the French academy.

4

The Intervention of Filmology

The philosophical project of Cohen-Séat's *Essai sur les principes d'une philosophie du cinéma* was to situate film as the object of a positive science. Its rhetorical project was perhaps even more ambitious; for it involved the persuasion of the academic establishment to adopt and pursue this new science of film. Cohen-Séat's appeal to the scholars of his day was thus as much a call to action as it was a philosophic treatise. His goal was the legitimation of a new field of inquiry and the institutionalization of a discipline. It was in this area that Cohen-Séat enjoyed the most immediate success.

In September 1946, concurrent with the publication of his *Essai,* Cohen-Séat founded the Association Française pour la Recherche Filmologique, with himself as secretary-general.[1] For the Directorial Committee of the Association, he assembled a number of renowned members of the French university. Mario Roques, Professor of the Collège de France and expert in Oriental Languages, was named president. The vice-presidents were the respected psychologist Henri Wallon, also a Professor of the Collège de France, and Léon Moussinac, then Director of the Ecole Nationale des Arts Décoratifs and soon to become the Director of IDHEC. The committee also included such professors of the Sorbonne as Gaston Bachelard, Raymond Bayer and Etienne Souriau, film directors René Clair, Jean Delannoy and Marc Allegret, technicians and trade union leaders Jean Grémillon, Louis Daquin and Henri Jeanson, scholar Georges Sadoul, and first president of the Association Française de la Critique du Cinéma Georges Charensol, as well as numerous counsellors and undersecretaries of the French government.[2]

This impressive list of names represented the breadth of concerns encompassed by filmology and played an important part in legitimating the new discipline both within the university and within the film industry itself. It also indicated a diversity which would pose its own difficulties in terms of methodologies and practice.

At the Constitutive Assembly of the Association, held November 4, 1946 at the Ecole Nationale des Arts Décoratifs, the question of emphasis was raised regarding the various fields to be covered by filmology. President Roques opened the proceedings by emphasizing the importance of film as a social fact, its unique conditions and the universality and intensity of its effects.[3] For Roques, filmology centered around the concerns of psychology and sociology; therefore, the cinematic fact assumed primary importance for him. "As for the rest," he stated, "the work is not just beginning; we have already studied, deconstructed and analyzed the filmic facts."[4] Viewing the aesthetics of the cinema as the province of technicians, he acknowledged the necessity of analyzing such questions, but argued that it was not the project of filmology "to aid the numerous personnel who create the cinematic material, the film. Nevertheless, it would be strange indeed if these studies did not aid the inventors and creators of cinematic material."[5] For Roques, filmology is a social science "which is not limited to developing man's knowledge of new conditions, but whose conclusions should inevitably apply to the knowledge we possess of many other attitudes and human situations."[6]

Roques's opening address was followed by a statement from Moussinac, whose school was hosting the proceedings. Moussinac politely emphasized the importance of the creative point of view for filmological study. It is the filmmaker, he argued, whose creations have provided the information to be analyzed; and the creation of the filmic fact is itself an empirical undertaking.

> At each instant a creator finds himself faced by the determined problems of creation, poses questions, asks himself how to resolve a certain problem; he does so in an empirical fashion according to his feelings, his experience, the understanding he has of the craft in which he is engaged, but often he cannot say and does not have the time to ask why he has resolved a problem in one way instead of in another.[7]

Based on information provided by creators and spectators, "the attention, the thought, the intelligence and the reasoning of specialists" could make an important contribution to elucidating the creative process and to explaining "the emotional reaction of the viewer in front of a film, to the extent that he will have a greater perception and knowledge" of the factors at work.[8] Implying a correlation between the purposeful act of creation and the purposefulness of the positive sciences, Moussinac concludes,

> it is extremely moving that men whose craft—I will say craft, for nothing is more beautiful than craft—is thinking, reflecting and putting all the knowledge they have acquired into their particular science have joined together in the service of a means of expression which is in a certain sense upsetting a number of our conceptions about feeling and understanding.[9]

The statements of Roques and Moussinac provide one of the earliest examples of the dichotomous trends which would continue to surface within filmology, and which correspond roughly to Cohen-Séat's division of filmic and cinematic facts. The important thing is that both Roques and Moussinac are careful to frame their arguments in a scientific context, although neither represents the point of view of traditional experimental science. This is an indication of the important rhetorical role played by filmology's scientific stance in providing a totalizing framework for the various concerns it encompassed.

As Professor Marc Soriano, editor of the *Revue Internationale de Filmologie,* explained the project set forward by Cohen-Séat,

> It is not merely a matter of M. Cohen-Séat elaborating certain reflections, however profound, on the subject of the new art, but of discovering the manner of grouping all the reflections which can be made about it—in sum, of creating a new science.

The neologism "filmology," he adds, embodies the project: "Double word, whose first part is new and whose second part is ancient, and which clearly indicates a matter of a traditional reflection upon a new object."[10]

The Association pour la Recherche Filmologique was founded as a locus for uniting film study under the banner of Cohen-Séat's new science. It set three major goals for itself, all of which were accomplished within a mere two years: (1) the publication of a journal as a forum for filmological research and writing, (2) the staging of an international conference which would bring together those interested in scientific film study from around the world, and (3) the creation of a Center for Filmological Research affiliated with the French university.

The last of these goals was achieved in September 1948, when the Minister of Education approved the attachment of the Institut de Filmologie to the Sorbonne, creating an official course of academic study in the new discipline.[11] In the interim since the publication of Cohen-Séat's *Essai,* the first issue of the *Revue Internationale de Filmologie* had appeared in July 1947 and the First International Congress of Filmology had taken place two months later at the Sorbonne.

Dividing the Field: First International Congress of Filmology

Held September 15-21, 1947, the First International Congress serves as a landmark in the establishment of filmology. Attracting scholars from Italy, England, Belgium, Switzerland and throughout Europe, the Congress not only indicated a widespread interest in the subject, but provided the first serious opportunity for discussing the organization of research in the various areas of concern. Since the Congress was composed largely of scholars representing a wide range of traditional disciplines, the temptation to categorize filmological research according to their various fields was quite strong. On the other hand, there was an understanding of the necessity for the new discipline to dictate its own categories to some extent. As Professor Gonseth of Zurich argued during the first meeting of the Congress,

The first temptation will be to say that traditional philosophy already designates categories relative to knowledge, ethics and sociology; that it is going to be necessary to examine filmology from these perspectives.... I believe that if philosophy is content with this categorization it remains inferior to the tasks set for it.... Philosophy would then be faced with fitting this unknown and still incommensurable fact, which is filmology, into more or less well-known categories. It would fix its interpretations within a framework already determined in advance, and it would probably be unable to distinguish what is essential and new, precisely those things which fascinate us and hold our attention.... In taking account of these new properties, it will be necessary to invent new categories. [12]

Cohen-Séat's call for a unified, systematic methodology served as a rallying point for the division of the field of study by the Congress, but his distinction between filmic and cinematic proved somewhat difficult as an organizing principle. The report on the Congress which appeared in the *Revue* describes the effort of putting Cohen-Séat's principle into practice.

Although at times misunderstood, the distinction of filmic and cinematic implies neither abstraction nor fragmentation; on the contrary, in affirming the singular character of the domain constituted by the human effects of the image, it involves the consideration of the filmic as a totality, as inseparable from the historical and technical framework which encompasses it, as irreducible to strict boundaries. But it is not sufficient to propose in an intuitive manner the specificity of the experience proposed for study. Moreover, a program of research cannot be the fruit of an isolated reflection; it involves the collaboration of specialists from each science, as of all those concerned with the problems of the cinema. In order to be systematic without surrendering to the mentality of the system, it will be necessary to unite the still unelaborated richness of cinematic expression with the rigor of psychological, sociological and philosophical methods. Only the encounters of interested researchers and specialists can reveal the filmic fact in its proper context, eliminating dogmatism by its discussion. [13]

The purpose of the Congress was to provide such an encounter between specialists in an attempt to create the new categories which everyone agreed were necessary.

In practice, the categories created for the Congress maintain the autonomy of the established disciplines, but group them topically, according to the goals established for filmology. Five categories were defined:

1. Psychological and Experimental Research

2. Research in the Development of Cinematic Empiricism

3. Aesthetic, Sociological and General Philosophical Research

4. Comparative Research on Film as a Means of Expression

5. Normative Research—Application of studies of the filmic fact to problems of teaching, of medical psychology, etc. [14]

Following this initial division, each of the five groups met separately to discuss their common interests and to plot a collective course of research and study. Each group then reported on their progress to the Congress as a whole.

Group 1, led by Henri Wallon, attempted to outline the psychological questions raised by the conditions of cinematic perception. According to Wallon, this involved the exploration of "an entirely new field of contacts between the perceiving subject and his milieu."[15] The viewer's perception of depth on the flat surface of the screen was discussed in light of a study by John Maddison of the British Central Office of Information, who noted that certain African "primitives" were unable to perceive screen depth. This suggested to the group the need for "a systematic study of variations in filmic perception according to age, intelligence, imaginative type and level of civilization."[16] Soriano raised the issue of the adaptations required by the viewer watching a film, especially with regard to reflex actions in response to filmic perception. Questions concerning the differences between objective perception and filmic perception, both in terms of time and space, were also deemed important for study.[17]

The second major area of consideration for Group 1 centered on the relationship between the audience and the film. Two aspects of this problem were defined by Wallon: the individual, i.e., "the relationship of the film to the intimate dispositions of the subject"; and the collective and social, i.e., "those types of assimilation and receptivity belonging to the milieux which the screen influences."[18] Here the concerns of Group 1, devoted to psychology and experimental research, clearly enter the territory of the psychiatrists of Group 5 in the former case, and of the sociologists of Group 3 in the latter.[19]

The sociologists of Group 3, also influenced by Maddison's study of filmic perception and African tribesmen, discussed the possible uses of film as a "test of culture," and thus as a research tool. From a completely different viewpoint, Siegfried Kracauer's study of the pre-Nazi German cinema, just published in English as *From Caligari to Hitler*, was discussed in terms of the use of film in the study of societies.[20]

The concerns of Group 5 also bore a relationship to the experimental and psychological approaches of Group 1, and to the intentions of Group 3 to utilize film as a method of testing. Group 3 devoted much of its discussion to the reactions of viewers who could not be categorized as average adult subjects, e.g., children, the mentally retarded, the pathological. Professors Poyer and Leuret, for example, proposed studies of the differences between the reactions of spectators of various intellectual levels and character types. Others suggested the importance of examining the correlation between the ages of children and their ability to understand the content of a film. A variety of other topics were discussed, ranging from the relationship of filmic rhythm and the "interior rhythm" of the subject, to the power of suggestion exercised by films upon children.[21]

Group 4, devoted to the comparative study of film as a means of expression, examined the questions raised by the unique mode of filmic communication. Roques proposed a basically philological and comparative examination of the language *(langue)* of film, intended to establish its history and to determine its semantics. Further, he suggested the importance of examining film as a "fact of language" *(langage)*, in the sense of such other non-verbal languages as gestures and mimicry, "languages whose workings are unknown to us, even though we know their effects." The main concern of Group 4, however, was the comparison of film with other arts—verbal, musical, plastic—in an attempt to note systematically the similarities and differences. Areas of proposed study ran from the examination of film adaptations and thematics to structural studies comparing filmic and literary syntax, and analyses of the use of music in films.[22]

Group 3, which included the topics of aesthetics, sociology and philosophy, represents what is perhaps the most curious of the five categories. In its report on the conference, the *Revue Internationale de Filmologie* acknowledged the "ambiguity of tasks" facing this group.[23] Since sociological, philosophical and aesthetic concerns all play a part in the considerations of the other four groups, Group 3 was left to more general "reflection" on the application of these fields of filmology. Led by Professors Bayer and Gonseth, the group considered such topics as the aesthetic categories specific to film and the characteristics of filmic "reality." Professor de Waehlens argued that the work of Husserl and Sartre concerning the object perceived and the mental image could be equally well applied to the filmic image. Roland Caillois attempted to demonstrate how the tragic mode in the cinema differs from its other literary manifestations since it depends less on verbal language to convey situations.[24]

The work of Group 2 in the "Evolution of Cinematic Empiricism" involved the practical task of organizing the means for an international exchange of filmological research.[25]

The concerns of the five groups overlapped almost constantly, placing the efficacy of the categories in question. As the *Revue* put it,

Even before the end of the Congress, the richness of points of view had begun to break down boundaries. The phenomenological problems relative to the filmic image applied to the research of Groups 1 and 5. The report of John Maddison, applying to both psychology and sociology, brought these two disciplines together in a method of inquiry. It was found impossible to separate in any rigorous way the viewpoint of expression as an aesthetic fact from that of expression as a language.... The abandonment of the normative viewpoint sent the pedagogues of Group 5 to the side of the researchers in Group 1 charged with historical studies on the cinema's past. Group 2... outlined a system for the international exchange of documents and bibliographic information covering all branches of filmology.[26]

Despite the difficulties in grouping, the interchange among various disciplines around the subject of the cinema meant that the Congress' work was a success. Although the participants remained closely attached to the concerns of their own work in their specific fields, the categories represented a new way of grouping these concerns, no matter how awkward.

Besides the presentation of a wide variety of issues and ideas, and the attempt to organize them in some workable form, the Congress initiated the creation of an International Bureau of Filmology charged with coordinating international research in the field, maintaining contact between researchers, and helping to create national filmological organizations in other countries. [27] In June 1948, this Bureau met to establish itself as a permanent organization. Locating its provisional headquarters at the Sorbonne, the Bureau assembled an international, though entirely French-speaking, group of officers, with Professor Gonseth of the Ecole Polytechnique Fédérale of Zurich as President, Professor A. Michotte van den Berck of the Royal Academy of Belgium as Vice-President, and Mario Roques as the designated officer. [28]

Filmology as an international movement flourished in the period immediately following the first Congress, making headway in a number of European countries. Almost immediately the *Revue* acquired an international slant, regularly offering articles from scholars in Belgium, Switzerland, Poland, England and Italy. On November 21, 1947, BBC radio broadcast a discussion of the Congress by John Maddison and Dr. R.C. Oldfield of the Institute of Experimental Psychology at the University of Oxford; [29] and in the Fall of 1948, at the same time that the Institut de Filmologie was officially attached to the Sorbonne, a similar Institute of Filmology was created at the Instituto de Investigaciones y Experiencias Cinematográficas in Madrid. [30]

Institutionalizing Film Study: Institut de Filmologie

On January 8, 1947, barely two months after its opening meeting, the Association pour la Recherche Filmologique founded the Institut de Filmologie as an organization for the scientific study of film. This was the first official step toward introducing filmology into the curriculum of the French university. By assembling a Board of Directors including Henri Wallon, Léon Moussinac, Etienne Souriau and Raymond Bayer, under the presidency of Mario Roques, the Institut guaranteed itself a legitimacy in the eyes of the academic community and the Minister of Education. [31]

Less than a year later, on September 20, 1948, the Minister officially approved the attachment of the Institut de Filmologie to the Université de Paris, under the Faculté des Lettres of the Sorbonne. Gilbert Cohen-Séat, though not a professor himself, was appointed official administrator of the

Institut. At the same time, an official two-year course of study in filmology was created, leading to a degree from the Université de Paris.[32]

The Institut was divided into four sections: (1) Psychological Studies, (2) Technical Studies, (3) General Filmology and Philosophy, and (4) Comparative Studies. Each section was presided over by an influential member of the board and included among its lecturers some of the most prestigious names in French academia. The section devoted to Psychological Studies was directed by Henri Wallon, who delivered lectures on film and child psychology. Other lecturing members of the faculty concerned with youth and education included Mme. Hélène Gratiot-Alphandéry of the Institute of Psychology, C. Lebrun, director of the Musée Pédagogique, and Dr. René Zazzo. Paul Fraisse of the Ecole des Hautes Etudes and Yves Galifret comprised a subsection on physiological and experimental psychology, which devoted its efforts to empirical studies of filmic perception. Another subsection treating medical psychology was comprised of Dr. Georges Heuyer of the Clinique de Neuro-Psychologie Infantile and Dr. Serge Lebovici of the Paris Hospitals. Finally, the lectures of Professors Georges Friedmann of the Conservatoire National des Arts et Métiers and of Henri Lefebvre of the Centre National des Recherches Scientifiques made up a subsection on collective and social psychology.[33]

Cohen-Séat himself headed the section on Technical Studies, which was devoted to a historiography of the cinema, treated in lectures by Cohen-Séat, Georges Sadoul and Léon Moussinac. Sorbonne Professor Raymond Bayer led the section on General Filmology and Philosophy, which included two subsections devoted to aesthetic/linguistic approaches to film: "General Morphology" and "General Aesthetics of Effects." These included lectures by Bayer, Cohen-Séat, Strasbourg Professor Pierre Francastel, soon to be recognized as one of France's most important theorists on the sociology of art, and Sorbonne Professors Pierre-Maxime Schuhl and Henri Gouhier. The area of "Filmic Anthropology" was represented by Sorbonne Professor Griaule, and included, under the subsection "Ethics and Ideology," a lecture by Maurice Merleau-Ponty on "The Signification of the Cinema." The final section, "Comparative Studies," directed by Mario Roques, encompassed a variety of lectures on comparative aesthetics by such people as Souriau, Sadoul and Roques.[34]

Each of the faculty members provided one or more lectures for classes held three times a week at the Sorbonne. Special work sessions were scheduled once a week, on Saturday mornings.[35] In addition, research laboratories were provided for the use of the Institut by the Ecole Pratique des Hautes Etudes, rue Gay-Lussac, and by the Henri-Rouselle Hospital, rue Cabanis.[36] Although the course of study in filmology was designed to take two years, many students took longer, due to the amount of practical and experimental work required of them. At the end of their coursework, students submitted a thesis prepared under the supervision of one of the professors and subject to approval by a jury of the Institut faculty.[37] One of the first such theses, prepared by a student of the Institut who graduated in July 1951, appeared in the *Revue* in 1952. Written by Jean Tribut under the direction of Souriau, the thesis was a study in comparative aesthetics entitled "Painting and Film."[38]

In April 1951, the Faculté des Lettres of the Sorbonne awarded its first Doctorat d'Etat, the highest degree granted by the French university, for film. The recipient was Marie-Thérèse Poncet, whose doctoral thesis was entitled *L'esthétique du dessin animé* [*The Aesthetics of the Animated Cartoon*].[39] Had the Institut de Filmologie not been attached to the Faculté des Lettres at this time, it is unlikely that such a thesis could have been presented for approval. With the support of Souriau, however, the thesis was passed with "very honorable" mention.[40]

Poncet's thesis demonstrated still a further debt to filmology. The first part of her study was entitled "The Cinematic Fact," in reference to Cohen-Séat's categories, and entailed a brief history of film animation from Emile Reynaud to Walt Disney, a study of the technical developments and evolution of animation as a means of expression, and an examination of the phenomena (persistence of vision, etc.) upon which this expression is based. The second part of Poncet's study, "The Filmic Fact," involved an analysis of specific animated styles and sequences according to a number of "values" suggested by the work of Souriau, who acted as her advisory professor on the thesis.[41] An accompanying study presented by Poncet, *Etude comparée des illustrations du Moyen-Age et des dessins animés* [*Comparative Study of Illustrations from the Middle Ages and Animated Cartoons*], further employed Souriau's comparative method.[42] Both Poncet's thesis and her accompanying study were published almost immediately; and in 1956, her third book on the subject, *Dessin animé, art mondial* [*Animated Cartoon, World Art*] appeared.[43] Poncet's subsequent writings on animated and "experimental" films continued to appear in such publications as *Technique Cinématographique* and *Image et Son* throughout the 1950s and 1960s.

From Poncet's aesthetic analysis of cartoons to the psycho-physiological testing carried on in the laboratories of the Institut, the first several years of the Institut de Filmologie offered the kind of variety encouraged by Cohen-Séat's *Essai*. During 1951-52, the fourth year of the Institut, lectures ranged from Georges Sadoul on the history and evolution of cinematic means of expression to René Zazzo on the correspondence between intelligence levels and the comprehension of films; from Henri Wallon on the perception of time and space in the cinema to Henri Gouhier on the comparison of acting in film and in the theatre; from Etienne Souriau on filmic forms and the comparative method to Georges Friedmann on film and sociology.[44]

As filmology began to focus its concerns more heavily on empirical/ experimental research in the years which followed, the range of topics offered at the Institut became somewhat narrower. Fewer but more in-depth classes were taught by a smaller and increasingly specialized faculty. A perusal of the subjects taught at the Institut in 1958-59, for example, reveals a preponderance of classes on experimental research and broader questions of mass communication. Cohen-Séat taught a class entitled "Techniques of Communication and Visual Information," and coinstructed a course with Serge Lebovici on filmological studies of perception and the affective reactions of viewers. A single course devoted to social, cultural, anthropological and historical considerations of the cinema was taught by Georges Friedmann, Georges Sadoul and Edgar Morin. Souriau provided the only course dealing with aesthetic and linguistic examinations of the "filmic fact," aided by Roland Barthes.[45]

The development of the academic curriculum of filmology can be traced quite closely in the issues of the *Revue,* which devoted much space to the Institut and its research, and which published a number of the lectures of the faculty in one form or another. In fact, it is the *Revue* which provides our clearest record of the development of filmology, both as a curriculum and as a problematic.

Defining the New Science: La Revue Internationale de Filmologie

While planning for the First International Congress, the Association pour la Recherche Filmologique devoted much of its effort to the publication of the first two issues of the *Revue Internationale de Filmologie.* The masthead of the *Revue* lists Cohen-Séat as Director, a title corresponding to his position as Secretary-General of the Association and as founder of the movement itself. The journal's editor was in fact a twenty-nine-year-old graduate of the Ecole Normale Supérieure and teacher at the *lycée* in Marseilles, Marc Soriano.

In an introductory article to the first issue of the *Revue,* dated July-August 1947, Soriano attempts to explain the goals of the journal. Returning to Cohen-Séat as a source, he comments on the *Essai*'s "remarkable humility": "a thousand questions are raised, a thousand appeals are launched in the direction of already established disciplines, but it is a matter of nothing but questions and appeals." One might ask, he continues, what kind of science it is

> which claims no formula, advances not even the slightest theorem, which refers endlessly to psychology and biology, sociology and aesthetics, seemingly resolved from the beginning to be nothing but a chapter added to the other sciences.[46]

The explanation for Soriano is simple: "Filmology is oriented in so many directions because its object of study is so vast." It is not filmology which must be humble; the established disciplines are in fact dependent upon it: "it must be admitted that filmology corresponds to a real need. The most eminent philosophers attach their research to ours, suggestions come to us from all countries."[47] In order to illustrate his point, Soriano cites a number of scholars interested in filmology in Britain, Belgium, the United States, Hungary, Poland, Czechoslovakia, Sweden, Switzerland, Italy and Peru.[48]

Anticipating the great strides to be made by the new-born science, Soriano clarifies the intentions of the journal:

> The *Revue Internationale de Filmologie* proposes to keep the public current with research undertaken and the results obtained by this ever-growing group of researchers. Nothing concerning the cinema will be alien to us. But our point of view is that of science; it will not be restricted to describing, but to understanding, to explaining that which enables us to foresee—for a more or less distant future—the hope, or if you prefer, the threat of [the cinema's] intervention.[49]

The first issue of the *Revue* reflected the eclecticism of filmology in its formative period, offering a variety of articles on topics which ran the gamut of concerns touched upon by the new discipline. Several of the articles attempted general introductions to specific branches of filmology, such as Henri Wallon's "Several Psycho-Physiological Problems Posed by the Cinema,"[50] Raymond Bayer's "The Cinema and the Human Sciences,"[51] and Etienne Souriau's "Nature and Limit of Positive Contributions of Aesthetics to Filmology."[52] The topics of other studies ranged broadly from an article by Georges Sadoul on the films of Georges Méliès and the beginnings of film language,[53] and an essay by Henri Agel comparing filmic and literary structures,[54] to a report by Dr. Jean Dalsace on the instructional uses of film in medicine[55] and film producer André des Fontaines's statement on those "industrial facts" of film production he considered essential for the filmologist.[56]

What links these widely different approaches is a common root in the project proposed by Cohen-Séat; and a perusal of the articles in the first issue reveals constant references to his *Essai,* which serves as a touchstone for defining filmology and for refining its conception for application.

The major concern in this regard is Cohen-Séat's distinction between the filmic fact and the cinematic fact, which is discussed again and again throughout the first issue. In his introductory article, entitled simply "Filmology," Mario Roques observes that the filmic/cinematic distinction is quite complex, and that the close interrelationship of the two types of phenomena is what gives the cinema its humanist potential, since "the individual filmic fact tends to become a social fact and this social fact extends from group to group, from country to country until it becomes a human fact."[57] Jean-Jacques Riniéri, on the other hand, emphasizes the distinction, substituting the polarity of the "aesthetic fact" and the "sociological fact" for Cohen-Séat's filmic and cinematic.[58]

The most perceptive and thorough critique of Cohen-Séat occurs in an article by Maurice Caveing, a young Marxist student of the Ecole Normale Supérieure. Caveing criticizes Cohen-Séat's inductive method of arriving at a "rational knowledge of the cinema."

> In defining the end and the objects of filmology [i.e., two types of phenomena: filmic and cinematic] at the very moment he constitutes it as a new problem, M. Séat [sic] has already launched it on a path where it will employ no other method than a quasi-undefined ennumeration of constantly changing materials, accompanied by the hope of a schematization which will be completed at a point in a still distant future.[59]

Thus Caveing criticizes the notion of a science arrived at by preconceived notions of categorization. He elaborates his argument by explaining how the study of a complex reality like the cinema cannot actually constitute a science in the sense of the natural sciences. Filmology, writes Caveing,

> consists neither of the delineation of an 'order of research' (which is what makes the facts which enter into this order seem ungraspable and innumerable), nor of the analytic reduction of the cinema to its simple 'elements' in order to reconstitute them rationally.[60]

Unlike the objects of natural science, film is "a human reality, which is to say an *anti-natural* reality in the sense Hegel employs the words."[61] For this reason Caveing argues for the abandonment of a purely empirical methodology in favor of a dialectical approach.

> M. Séat indicates the need for a '*totalization* of the cinema.'... Yet for a method whose principle is abstraction, totality is revealed only in terms of a total which is all ennumeration and addition. If one wishes to grasp the essense of the cinema, it is necessary not to move toward totality, but to pose it from the beginning and to keep it present at all stages of research. In other words, this totality is itself dialectic.[62]

More than any other critique of the *Essai*, Caveing's article identifies the assumptions underlying Cohen-Séat's approach, criticizing the fact that, "far from conveying any hope for a solution, his distinction does nothing but pose the problem."[63] Caveing's objection arises from the way in which the question has been phrased:

> We are not contesting this view as one contests a definitive theory: M. Séat gives us no such thing. We contest it inasmuch as it may become what M. Séat proposes: that is, a working hypothesis. We contest it as a method. This method is abstraction: it consists precisely of isolating, if only as a working hypothesis, a moment of a real process—which is not concrete unless taken as a whole—in order to create an object of study. An essentially fruitless method, despite all the later attempts to *recompose* the matrix of the process and to systematize the results: in the interval, the essence of the process, that is the very object of research, has vanished.[64]

Caveing's critique, the most pointed and specific to appear in the *Revue,* was never explicitly answered, although two issues later Cohen-Séat tacitly acknowledged the article when he wrote,

> ... one cannot make [the cinema] an object of study unless one first takes it as a whole, indistinctly, in all the reality of its own existence. Although some aspect, some particular or partial characteristic may fall more easily into some traditional category, one cannot separate it from its origin. Moreover, the cinema cannot be considered only in its current state and at the present moment; it is also necessary to consider it organically, in terms of the way in which it has become what it is.[65]

Jean-Jacques Riniéri's comments on Cohen-Séat also reflect a Marxist perspective, but one tempered by Christian and humanist biases, and therefore more sympathetic than Caveing's. Riniéri compares Cohen-Séat's projection of a "universally homogenous" evolution of the cinema to the Marxist conception of history:

> ... that it is man who makes his history, who forges his destiny, but that he has a calling, which is to say that reflection can discern in the course of history certain privileged directions or trajectories according to which practice must be oriented if it is to be constructive and fruitful.[66]

Thus Riniéri supports Cohen-Séat's scientific positivism by linking it to the idealism attached to Marx's economic determinism. Noting that filmology also ascribes to the Marxist tenet that "practice is inseparable from theory," Riniéri emphasizes the social mission of filmology while denying any direct attempt

> to dictate conduct to the men of the cinema. Our efforts must first provoke research; and it bears repeating that it is still not a question, and may not be for some time, of providing solutions, but of revealing new problems. That is, once man himself is at stake—and we have tried to demonstrate that he holds the most important position in the cinema—research cannot be purely disinterested.[67]

Curiously, Riniéri was not the only writer at this time to assert that filmology had no intentions of placing demands on the producers of films. In his statement to the first meeting of the Association, Roques also asserted that filmology did not intend to affect the work of industry personnel directly, but merely to present them with information on the effects of their work.[68] The opening article of the second issue of the *Revue* further asserts this detachment from the industry:

> Against all attacks on an imaginary imperialism, filmology needs no defenders. Its object is not the technique of the screen, and it has no intention of imposing itself as some kind of judicial council for filmmakers. The very definition of the filmic fact restricts the field of the new-born science to the human effects of the image; and it is no wonder that to accomplish

this study specialists have gathered from throughout the human sciences.... Their ambition is not the ability to instruct the filmmaker. It is a matter of studying the viewer. Their viewpoint is that of the patient.

The human sciences do not create their object, and that is what makes them so urgent. We suffer before we acknowledge the existence of medicine and we do not await the psychiatrist in order to dream.... It is the sick man who brings us to discover man.... Perhaps the filmic fact, by the collective dimension it entails, requires an even greater urgency.[69]

Clearly the rhetoric of this passage equates the film viewer with a sick patient awaiting the doctor, and the cinema with the illness which requires immediate professional attention. Yet to follow this logic one step further, in light of the hands-off attitude towards the industry, it seems that the writer is suggesting that the goal of the filmologist is to study the disease and possibly to treat the patient, but not to interfere with the cause of the illness. It is an indication of the curious position occupied by filmology, with its conflicting commitments to scientific detachment and social action.

The second issue of the *Revue,* dated September-October 1947, appeared at approximately the same time that the First International Congress took place. A number of the articles appearing therein are papers which were delivered at the Congress, and they are arranged according to the Congress' five categories. Group 1, "Experimental Research," is represented by articles from Georges Poyer, Professor at the Sorbonne, on "Differential Psychology and Filmology,"[70] and by Marc Soriano's "Methodological Problems Posed by the Cinema Considered as New Psychological Experimentation."[71] No articles appear under the "Cinematic Empiricism" heading of Group 2. Group 3, "Aesthetics, Sociology and General Philosophy" is by far the most strongly represented group, accounting for almost half of the articles in the issue. These include papers from Poland, Belgium and Switzerland, as well as three articles prepared by students of the Ecole Normale Supérieure who had studied in a special filmology group which had existed for almost a year prior to the official attachment of the Institut de Filmologie to the Sorbonne. The category for "Comparative Studies," Group 4, includes an article by linguist Marcel Cohen on "Writing and Cinema"[72] and a call for an "abstract cinema" by Sorbonne Professor Pierre-Maxime Schuhl.[73] The fifth group, "Normative Studies," is represented by one article on the educational value of the cinema[74] and two papers on film and the practice of psychoanalysis.[75]

The third issue of the *Revue,* a special double issue numbered 3/4, appeared one year later, in October 1948. An opening statement from the editors briefly notes the changes which had taken place since the second issue:

Since the First Congress of Filmology, circumstances have changed profoundly. In a matter of a few months, the Center for Filmological Research and the Institut de Filmologie at the Université de Paris have been created. For its part, the definitive establishment of the

International Bureau is a *fait accompli*. These events were foreseen. The speed with which they have taken place, however, was not exactly predicted. Indeed, the best of plans, envisioned for a slightly more leisurely evolution, have been upturned.[76]

The most immediate result of this activity in terms of the *Revue* was a delay in publication and a resulting double issue.

This third issue also reflects a shift in interest toward more strictly empirical studies, which is indicated by the editors when they proclaim that "the properly scientific documentation of the Bureau will occupy a predominant place in the upcoming issues of the *Revue.*"[77] Although many of the articles in issue 3/4 were also prepared for or grew out of the International Congress, the Congress' five categories were abandoned. In addition, the preponderance of studies on aesthetics, sociology and philosophy in the second issue has given way to a majority of articles devoted to phenomenological studies of filmic perception, including two of the most significant papers on this subject ever to appear in the *Revue:* A. Michotte van den Berck's "The Characteristic of 'Reality' in Cinematic Perception,"[78] and Dr. R.C. Oldfield's "The Visual Perception of Images in the Cinema, Television and Radar."[79]

The increased emphasis on experimental scientific research continued until 1954, when it became almost the sole interest of filmology reflected in the *Revue,* indicating the end of the eclectic, formative period of the movement. Describing this perceived tendency in 1948, the editors noted that the *Revue* "would assume a more and more specialized character...further from the public and, from a certain standpoint, from the ordinary problems of the cinematic spectacle itself."[80] Once again, the demands of science move filmology further from social action, which nevertheless remains something of a *raison d'être.*

The next three issues, which appeared at a rate of one issue per year, clearly demonstrated this trend. Of the 14 articles included in the fifth issue (October 1949), 10 were devoted to perceptual studies, experimental psychological research employing film, and psychoanalytic perspectives on the cinema. Only two articles represented the approach of comparative aesthetics, with individual essays devoted to pedagogical and linguistic concerns. A large portion of this issue reflects the work of a filmological conference held in June 1949 at Knokke-le-Zoute, Belgium, including a list of research proposals which emerged from the meetings. Professors Michotte van den Berck and J. Colle, both of the University of Louvain, René Zazzo and Paul Fraisse of the Ecole des Hautes Etudes, Henri Wallon and Yves Galifret of the Collège de France, and Mme. H. Gratiot-Alphandéry of the Paris Institute of Psychology, all proposed empirical studies of the perception and comprehension of film, with a special emphasis on young viewers. In addition, at least two sociological studies requiring survey methods of audience samples were proposed.[81]

In keeping with this empirical emphasis, the fifth issue begins with a readers' questionnaire in both French and English, intended "to collect information of extant investigations on filmology and on Institutes, Associations, etc. who could do such research."[82] Included in this questionnaire is a very clear statement of the project of filmology as it was understood three years after the publication of Cohen-Séat's *Essai*:

> [The objects of filmology are] the reactions of the audience during the film and also, naturally, the conditions which produce those reactions. By 'audience' we do not mean only a collection of individuals sitting in front of a screen, but also the groups on which the film can have an effect, either directly or indirectly, through the 'atmosphere' it creates.
>
> Those effects or those conditions can be physiological, perceptual, intellectual, aesthetic, ethical or social.[83]

Still acknowledging the importance of a number of fields of study, filmology in 1949 nevertheless placed a primary emphasis on the empirical study of the film viewer.

The emphases of the sixth issue (1950) were clearly sociological and psychological, although individual articles maintained a certain variety of approaches, ranging from Kracauer's analysis of national stereotypes in Hollywood films[84] to the use of film by René and Bianka Zazzo as an experimental tool for testing the level of comprehension among adolescents.[85]

Issue 7/8 (1951) included a major article by Souriau on the "filmic universe" and the vocabulary of filmology,[86] with the remainder devoted to pedagogical issues and reports on psychological and perceptual tests. The first illustrated number of the *Revue*, this issue provides eight pages of plates to accompany a photographic (but non-filmic) study of composite portraits and the typology of faces by David Katz of the University of Stockholm,[87] and four pages of electroencephalograph readings attached to a report on the testing of the effects of rhythmic, intermittent light impulses on the central nervous system.[88]

The year 1952 saw a resurgence of activity in the *Revue*, with three issues (9, 10 and 11) appearing in a single year. Each of these issues seemed purposely devoted to a different aspect of the filmological project. Issue 9 (January-March 1952) was entirely concerned with psychological research and with the use of film in teaching. Three of its six articles were reports on psychological tests regarding the comprehension of the film story by children,[89] the memory of a film retained by the viewer,[90] and the reactions of maladjusted children to the film.[91] Issue 10 (April-June 1952) marked a definite departure from the trend of the past several issues. The first of its four articles was an overview of the application of sociology to the cinema, written by Georges Friedmann and Edgar Morin.[92] The other three articles were specifically concerned with comparative aesthetics and included a general essay on the subject by

Souriau.[93] It was the first time since the second issue that aesthetic concerns dominated the pages of the *Revue,* and it would also be the last. Issue 11 was entirely devoted to reports on international filmological research in Italy, Great Britain, the United States and France. In his introduction to the issue, Cohen-Séat remarked on the rapid dissemination of filmology:

> Everywhere "the slowness with which the thinking of governments," according to the formula of Henri Laugier [in his introduction to Cohen-Séat's *Essai*], "adapts itself to the technological progress of scientific civilization" seems little by little to have undergone a sort of acceleration. On the other hand, we have seen the sudden rise of all sorts of enterprises aimed at defining, in one important area or another, a course of action regarding the cinema. In brief, the inventory of active curiosity about the problems which concern us has for some time shown considerable changes.[94]

In terms of practical social action, Cohen-Séat expresses a belief that the problems raised by filmology "are on the way to overcoming the last obstacles on the level of public policy, before becoming what they always were: problems of civilization, and as a result, 'political' on the highest scale." Given the readiness of the public powers to intervene in the course of the cinema's evolution, he adds, "one can imagine nothing more grave than the lack of precise facts or ill-founded information."[95] Thus the project of filmology was defined once again as the provision of hard, scientific data upon which policy could be based.

Cohen-Séat's assessment of filmology at the end of 1952 was reflected quite strongly in the three issues of the *Revue* appearing in 1953. Issues 12, 13 and 14/15 concentrated entirely on reporting the "precise facts" derived from experimental research and empirical studies, and on discussing issues of social control in order to determine the course of action to be taken by filmology. Of the six articles appearing in issues 12 (January-March 1953) and 13 (April-June 1953), five reported on studies of filmic perception, memory and identification. The sixth article, written by Edgar Morin, provided statistics on the international film audience.[96] The topic of issue 14/15 was censorship and the social effects of the cinema. Articles ranged in opinion from London Professor Gertrude Keir's "The Role, the Necessity and the Value of Cinematic Censorship"[97] to an essay by Morin in which he argues the lack of any conclusive data to support the so-called "dangerous effects" of the cinema.[98] The questions raised in this debate were directly related to the concerns of filmological experimentation on the effects of film on the viewer. By issue 16 (January-March 1954), the concerns of the journal seem clearly united by a common social project and a common task of compiling empirical data, a task to which nearly all subsequent issues of the *Revue* were devoted.

The publication of Etienne Souriau's *L'univers filmique*[99] in 1953 provides a further indication of a definitive split in filmology. Representing the aesthetic and comparative branch of the Institut de Filmologie, which had moved its base from the Faculté des Lettres at the Sorbonne to the Institut d'Art on the rue Michelet, Souriau's anthology included articles by seven other scholars including Henri Agel and Jean-Jacques Riniéri,[100] none of whose writings would ever again appear in the pages of the *Revue*.[101]

Only in the oversized issue 20/24 (1955), reporting on the Second International Congress of Filmology held at the Sorbonne February 19-23, 1955, did the *Revue* again broaden its concerns even slightly. Although the Congress included such "non-scientific" film scholars as Georges Sadoul, Léon Moussinac and André Bazin,[102] the areas of research treated there indicate that the narrowed scope of interests in the *Revue* quite accurately reflected the direction of the Association and the International Bureau. This shift is evident in the difference between the five categories of research specified by the First Congress and the seven groups represented at the Second:

Group I:	Problems of Cinematic Projection and Psycho-physiological Effects
Group II:	Study of the Reactions of Viewers to Projection and Its Effects on Their Behavior
Group III:	Sociological Problems of the Cinema
Group IVa:	Film in Teaching
IVb:	Film in Professional Training and Work Study
IVc:	Film as an Instrument of Scientific Research
Group V:	The Integration of the Cinema in Social Life and Leisure: Normative Problems
Group VI:	Comparative Problems of the Cinema and Other Forms of Expression
Group VII:	Comparative Problems of the Cinema and Television[103]

The emphasis had clearly become the empirical treatment of psycho-sociological questions: the testing of effects on the viewer and the practical application of film toward desirable ends. General reflections on aesthetic and philosophic questions were eliminated, and only Group VI represented an area which would include the branch of filmology associated with Souriau. Even so, the parallel Group VII, comparing film and television, suggests a shift of interest in the comparison of film and other forms of expression, from aesthetic issues to issues of mass communication.

Following this Second Congress, the leadership of the filmological movement shifted from France to Italy, where the method of experimental psychology took precedence.[104] The *Revue Internationale de Filmologie* continued publication in France through issue 39, dated October-December

1961. That same year the First International Congress of Research on Visual Information took place in Milan, where the remaining filmologists assembled to expand their project officially to include the scientific study of mass communication.[105] In 1962, the *Revue* became *Ikon,* and its headquarters were transferred from Paris to Milan. Strongly grounded in an experimental/empirical methodology and a concern for the practical application of communications research, *Ikon* has maintained the subtitle *La Revue Internationale de Filmologie,* and continues to publish articles in Italian, French and English to this day.

Critiquing Filmology: Views from outside the Circle

Once filmology had become institutionalized in France as an academic discipline and as a methodology, the reactions of the film community were extremely mixed. Except for a few articles appearing outside the *Revue* but written by those within the filmological circle,[106] most of the commentary on filmology found the new enterprise somewhat questionable. Some seemed pleased by the legitimation of film implied by the success of the movement, while remaining suspicious of its methods. Others praised the filmologists with only the slightest reservations. Still others found the notion of a science of film either laughable or threatening.

One of the earliest articles on filmology in a popular periodical appeared in the October 7, 1947 issue of *L'Ecran Français,* a weekly trade paper devoted to the film industry in France. Taking the opportunity of the First International Congress to discuss the new science of the cinema, author Jean Vidal traces the year-long history of the movement, attempting to present for the general public a straightforward explanation of the problematic posed by filmology. Quoting Wallon and Cohen-Séat on the subject of the movement's scientific basis, Vidal questions whether filmology can become "an independent science or if it will simply embrace a certain number of already known facts which are emphasized by the cinema."[107] Vidal finds filmology's orderly approach to the cinema and its preference for concrete facts over abstract speculations encouraging; nevertheless, he expresses concern about the practical applications of so admittedly erudite an activity.

> Our only worry is that, from the outset, [filmology] adopts a highly confidential character; that it professes an annoying penchant for the solemnities of the Sorbonne, university diplomas, philosophical hermeticism; that it displays little enthusiasm for the prospect of associating itself with the work of the cinema's practicians.[108]

Thus, Vidal's enthusiasm for the serious treatment of the cinema is somewhat tempered by a suspicion of filmology's status as a science and by a distaste for its aloofness.

These criticisms were elaborated even more strongly the following year in André Lang's book *Le tableau blanc*. Given the similarities between Lang's stance and that of filmology regarding the social role of the cinema, *Le tableau blanc* displays a sympathy for the mission of the new science, while being quite critical of the haughty, philosophical tone of Cohen-Séat's *Essai*. As Lang puts it,

> It is a book of philosophy written for philosophers. One of those books which is indecipherable to the profane film lover and which the critical establishment has treated with great respect, undoubtedly to excuse their not having read it carefully. [109]

Lang's primary quibble with filmology concerns the relationship of theory and practice; that is, he questions whether there are any practical applications for its philosophical project.

> It is obviously flattering to the cinema to see philosophers thinking about it and translating it into their own language. But the practical interest of such an examination is still unclear. We must wait for the next two volumes [of Cohen-Séat's *Essai*] to better explain (and I say it without irony) what 'filmosophy' can do to help solve the problems raised by the existence of the cinema. [110]

Of course, Lang's question was never answered in the way he had hoped, for the projected volumes of Cohen-Séat's *Essai* never appeared. Nevertheless, as filmology moved away from its eclectic stages in the early 1950s, becoming less philosophical overall and more empirical, its practical applications became somewhat clearer, mainly in its emphasis on the pedagogical uses of the cinema.

Lang's final word on filmology is hopeful. "As much as one fears that the filmologists will remain prisoners of their terminology," he writes,

> we must wish them good luck, and M. Cohen-Séat must be saluted for his ambitious attempt which cannot help but—sooner or later, no matter what reactions it may provoke—have beneficial results. [111]

A rather different attitude was taken in the attack on filmology launched in the pages of *Cahiers du Cinéma*. Under the editorial direction of André Bazin, *Cahiers* began publication in 1951 as a journal of film criticism for film devotees, and quickly became the major forum for a new generation of cinephiles to display their fascination for the unsung classics of world cinema to the detriment of contemporary French films. The bias of *Cahiers* was humanist and aesthetic, and its emphasis on film authorship indicated an approach to art drawn from the traditional tenets of the humanities. Bazin and the writers for *Cahiers* and its rival journals such as *Positif* represent a postwar resurgence of interest in the cinema contemporary with the development of filmology, but entirely separate from it.

As a result of their radically different approaches to the same object, *Cahiers'* assault on filmology is perhaps the most scathing to appear. Written by Florent Kirsch and ironically entitled, "Introduction to a Filmology of Filmology," the critique appeared in the fifth issue of *Cahiers,* during its first year of publication. Acknowledging the "material and moral success" of filmology, its legitimation within the academic institution and its support by a distinguished group of scholars, Kirsch expresses less concern with the "content" of the new discipline than with the means of its rapid and unprecedented acceptance.

> Even before the university administration had decided to install projection facilities in its amphitheatres—no better equipped in this respect than they were in the Middle Ages—the Institut de Filmologie was already holding classes there. Where the tenacious conviction of several thousand French schoolteachers has yet to succeed in introducing the cinema into the pedagogy of the primary schools, M. Cohen-Séat has, without apparent difficulty, convinced the upper echelon of higher education, the ministerial offices and the students of the rue d'Ulm. Better still, he has managed to extend this movement internationally, arousing enthusiasm from Buenos Aires to Moscow. ... To attribute such a general success against the prejudices of the universities, political obstacles and personal reticences solely to the diplomacy of M. Cohen-Séat defies all probability.[112]

Twice before, Kirsch notes, the cinema enjoyed the favor of French intellectuals: first with the *Film d'art* during the first decade of the century; then during the 1920s, with the activities of the avant-garde. In both cases, intellectuals were placed in the position of supporting a transformation of the cinema, running headlong against the inertia of the film industry. What Cohen-Séat understood, explains Kirsch, was that an intellectual movement like filmology could not hope to succeed this time "except by avoiding any confusion between the study and the production of the 'filmic object.'"[113] The success of filmology was therefore a product of the disjunction of theory and practice.

Cohen-Séat's first tactic, according to Kirsch, was to assure the intellectuals "that filmology was nothing but a new synthesis of classical disciplines, of grammar and sociology."[114] Thus the scholars whose knowledge lay in the various traditional fields of the university were justified in turning their attention to a subject they knew little about. In this way, Kirsch explains, Cohen-Séat "makes indifference an intellectual virtue, misunderstanding a factor of scientific prudence, and near ignorance an *a priori* condition."[115] Moreover, Cohen-Séat's appeal to the intellectuals "calms professional scruples by radically distinguishing between the practice of filmology and a knowledge of the cinema."[116]

> There is no need for a distinguished filmologist to have any . . . familiarity with the classics of the screen. . . . Far from such ignorance being a debilitating obstacle, filmology makes it a virtue. Of course, it is not forbidden for filmologists to attend the movies, but it is not particularly recommended either, since such superfluous baggage might risk obscuring the new-born science. Filmology is the study of film-in-itself, independent of its history and its works. Nothing indicates that Pavlov liked dogs. If certain studies someday require of those who undertake them a minimum of attendance in the darkened movie houses or even in the ciné-clubs, this will indicate nothing but a kind of accidental case, as when the professor of sociology is obliged to smoke a peace-pipe with a Sioux chief. . . . the cinematic virginity of the scholars, which is made to seem so desirable, is a symbol of the new science, of the rigor of its method and the antisepticness of its laboratories.[117]

Kirsch supports these claims by pointing out that Cohen-Séat's essay on the cinema

> carefully eliminates all film titles, any reference to a precise cinematic event, and the slightest reference to the name of even the best known movie star; we are referred to Plato, Bergson, Euripides, Shakespeare, Molière or Tabarin, but restricted to only the hint of allusions to the names of Lumière, Méliès and René Clair.[118]

Kirsch attacks this obtuseness of Cohen-Séat as an overcompensation of two "inferiority complexes": "that of the university concerning the cinema, and that of the cinema with regard to the other arts, which have long been recognized and consecrated by official instruction."[119] Ultimately, says Kirsch, Cohen-Séat plied the intellectuals with flattery by adopting their terminology and by confirming their "conviction that the practice of philosophical rhetoric is infinitely more useful than a familiarity with the cinema."[120]

Representing the viewpoint of those most impassioned by the cinema as an art form and those most proud of their encyclopedic knowledge of films, Kirsch's essay is a frontal attack by that faction of the film community most hostile to the project of filmology. The filmologists were seen not only as dilettantes to be ridiculed, but as a threat to the cinephile's position. It is with this threat in mind that Kirsch concludes the attack:

> It should be astonishing that these truths are only now being spoken publicly, were it not that a complicity of silence exists on this subject, confirming the sociological character of the phenomenon. From the first symptoms of its success, filmology has not convinced only by its success: it has resorted to a reign of terror. . . . Filmology has quickly acquired the authority of a secret society already filled with the highest dignitaries. Chances are that M. Cohen-Séat had more difficulty in selecting than in convincing.[121]

Retreating only slightly, Kirsch admits that filmology might, at some future date, display some real value, especially in terms of opening the cinema as a legitimate field of inquiry for students. Nevertheless, the obstacles to such progress are viewed as precisely those elements of Cohen-Séat's rhetoric which led to filmology's unprecedented success.[122]

When four years later *Cahiers'* rival film journal *Positif* reported on the Second International Congress of Filmology held in February 1955, it was with less urgency and less bitterness than Kirsch, but with equal irony. Comparing the filmologists to the blind men examining the elephant, Xavier Tilliette, author of the *Positif* article, concludes that, if not completely blind, the filmologists were very often quite myopic. "The cinema," he explains,

> serves as a pretext for learned elucubrations, if not digressions by scholars who, coming late to the cinema or cultivating it for their relaxation, intrepidly apply their techniques and experiments to some aspect or other of the cinematic—or better, filmic (according to the distinction dear to M. Cohen-Séat)—reality. [123]

Reiterating the suspicions expressed by Kirsch regarding the dilettantism of filmology, Tilliette wonders less at the success of the movement than at the absurdities of filmological research.

> It is quite interesting to know that films have been projected to dogs similar to those of Pavlov, or that one can divide up the *Aeneid* like a screenplay, but ultimately this doesn't carry us too far. The hybrid character of this research and work is indicated by the copious reports of this latest Congress and of filmology in general, which has yet to find its place in the sun. [124]

Tilliette is quite willing to acknowledge that "a lot of ingenuity was deployed in most of the reports," but he seems most encouraged by the participation of such critic-historians of the cinema as LoDuca, Agel and Amédée Ayfre, [125] who actually comprised a very small proportion of those at the Congress. Of the 62 reports presented, only 5 could be said to represent aesthetic and critical concerns. [126] Nevertheless, it is clear that Tilliette no longer perceives filmology as a threat in the way Kirsch did. In fact, the inability of the movement to maintain the momentum of its first years is understood as a kind of failure.

Cahiers also ran an article on the Second Congress which was not only more sympathetic than that of *Positif,* but which marked a total reversal of opinion since the time of Kirsch's attack on filmology four years earlier. Written by Amédée Ayfre, whose paper on the aesthetics of Italian Neorealism had been one of the handful of critical-aesthetic studies presented at the Congress, the *Cahiers* article attempts to assess and to reconcile some of the differences between the cinephile and the filmologist. Instead of attacking Cohen-Séat, Ayfre explains the rhetorical project in which the founder of filmology had been involved:

> ... ten years ago, when M. Cohen-Séat laid the first stones of the edifice of filmology ... [he] purposely accentuated the most severe aspects of its facade in order to encourage serious scholars, his colleagues at the university. A laboratory is not a place of pleasure. An institute

of filmology is not a cinema. But on the other hand, he knew every other aspect of the cinematic problem all too well not to note the impossibility of absolutely disinterested research and the necessity of uniting theory and practice.[127]

Ayfre's claim that filmology sought such a unification directly contradicts Kirsch's observation that the separation of theory and practice was the very foundation of Cohen-Séat's project.

Ayfre presents the schism in the film community, between the cinephile readers of *Cahiers* and the filmologists attending the Congress, in terms of a caricature growing out of such articles as the one by Kirsch.

For the cinephile, the filmologist was an old university professor who had certainly seen no more than five or six films during his entire existence, but who quickly discovered at the end of his life that, if he was a philologist, the cinema could be compared to a language, or if he was a psychobiologist, one could consider the cinema as a stimulus and scientifically study its effects on viewers. Any piece of celluloid would do as experimental material and no particular knowledge of cinematic history or aesthetics was required. What was required was a knowledge of philology or psychobiology. These disciplines—and perhaps a few others, provided they had a chair at the Sorbonne—demonstrated to the ignorant that everything previously said or written—supposing it was known that something had been written—was strictly worthless, and should in any case be thrown into question until the scientists had delivered their conclusions. Henceforth, nothing serious could be written on the cinema unless it was duly certified by filmology.

It is understandable that the young cinephile who knew every detail of the succession of diverse cinematic schools from Lumière to Clouzot, who never confused Elia Kazan and Laslo Benedek, who could recite the credits of *Le jour se lève* and the filmography of Pudovkin by heart, who had read every volume written by Sadoul, the English editions of Eisenstein, the major texts of Bazin, and who subscribed to *Cahiers du Cinéma*—it is easy to understand, as I said, that this young cinephile, faced with the image he had of the filmologist, could have no doubt of his own superiority. It was clearly he who grasped the true cinematic culture and not this pedantic and tiresome newcomer, this pseudo-scholar who didn't even bother to situate his subject before embarking on the aspect to which he wished to devote his research.[128]

The satiric overtones of Ayfre's assessment suggest that the cinephile no longer took the threat of filmology quite so seriously by 1955. For by the time of the Second Congress, the increased specialization of filmological concerns suggested that the science of the cinema was not to become the monolith feared by such critics as Kirsch.

In fact, in the years to follow, filmology received less and less public attention. Those articles which did treat the movement were explanatory in much the same way as the first articles to appear on the subject a decade earlier. A 1957 article entitled "Do You Know the Institut de Filmologie?"[129] and a 1959 report called "Filmology: What is It?"[130] both of which appeared in film-related journals, indicate that public awareness of filmology, even among those most likely to know about it, had waned severely.

Part II

Theory and Practice of Filmology

5

The Filmic Fact: Aesthetic and Linguistic Considerations

As originally defined by Cohen-Séat, the filmic fact "consists in expressing life, the life of the world or of the mind, of the imagination or of beings and things, by a *determined system* of the combination of images."[1] In this sense, the filmic fact is not simply the material of the film itself—the celluloid, the individual shots, the projection at 24 frames per second—but the combination of these elements as a system of expression. It is to this extent that the study of the filmic fact encompasses both aesthetic and linguistic considerations.

Examining Cohen-Séat's conception in 1947, Marc Soriano attempts to clarify the relationship of the filmic material to the system which organizes it:

> The filmic fact is the realm of the image and the sounds which accompany it . . . considered independently of the audience for which it is destined. . . . That is to say that the filmic fact is of the technical order and that it remains in the realm of the celluloid. [Cohen-Séat] does not attempt to deceive himself about the arbitrariness of such a choice, that this light and sound signify nothing without the public who sees and listens.[2]

Yet isolating the filmic fact from sociological and psychological considerations enables the examination of the formal and systematic elements of the film. As Christian Metz would later explain,

> The importance of this distinction between the cinematic and the filmic facts lies in the fact that it allows us to restrict the meaning of the term 'film' to a more manageable, specifiable signifying discourse in contrast with 'cinema' which . . . constitutes a larger complex. . . . [3]

It is precisely the signifying elements of film to which Cohen-Séat refers in Part II of his *Essai* when he writes that the filmic fact refers to "all the elements of film susceptible of being taken for its signification as a sort of absolute, from the point of view of intelligibility or from the point of view of aesthetics."[4] Thus, he refers to such filmic elements as the shot, which "offers a certain practical unity, " and the sequence, "which presents itself rather naturally as a kind of whole."

On this point Soriano poses a rhetorical question:

> the filmic fact, you say, is of the order of the image; now you define it as a unity of signification. In that case, signification supposes a mind which conceives it, not purely as an image, but already interpreted. Thus, the filmic fact is already confused with the cinematic fact, which assumes the presence of an audience which conceives and interprets.[6]

Still, Soriano defends this distinction on the basis that Cohen-Séat's definition is "conventional":

> What is assumed by the filmic fact is elementary; it is the naked and purely logical line which brings together a limited number of images. It does not imply this fringe of interpreting the transference of feeling created by the presence of the audience. Thus the filmic fact can be posed as an autonomous unity, without becoming confused, due to its purely relational signification, with the cinematic fact.[7]

In 1971, Christian Metz explored this precise point in *Language and Cinema,* concluding that the signifying system of film is a part of the cinematic fact, but a very special part which he calls the "cinematic-filmic," in opposition to the "cinematic-non-filmic" aspects of the cinema as a social and economic institution.[8] Soriano acknowledges that the isolation of the filmic fact involves an artificial distinction which removes the phenomenon from its context. Nevertheless, both Soriano and Metz find the filmic fact a useful methodological distinction which allows the examination of film both as art object and as signifier.

In order to appreciate the filmological treatment of the filmic fact as aesthetic object and as a signifying discourse, it is necessary to understand the rigorous method which characterized and linked the approaches of aesthetics and linguistics during this period. Of key importance in this respect is the work of the most influential figure in this field of filmology, Etienne Souriau, whose rigorously "scientific" approach to aesthetics provided the thrust of filmology's approach to the filmic fact.

The Aesthetic Method of Etienne Souriau

Etienne Souriau was born in Lille in 1892, the son of philosopher and aesthetician Paul Souriau. In 1920, he graduated from the Ecole Normale Supérieure with a degree in philosophy, and five years later received his doctorate. He taught philosophy at Aix-en-Provence and Lyon from 1926 to 1941, at which time he became a lecturer in philosophy at the Sorbonne. In 1945 he succeeded Charles Lalo to the Sorbonne's chair of Aesthetics and Science of Art. Three years later, he founded the *Revue d'Esthétique* with Lalo and Raymond Bayer, and remained the director of the publication until his death in 1979.[9]

Souriau was firmly committed to a science of art and his work represents one of the most consistent, ambitious and rigorous attempts of the period to systematize aesthetics. Best remembered for his notoriously titled *Les deux cent mille situations dramatiques* [*The Two Hundred Thousand Dramatic Situations*], [10] in which he calculates precisely 210,141 situations in the classical theatre arising from six elements and five methods of combination, Souriau combined a desire to provide a rational, scientific system for studying aesthetic facts with a philosophical stance related to, but ultimately quite different from that of existential phenomenology. As F. Sciacca pointed out in 1954, Souriau was "independent of all existing schools, but nevertheless involved in the contemporary problematic." [11]

Souriau's most fully realized explication of his aesthetic method, *La correspondance des arts*, appeared in 1947, contemporary to the birth of filmology. In this work, he proposes the comparative method as the means by which the various arts may be categorized and their common elements isolated and studied. Souriau recognizes nine basic arts, of which the cinema is the newcomer, but an undeniable part of the group. [12] Each of these arts represents a different mode of existence, a different "universe" of art. In one of several definitions of art he offers in this work, Souriau writes:

> ... art is what a symphony and a cathedral, a statue and an antique vase have in common; it is what allows a comparison between painting and poetry, architecture and dance.... [13]

For Souriau, art is the *activity* common to these works, and that activity is *instauration,* a term central to his philosophy.

As explained by Luce de Vitry-Maubrey in her study of Souriau's philosophical work, instauration is "the ensemble of processes which result in establishing a being whose presence, solidity and autonomy of existence are incontestable." [14] In the case of aesthetics, this being (*être:* existence; entity) is the work of art itself, which is the result of the "instaurative activity"—a term employed by Souriau as another definition of art. The instaurative activity, he writes,

> is the ensemble of approaches—oriented and motivated—which tend expressly to conduct a being [*être*] ... from birth or from an initial chaos to complete, singular, concrete existence, attested by its indubitable presence. [15]

Therefore, instauration refers less to the processes employed than to the directive force behind them. As Souriau explains,

> ... it is less a question of the ways in which these approaches are executed in practice than of the mind which animates them.... Art is not only what makes the work; it is what guides it and orients it. [16]

Here Souriau's concept of instauration bears a striking resemblance to the notion of "intuition" forwarded by Benedetto Croce in his turn-of-the-century treatise *Aesthetic as Science of Expression and General Linguistic.*[17] Croce's thesis that "the artist's creative act is the intuition of a novel form which is independent of the manipulation of the materials which embody the intuition"[18] is shared by Souriau to the extent that the latter views instauration as a kind of universal positive principle. That is why Souriau prefers the term "instauration" (a synonym of "institution" and "establishment") to the more familiar concepts of "invention" or "creation." As Vitry-Maubrey explains,

> Certainly, in all instauration there is invention and creation. But creation, strictly employed, indicated the art of pulling something from nothingness, an act which cannot be understood except in terms of divine power. Whereas an instauration is accomplished by employing materials of varying richness, where 'materials' refers to data which can be entirely psychic. Thus, the poet does not, properly speaking, create his poem, for he first employs 'the words of the tribe,' and then his lived experiences, his feelings, his dreams. . . .[19]

Daniel Charles explains instauration as "the movement by which man—if he does not create, in the strictest sense of the word—discovers and actualizes certain types of pre-existent morphemes, accomplishes what nature has sketched or outlined, brings to realization that which is everywhere latent *(inchoatif)*."[20] These morphemes are the "materials" to which Souriau refers, and they are essential to the process of instauration, which "governs man by means of things and things by means of man."

Souriau's notion of instauration bears certain similarities to the basic concepts of phenomenology,[21] especially to the extent that phenomonology has been called the "philosophy of creative intuition."[22] From Edmund Husserl to Henry Bergson, phenomenology maintains the view that "man is the being by which the world is partly revealed, and in some ways created, known and given meaning."[23] Beginning from the premise that the world exists prior to any attempts to understand it, phenomenology embarks upon the task of apprehending it intuitively, free from all *a priori* conceptual constructs. Central to this approach is the idea that the "apprehending subject is an intentional consciousness."[24] The creative intuition of this intentional consciousness resembles Souriau's notion of "instaurative wisdom," which he explains is the "intuitive acquisition and possession, and the active and concrete usage of directed knowledge."[25] For Souriau, as for phenomenology, man is not the creator of the world, but the consciousness by which the world is *realized.*

Vitry-Maubrey points out that Souriau was a philosopher before he was an aesthetician, and "it is the search for a solution to the problem of knowledge which led him to meditate upon art (and not inversely)."[26] The basis of Souriau's philosophy was the instaurative dialectic, "in which the *making* of art offered itself to philosophical thought as the model of a realization of the real *in* and *for* the work, by the instaurative process."[27] It is in this sense that art, the instaurative activity, is directed toward the realization of a being, for "the work of art is a unique being, as unique as a human being in its singularity."[28]

Souriau explains this aspect of art in terms of the idealist concept of finality, which refers to the desired end of any positive activity. Thus, the directive, intentional aspects of the instaurative activity dictate the finality of art.

> But this means nothing unless it is clear that this is a very specific type of finality—one whose expression is an existence, and more particularly the existence of being, a singular being with all that word implies of richness, of originality, of the unique power it possesses, of irreplaceable and present being.[29]

Art differs in this way from most human activities, which are oriented toward events. Art is directed toward the production of beings, and thus toward ontology.

> This distinguishes art from technique.... And this criterion of ontological finality which defines the instaurative activity is sufficient to distinguish the two types of activities. Undeniably, they cooperate; they are mixed. But in precisely this manner, they may be analyzed and separated according to their dosage. For if all art has its techniques, almost all technique can be elevated to an art.[30]

Given a definition of the arts as those human activities which "are expressly and intentionally creative of things, or more generally of singular beings, whose existence is their end,"[31] Souriau is able to propose measuring the *amount* of art in a given object, distinguishing it from technique or from any other human ends. This project he proposed as early as 1929 in *L'Avenir de l'esthétique*[32] *(The Future of Aesthetics)* and reprised in his first major article on filmology.

Souriau rejects the criterion of beauty in defining the finality of art, since beauty is a subjective value which depends upon an impression created in the subject.

> To define art by this final impression is to go in a circle. When we say that art has for its direct, constitutive goal at least the sufficient, and if possible, the full, ardent and triumphant existence of a singular being—its work—the circle disappears.[33]

Here Souriau carries the positivist line of existential phenomenology past the point of the notion of intentional consciousness. As Mikel Dufrenne explains Souriau's logic,

> That life is an accomplishment of nature, and art an accomplishment of life—this introduces another theme: that the contemporary emergence of man and of the world is also an

accomplishment of nature; and that it was necessary that man be born in order to give birth to the world, in order to realize the truth at work in the cosmos.[34]

Such a conception fits well with the existentialist notion that the world and the mind are both of nature and thus participate in its laws. Yet Souriau's positivist understanding of these laws leads him away from the phenomenological project of the description of essences free of all *a priori* conceptions. Instead he subscribes to a scientific positivism, which demands analysis and categorization, a project rejected from the inception of phenomenology by Husserl:

> ...when it comes to the psyche, to subjectivity understood as individual subjectivity, or an existent in isolation, or as involved in history and in a social community, it is clearly absurd to confer upon it an objectivity similar to that of the natural sciences.[35]

Souriau's systemization of aesthetics requires a certain empirical objectivity clearly at odds with this tenet of phenomenology.

Souriau's science of art is based upon his conception of the art work as a unique, singular being:

> Each of these works is also a whole world, with its spatial, temporal and also its mental [*spirituelles*] dimensions—real or virtual, inanimate or animate, human or superhuman—with the universe of thoughts that it awakens and animates within the mind. And it is this universe which comes together in the being, the presence.[36]

Each art comprises its own universe, its own cosmological unity, which is a mode of the instaurative activity. The fine arts are thus "activity-types" which

> have no other characteristic than that of being more concentrated, purer and more immediately oriented toward autonomous productions of a certain gratuitousness and a certain existential purity. Around them is a halo of less pure activities, involving less complex requirements, creating works whose usage is not limited solely to the status of having been made for art....[37]

In this way, the hierarchy of the arts is established by Souriau in terms of purity of essence. It is a further indication of the desire to quantify art based on instauration and finality.

Yet all the arts, and all the works of art which fulfill the definition, are a part of a larger "cosmic unity" or, in Souriau's terminology, "a gigantic *plérôme* of diverse beings."[38]

> I maintain that it is a whole world; and it is from this world that we must derive a hierarchy, a morphology, and constituent norms—I would gladly say, its comparative anatomy and physiology.[39]

It is therefore the comparative method which forms the basis of Souriau's science of aesthetics. In pursuing this method, he emphasizes the importance of the *correspondence* between various art works—that is, the commonality of the instaurative activity as manifested in each. Explaining the project of the science of aesthetics, Souriau writes,

> If we wish to penetrate to the heart of each art, to seize the primary correspondences, the considerations whose principles are the same among the most diverse techniques, to discover laws of proportion or schemas of structure as valuable to poetry as to architecture, or to painting as to dance, we must institute a whole new discipline . . . and one which is truly scientific.[40]

Souriau's proposal of a system of correspondences in the arts and his aspirations toward discovering its laws and structure represent a clearly positivist undertaking. At the same time, it is a project which closely resembles the activities which would soon be classified as "structuralist." On this subject, Robert Scholes writes,

> The perception of order or structure where only undifferentiated phenomena had existed before is the distinguishing characteristic of structuralist thought. In this mental operation we give up our general sense of all the observable data in exchange for a heightened sense of some specific items. These fewer items, which we now see as related, forming a system or structure, give us a greater conceptual power over the material under scrutiny. From one point of view, all such operations are reductive: we give up a sense of some 'whole' in order to perceive some formal relation of 'parts.'[41]

In his search for correspondences, Souriau is willing to acknowledge a reductive aspect to his comparative aesthetics, much as Scholes does with structuralism. As a result, Souriau never insists that his method can answer all the questions raised by art.

> . . . we pretend neither to impose a method nor to argue the prerogative of a specific theoretical conception. Nor do we maintain that comparative aesthetics is the unique or sole method which is worthwhile in aesthetics. A variety of methods and viewpoints are legitimate to this exciting study in which psychology may participate as well as sociology, and the science of forms as well as metaphysical meditations on art.[42]

Souriau's conception of aesthetics is primarily structural and scientific; yet it reflects a relativism which conceives of science as a philosophical unity analogous to the cosmological unity of the art work. As René Passeron explains Souriau's philosophical stance on this issue,

> . . . each philosophy in its singularity is endowed with universality since, thanks to it, all men may come to the viewpoint which it opens onto the world. It is at once a universe which is singular and universal; and it is thus that philosophy has the characteristics of a work of art:

"this universe is exactly like a law for a certain type of realization"[Souriau, *L'instauration philosophique,* p. 365]. Diverse philosophies are no more mutually exclusive than diverse works of art.[43]

This relativism clearly informs the first article written by Souriau for the *Revenue Internationale de Filmologie.*

Etienne Souriau and Filmology

In the article "Nature and Limit of Positive Contributions of Aesthetics to Filmology," which appeared in the first issue of the *Revue,* Etienne Souriau attempts to assess the role of his own discipline in the development of the new science of film, without asserting aesthetics as the sole, or even the preferred method of approach. Noting that films serve a number of ends (economic, didactic, etc.), he asserts that aesthetics is applicable to film only insofar as it is "finalized toward an artistic character."[44] This is neither a matter of evaluating the "artistic intention" of a work, nor is it a matter of evaluating its artistic quality.

> It is knowing to what extent these results arise from the quantity of real art effectively put into the work; of that art, I say, quantitatively evaluated (even measured) according to rigorous objective and technical methods. Undoubtedly, this will not be easy.[45]

In this sense, the work of aesthetics is to identify and tabulate the "fact of art." Representing only one part of the filmological field, aethetics then functions in coordination with other disciplines, each with its own defined end, each adding information which is accessible only through its specific methods.

To illustrate the way in which aesthetics works with other disciplines, Souriau asserts the example of psychology.

> If, for example, psychology tells how the feelings—even aesthetic feelings—are provoked, promoted and excited, such as those for the beautiful, the sublime, the comic, the ugly, the ridiculous, the nostalgic ... or what kinds of laws of sensation and perception intervene in the contemplation of a moving, luminous or colored image, it cannot tell us in what way these feelings or these laws can and should be employed in the overall orientation so that this ensemble constitutes an authentic work of art.[46]

In much the same way, Souriau continues, aesthetics has a contribution to make to the sociological perspective.

> ... sociology can easily study how individual psychological reactions in the movie theatre are modified by the fact of the collectivity of the public, even how judgments—or more exactly 'opinions'—are formed regarding the value of the work presented; but not how all these facts may be controlled, employed and even directed in view of the accomplishment of the artistic mission.[47]

Souriau then demonstrates the role of aesthetics in descriptive filmological analysis by defining two degrees of filmic form: the first degree refers to those formal qualities of the image on the screen (composition, proportion, balance, contrast, shape) independent of all signification; the second degree refers to "morphological appearances," including not only the illusions of volume and depth, but also the representation of people, objects, places, etc.[48] Between these two degrees of form, Souriau posits five principal correlations: (1) *juxtaposition* or *coexistence*, in which first degree form functions independently from the representation, creating, for example, a pleasing composition of light and shadow; (2) *representative evocation*, where first degree form enhances the representational level, as in the use of a high angle shot to achieve a certain effect; (3) *harmonious relationship*, in which the formal qualities of the image and the representation enhance one another, as in the illusion of texture; (4) *contrast*, where the first and second degrees of form contradict one another, for example, in an artistic heightening of pathos or irony; and (5) *symbolic*, where the formal qualities of the image overlay the representation with a further signification.[49]

In addition, with regard to the viewer's perception of movement and time in the cinema, Souriau distinguishes between "objective time," referring to the actual time elapsed during the projection of a film, and the time of the "filmic universe," or the fictional time of the narrative as it is presented to the viewer.[50] This distinction bears important similarities to Bergson's distinction between exterior time, which is relative, and interior time, which is absolute. For Bergson, the reality seized "through intuition is the reality of our inner self flowing through time, making time."[51] On a philosophical level, then, Souriau's distinction between filmic time and objective time relates the filmic universe to unified, interior time, and enhances his definition of the work of art as a being realized by the instaurative process.

The ways in which the mind relates these various levels of the filmic fact— which are distinguished, Souriau asserts, only by the science of aesthetics—is the province of psychology. Film takes the interior mental processes of the viewer in hand and directs them according to "constant psychological laws, laws which it utilizes without breaking."[52] It is for psychology to clarify these laws, to study the effects of filmic rhythm, and to reveal the "final affective impression" (we might say "gestalt") of the film upon the viewer. Emphasizing the importance of experimental psychology, he concludes, "it will be necessary to undertake investigations of the viewer's psycho-physiological state (skin, blood pressure, reaction time, etc.) before and after the projection of a given film."[53] Such data would provide important information for the further work of aestheticians.

As for the relationship between aesthetics and sociology, Souriau suggests the example of the formulation of opinions by the film audience which are independent from "the real artistic value of the film, or more exactly, the quantity of art put into the work."[54] With this in mind, he takes the example of an audience's perception of the "photogenic" quality of a film actress, which includes at least four separate factors: (1) the average consensus regarding a woman's beauty held by a society; (2) the actual physical qualities of a given actress, in comparison with the social consensus; (3) the physical qualities of the actress with regard to the camera's point of view, including such factors as lighting, makeup, costume and decor; and finally (4) the judgments of the audience during the projection of the film, bearing less on the character played by the actress than on a perception of the model who plays that character.[55] The criteria by which the audience's opinions are formed combine both aesthetic and sociological factors; neither field alone could therefore provide an adequate understanding of the question.

If filmology is to approach its subject seriously and comprehensively, Souriau concludes the article, it is "obliged to take into consideration the artistic *finalization*, to the extent that it is actually present in a film."[56] For if film has

> eternal value, the value of permanence and of indefinite survival . . . it depends precisely and exclusively upon the value of art. Among all the values (economic; psychological, in terms of feeling; sociological, either in terms of amusement or as a didactic or practical tool) which the filmic reality may have, the single value which is unconditional, absolute and indefinitely valuable is the value of art.[57]

Granted this artistic value of film, it still remains for Souriau to define the specific artistic qualities of the film, for "each art has its own domain, its own means, and its specific ends."[58]

Souriau pursues this question in an article appearing in the *Revue* some five years later, "Filmology and Comparative Aesthetics," which begins with a strong methodological assertion:

> The Science of Art is a positive discipline. And one of its most powerful methods, both for apprehending facts in their most delicate yet concrete terms, and for penetrating nature and significance in depth, is the comparative method.[59]

In pursuit of this definition by comparison, Souriau provides an "experiment" in which he analyzes the "translation" of a given subject in film and in another art form. He elaborates on this notion of "translation" in a 1967 preface to his *La correspondance des arts:*

> Without adopting too lightly the currently popular theory that art is a language, we can nevertheless note an analogy between the diversity of artistic endeavors . . . and the diversity of languages, in the philological sense of the word. By employing the word 'comparative' to refer to that which seeks resemblances and differences between a statue, a cathedral, a

symphony or a vase, we have simply sensed and admitted that there was some analogy between the translation of an artistic idea in painting, in music and in sculpture, and the translation of a literary idea—for example, poetic—into French, English or German. Each language brings with it its own resources and inadequacies, and treats the subject according to its own means.[60]

Based on this notion, Souriau can assert that

...the adaptation, the transfer and the transformation into a filmic work of a work originally in another art form constitutes a concrete filmological experiment whose examination opens important paths and, of course, laws and structures proper to the filmic universe, as motivations of filmic reactions.[61]

Souriau's experiments in this article involve the analyses of translations between film and the theatre, the novel, painting, choreography and such spectacles as the circus and the music hall. Admitting that such comparisons are both fundamental and general, he calls for a

great number of filmological studies to be done on the bases indicated above, in the form of *monographs* studying in detail (which we cannot do in this already lengthy study) a certain precise case of adaptation, by carefully noting all the transformations required by filmic recreation, and by researching, one by one, all the aesthetic and technical reasons. Except for the introspection practiced by the artist on himself, it is the only truly experimental process which can be employed in apprehending the fundamental processes of *cinematic thought*.[52]

A year later, in his anthology *L'univers filmique,* Souriau nevertheless published the results of still another type of filmological experiment on "Rhythm and Unanimity," this one bearing directly on the reactions of an audience to a specific film and employing the empirical methods of the psychologist and sociologist to do so. Noting that the film audience is often considered as a single being with collective, normative reactions, to which all individual variations are viewed as "aberrant," Souriau describes a test intended to provide data for determining whether the collective reaction is "a simple addition of individual reactions or a sort of global unanimity."[63] The test sought to compare the reactions of individual viewers to the rhythm of a film, thus studying the correlation between filmic time and individual interior time.

Fourteen subjects—all students of the Institut de Filmologie—were shown the film *Le Ciel est à vous.* At regular intervals of 20 seconds a number was called out and the subjects were asked to note whether the film at that point seemed too slow, too fast or just right. The responses were remarkable for their similarity. Often, when only a part of the group noted that the film seemed too rapid, for example, the next notation would confirm this judgment with a unanimity among the group.[64] Despite the number of variables unaccounted for and the obvious similarity among the group of student subjects, Souriau asserts the remarkable correlation of perceptions of filmic rhythm, especially in those sections where the rhythm was judged by the group to be just right. For Souriau, this unanimity suggest an ideal shared by individual viewers which corroborated "rather powerfully the idea of effective instauration of a common psyche by means of seeking and obtaining an appropriate rhythm."[65] This marks the only occasion on which Souriau attempted to prove the assertion of ideal cinematic form through the empirical testing of an audience.

In fact, Souriau was largely outside his fields of expertise when it came to such an experiment. His understanding of the science of art involved the methodical comparison and analysis of art works; and it was the rigor of his method and the strictness of his terminology which made this pursuit "scientific." As he wrote in the pages of the *Revue,*

> ... if a science is not uniquely, according to the celebrated formula of Condillac, 'a well-made language,' it at least requires and supposes such a language. To refuse the effort necessary to establish this language, to adopt it, to take it and to use it in a correct and normal manner is to be condemned in advance to the realm of badly posed questions, vague researches without positive results, poorly drafted observations, and provisional and confusingly heuristic studies.[66]

This statement appears as an introduction to one of Souriau's best-known and most influential articles on filmology, "The Structure of the Filmic Universe and the Vocabulary of Filmology," which was originally delivered as a lecture at the Institut de Filmologie in 1950. Here Souriau undertakes his most thorough analysis of the filmic universe, providing a rigorous definition of seven levels of filmic reality.

His definition of the filmic universe goes beyond the mere distinction of the cinematic art from other arts. Each film, he asserts, creates its own universe, with its own rules, systems of belief, characters, settings, etc. This is just as true of a Neorealist film like *Bicycle Thief* as it is of a fantasy film like René Clair's *I Married a Witch*. Souriau refers to this unique realm specific to each film as its "diegesis," a term he borrows from Aristotle, and which Souriau uses to include all the elements of story and narration.[67] In contrast to the film's "diegesis," Souriau poses the reality of the "screening space," which encompasses everything given within the film frame itself, "the play of light and darkness, the forms, the phenomena which are visible there."[68] This distinction is almost identical to that made in his earlier article between first and second degree form. Yet here Souriau expands his analysis of filmic reality much further.

First, he defines *afilmic reality,* which is the real and ordinary world independent of the film, everything outside of that which is encompassed by filmic reality. Such a definition is necessary, Souriau argues, since it is "constantly necessary to refer the filmic universe to this type of reality ... and this term will make verbalizing this reference easier."[69] He then distinguishes from the afilmic the level of *profilmic reality,* which is the reality photographed by the movie camera. "All that I see on the screen (even an animated cartoon) has been created by the photography of a real, physical object," Souriau observes. "It is this object which I call profilmic."[70] Thus, he begins by defining two levels of reality exterior to the film itself.

The third type of reality he refers to as *filmographic,* which encompasses the film as a physical object, "existing and observed on the level of . . . the celluloid."[71] The filmographic therefore includes all techniques, such as editing, which affect the film as material object. This level of the film is distinct from the fourth, the *screenic* or *filmophanic reality,* which involves the projection of the film on a screen. It is the filmophanic level, Souriau notes, upon which the great majority of filmological study is focused. The study of filmic time, for example, is "the result of the dual factors of the filmographic material and the movement of the projector," and therefore falls within the realm of the filmophanic.[72]

Probably the most important distinction Souriau makes is the one which begins his analysis of the levels of filmic reality: the distinction between the filmophanic (screenic) level and the *diegesis,* which is the imaginary world created by the film, encompassing "everything which concerns the film *to the extent that it represents something.*" Therefore, the fifth level of filmic reality is the *diegetic,* "that type of reality *supposed* by the signification of the film."[73] Souriau offers the following examples of the contrary, yet coexistent realities of the profilmic and the diegetic:

> Everyone understands what is meant when we say that, in the studio, these two sets (for example, the chateau and the shack) are next to one another, but that in reality (in the story) they are 500 meters apart; that the scene of the brawl and that of the lovers' rendezvous in the shack were shot on the same day, when in reality (in the story) they are supposed to have taken place a year apart.[74]

This distinction is essential in discussing the filmic fact, for only by positing a diegetic reality can Souriau move from a discussion of the material components of the film to the level of filmic signification, which occurs only in conjunction with an audience.

The sixth level of filmic reality defined by Souriau moves one step closer to the audience. These are the elements he refers to as *spectatorial facts,* including "all subjective phenomena brought into play by the psychic personality of the viewer."[75] Once again employing the example of filmic time, he distinguishes between "filmophanic time," which is objective and measurable, and "spectatorial time," which is subjective and which refers to a personal perception of the pacing of a film.[76] It is therefore the spectatorial factor which concerns Souriau in his empirical study, "Rhythm and Unanimity." Given a normative interpretation of filmic signification, he continues, "errors" of interpretation fall within the realm of spectatorial factors.[77] Furthermore, spectatorial phenomena last beyond the length of the film itself and encompass the reactions of the viewer to a particular film and its conscious or unconscious effects upon him/her. Such phenomena also begin prior to the projection of a film, as when an advertisement arouses the interest of the viewer and affects his/her attitude toward the film.[78]

Souriau's seventh and last level of filmic reality is *creatorial,* referring to considerations of the creator(s) behind the film. Admitting that concerns about the filmmaker's intentions are, strictly speaking, outside the filmic universe, he nevertheless asserts the creatorial level as a point of reference.

> It is a matter of a sort of residue or refuse, which is also subjective: for example, everything which might be in the mind of the film's creator, which was not achieved, which did not succeed, which is not available in the objective givens of the film, nor in spectatorial subjectivity.[79]

The inclusion of this level is important to Souriau since it corresponds to the intentionality of the instaurative process and to the film's finalization. That is, it includes considerations of the film's economic, propagandistic, pedagogical or artistic ends; and it is therefore a factor which enters into the calculation of the quantity of art in a film.[80]

Souriau's analysis of the levels of filmic reality is almost certainly his most significant contribution to filmology. Reiterating certain points in a later article in *L'univers filmique,* he develops several hypotheses based on his distinctions. For example, he discusses the general attempt of films to correlate perceptive (spectatorial) rhythms with representative (diagetic) rhythms, concluding that the "psychic allure" of film arises largely from the fact that its rhythm is "finalized" as a "psychic rhythm."[81] In addition, he observes the differences between the perception of the viewer and the view offered to the eye by the camera. The camera's view, he observes,

> functionally and perceptually assures a harmonious relation between the filmic universe and the "I" of the viewer. But here there is not only an operative act.... There is a constitutional finality which animates and orders the universe.... [Everything] is ordered and presented, hidden or revealed, relative to our point of view.[82]

Carrying this analysis of the viewer's relationship to the screen further, he notes that the view offered the audience is constantly displaced by editing; yet these displacements are "never interpreted as diegetic events,"[83] but as a part of the rules of film signification, which, as Metz notes, is a direct prefiguration of the semiological notion of the code.[84]

Souriau's work on film forms the core of filmology's aesthetic and linguistic analyses of the filmic fact, dominating virtually every other aesthetic study appearing in the *Revue*. This was due largely to Souriau's rigor and the precision of his analytic method, as well as his preeminence in his field. As Metz has written of Souriau,

> The cinema was not one of his primary preoccupations; he was not a specialist . . . nor did he regard himself as such; he did not devote very many or very lengthy articles to the problems of film. But their quality—as with that of everything he did—resulted in the fact that what was a small thing for him was no small thing for the theory of the cinema.[85]

Aesthetics and the Filmic Fact

As the most influential and productive of the aestheticians who turned their attention to filmology, Etienne Souriau's ideas and methods would permeate much of the research of the filmic fact undertaken by others, although the articles on film aesthetics in the first several issues of the *Revue* are notably eclectic and varied. Still, the comparative aesthetic method proposed by Souriau in the first issue provided the clearest path for others to follow and had the legitimating advantage of a scientific basis. One writer who followed Souriau's lead was Roland Caillois, who examined the correspondences between the filmic work and the theatrical work in two articles, "The Tragic on Stage and on the Screen," and "The Cinema, Murder and Tragedy." In the former article, he explores the "translation" of the genre of tragedy in the theatre and the cinema, noting that it is verbal language which conveys tragedy on stage, while the cinema depends on the tragic image. On stage, the tragic character is seen in the process of taking action, which "makes his behavior readable without introducing us into the soul of the character." Using Fritz Lang's *Woman in the Window* as an example, he observes that the cinematic convention of point-of-view shows us the situation through the eyes of the character in the midst of action.[86] Continuing his examination of film and tragedy in a second article, Caillois observes that, due to the new relationship between the audience and the character, "death in the cinema in not tragic, but only pathetic." Because "the cinematic world is a photograph of the real world," he explains,

> death regains its physical qualities; thus the emphasis on pain, torture and physical cruelty in general. . . . Therefore, it seems that in a world represented as real—which wants to give the illusion of being real—determinism takes the place of the essential role played by Destiny in the spiritual universe of tragedy.[87]

It is interesting that Caillois carries his comparison one step further, in order to lend his aesthetic analysis some sociological significance. He observes that the new myths perpetuated by the cinema, combined with the filmic image, are in fact dangerous, since "the cinema shows us that it is easy to kill, that in any case murder is a solution which exists to resolve certain practical problems."[88]

Also in keeping with Souriau's project are the early articles by Henri Agel, a young writer who would soon become one of the primary exponents of the phenomenological study of film, along with André Bazin. Agel initially turned his attention to the comparison of film and literature. In his first *Revue* article, "Cinematic Equivalences of Literary Composition and Language," he cites passages from the *Aeneid* and from Lamartine which correspond to cinematic conventions such as the "dolly-in" and "dolly-out."[89] The second part of this study, "On the Utilization of Cinematic Syntax in the Explication of Classic Texts," emphasizes the social applications of this method as a teaching tool. Acknowledging that cinematic syntax is far more familiar to the average student than are the classics, Agel suggests that

> if this method is used only when appropriate and with discretion, we have the right to hope for an easier awakening of aesthetic sensibilities in young brains.... The interest and fruitfulness of this method lies in the relationship of the two arts. The mind is forced to discern, bit by bit, the laws and movements of which an intimate knowledge is the foundation of all culture.[90]

Like Souriau, Agel subscribes to the notion that an idea is "translated" in different works of art according to the specific techniques of each. His use of the term "syntax" also indicates the influence of structural linguistics, one of the best organized of human sciences at this time, in establishing a vocabulary for the discussion of filmic expression. A more precisely linguistic analysis of cinematic syntax would await Christian Metz in the 1960s, but Agel already seems to foresee the importance of a rigorous definition of filmic language and rhetoric when he writes,

> To speak of the poetic film: is this the proper way to situate the question? Must we not first study what a *cinematic poem* might be? Here, it is the syntax of the cinema, and the modes proper to its expression, which must be considered first.[91]

For Agel as for Souriau, the key consideration remains the correspondence of the arts, the similar impulse (Souriau's "instauration") manifested in different ways by the cinema, by classic literature and by poetry. It is in this way that Agel can argue the efficaciousness of using recognizable cinematic forms to awaken the aesthetic sensibilities of young students.

More than Souriau, however, Agel emphasizes the social and humanist role of film aesthetics; and Agel's understanding of artistic finality is far more strictly a product of his Catholicism. His 1952 book, *Le cinéma, a-t-il une âme?* [*Does the Cinema Have a Soul?*] begins with the sentence, "For all men who are not absolutely materialist, a number of psychological, moral and ethical givens are charged with a certain coefficient, either visible or latent, which, for lack of a better word, we are obliged to call 'spiritual.'"[92] For Agel, the work of art—

and specifically the cinema—is an opening to this spirituality, and it is this thesis which he develops here and in *Le cinéma et le sacré,* published the following year.[93]

In his discussion of Agel's film writing, Dudley Andrew defines Agel's position as "essentialist,"[94] which is to say that Agel privileges the work of art above the material conditions of its production. As Andrew points out, Agel shares the phenomenological stance of Merleau-Ponty which argues that

> art is a *primary* activity, a natural, immediate and intuitive way of understanding life. All theory is *secondary,* placing primary activities within a schema constructed to make their interrelationships clear.[95]

For Agel, the primary value of art is a link with nature, with existence and with the sacred. Although the rhetoric differs somewhat, his position is similar to Souriau's notion of art as an instaurative activity which makes use of material means, but which is itself directive and finalized toward the creation of an object or being.

Agel's concerns with ethical and spiritual questions situate his work as an interesting bridge between the positivism of Souriau and the humanism of Cohen-Séat. Twelve years after the publication of Cohen-Séat's *Essai,* Agel would reiterate the mission of the cinema in terms almst identical to those originally employed by the founder of filmology:

> Either the cinema will be split by particularism and it will become a failure, or it will attain universality and its role will become fundamental, since it will cement the unity of humanity by carrying forward a 'universal characteristic.' In this perspective, it will become a privileged instrument in the hands of tomorrow's man for constucting his destiny. The cinema would then bring to full existence an 'imaginary civilization,' that is, a civilization which is dreamed and deliberate.[96]

Agel's aesthetic analyses are therefore directed by a desire to see the cinema achieve its proper humanist mission. This means that, for him, there is more involved in the filmologist's work than a scientific quantification of the art in a film. Instead he asserts a social and ethical importance for judging and encouraging the spiritual value of the art work.

> We must still distinguish between works which are nothing but a bitter statement of social reality and those which attain the intemporal pathos and that clarity of inspiration thanks to which drama is elevated above the worldly level.[97]

Therefore, it is not Bazin's phenomenological observation of the ontological connection between the photographic image and the reality photographed[98] which inspires Agel's belief in the cinema's power to apprehend existence; it is the spiritual power of the art work itself which transcends the realist aesthetic.

As Agel writes in his article "Poetic Finality," which appeared in *L'univers filmique:*

> Nothing is less realistic than this art which, by its very technique, delivers everything but the reproduction of the exterior world: the simple fact of its passing onto celluloid is the first stage of this transfiguration; then comes a transposition either into black and white or into colors more vivid or subdued than those in our experience; then there is light, the play of illumination, which heightens or darkens shapes; followed by a diversity of planes (the orchestration of a scene), the framing, the montage, and often the music. Each of these elements imposes upon our always confused and summary apprehension of the world a plastic density and a significance which is precisely what gives the cinema its power.[99]

Thus Agel's position has less in common with the phenomenology of Bazin than with Rudolf Arnheim, who had already observed that the artistic qualities of the cinema were precisely those differences between the film and the world as normally perceived.[100] For Agel, as for Arnheim, the cinema accomplishes an artistic transformation by means of "a metamorphosis of the ordinary givens of perception,"[101] which is, for Agel, what provides the cinema its access to the spiritual. "Even without poetic ambition, and solely by the act of transcribing and orchestrating certain scenes in cinematic terms," he writes, "the authors of films are liberated from the opacity of our universe and we are engaged in a dreamlike and disconcerting world."[102]

It was the definition of this world, Souriau's "filmic universe," which occupied most of the attention of the aestheticians who wrote in the first several issues of the *Revue.* In general, these studies examined the formal qualities of film from the standpoint of what the cinema *should* be, whether in psychological, sociological, aesthetic or philosophical terms.

In his article "For an Abstract Cinema," in the second issue of the *Revue,* Sorbonne professor Pierre-Maxime Schuhl observes that "new inventions, at their outset, are often assessed according to anterior techniques, before conquering their own originality."[103] The cinema, he notes, still remains a prisoner of the functions of photography and portrait art. On the other hand, painting, liberated of its representative function by photography, has been allowed to become decorative and abstract. In the same issue, Jean Lameere makes a similar observation about traditional conceptions of film when he notes that films are frequently judged in much the same way as novels and plays, according to the psychology of the characters, instead of in terms of "rhythms and other plastic qualities."[104] Both authors suggest the possibility of the cinema becoming something it is not, though neither becomes more precise than the term "abstract," employed by Schuhl. In both cases, however, the emphasis is clearly formal; and, to this effect, Lameere cites Raymond Bayer, who situates the question of beauty as "uniquely a matter of rhythms and structural equilibriums common to a number of diverse forms."[105] These are the qualities which Bayer judges to be properly aesthetic; and according to

Lameere, the greatest danger to the cinema as an art form is therefore "the excess of 'realism.'"[106]

François Ricci's article, "The Cinema Between Imagination and Reality," which also appeared in issue 2, takes a stance in opposition to Schuhl and Lameere. Ricci writes of the evolution of the cinema toward the real in much the same terms as André Bazin in his article "The Myth of Total Cinema," which had appeared the year before.[107] Noting that the addition of motion to the photograph, and of sound and color to the cinema has contributed to an increasingly literal imitation of the world, he criticizes those who would deny the realistic tendency of the cinema.

> . . . it is not without paradox that one pretends to defend an art by condemning its logical evolution: born of a desire to aid and compensate the imagination by a mechanical artifice, how can the cinema not await new means of science for more completely satisfying this desire?[108]

Even in the cases of poetic or fantasy films, Ricci continues, "there is a realism more perfidious than that of the most literal documentary, for it is the irreal that it realizes."[109] Here, Ricci's argument touches upon psychoanalytic considerations, comparing the film to the dream and describing the psychological link between the viewer and the screen. It is the essence of the cinema, he writes, "to imagine for me, to imagine in my place and at the same time *outside of me,* with an imagination more intense and precise, and also more convincing, because it is not governed by my will."[110] Given the cinema's function as a dreamlike substitute for reality, Ricci notes that, in sociological terms, the marketing of film as a commodity has fulfilled the wish of the consumer by producing fantasies of happiness. "The success of Hollywood is no accident," he observes. "It signals the path of the norm—which is to say, of course, the most banal, the most simply mediocre—but nevertheless a reference point which is important to keep in mind."[111]

Given the sociological and scientific concerns of filmology from its very beginnings, aesthetic studies remained in a rather precarious position throughout the development of the movement. As is clear in several of the studies above, many of the aesthetics articles which appeared in the *Revue* felt an obligation to ground themselves in either psychological or sociological contexts. For the most part, however, Souriau's methodology and his preeminence provided both their justification and their single strongest point of reference. Yet as soon as aesthetic studies turned their attention to the film audience, they entered the realm of psychology and sociology; and once they concerned themselves with cinematic expression, they raised a whole range of questions touching upon film and communication. As a result, the majority of specific studies of the filmic fact, whatever their points of origin, tended to raise questions of film and language.

Film and Language

In his introductory article to the first issue of the *Revue,* Mario Roques asserts the importance of the question of film and language. "In essence," he writes, "film as we understand it is an intention, a will to communicate feelings and thoughts, quite precisely a language, for there are not only phonetic languages."[112] As employed by Roques, language *(langage)* refers to a variety of sign systems, including the languages of mime, of gesture and of posture. These languages he believes to be essential to an understanding of the meanings attached to the behavior of characters on the screen. Other languages are equally important to the cinema; the language of set decoration, the language of symbols and, of course, the language of techniques belonging exclusively to film. In Roques's discussion of cinematic expression, we can observe a subtle reorientation of aesthetic concerns in the equation of expression and communication. By emphasizing the artistic "will to communicate," Roques does not deny what Souriau would refer to as the instaurative activity; instead, he simply places an emphasis on the *systems* by which works of art are expressive.

Neither Souriau nor Cohen-Séat were comfortable with the term "film language." Souriau displayed little interest at all in a linguistic analysis of the film, although his rigorous analysis of the filmic fact and its levels of reality provided the very basis for such an approach. As Christian Metz noted in his own carefully plotted linguistic analysis of film, *Language and Cinema,*

> Filmology, under the influence of Etienne Souriau, had already undertaken the task of isolating and circumscribing that aspect of film which is pertinent to us here, and had coined the term *filmophanie* (or 'filmophanic level') to designate the film functioning as an object perceived by an audience for the duration of its projection. It is the 'filmophanic' film, and it alone, that we shall call 'film' [for the purposes of Metz's book].[113]

Although Souriau never expressed any intention of placing the film under linguistic analysis, his concern with the "translation" of an idea between media, his attention to structural similarities between art works (especially in *Les deux cent milles situations dramatiques*), and most notably, his interest in the elements of filmic "punctuation" bear strong similarities to the methods of semiology.

Souriau's anthology *L'univers filmique* contains a number of articles which analyze the aesthetic elements of film with respect to their signification. François Guillot de Rode's article on "The Sound Dimension" traces the development of a sound-film aesthetic, and the differences in the means of conveying information in the silent film and the talkies.[114] Jean Germain, professor of music at IDHEC, contributed an article on "Music and Film," in which he analyzes the soundtrack of two sequences from *La bataille du rail,* distinguishing between the uses of noise and music.[115] Such analyses were not new in 1953. In fact, beginning with its first issue in 1946, *La Revue du Cinéma* ran a three-part article by Pierre Schaeffer on "The Non-Visual Element of the Cinema,"[116] and its Autumn 1949 issue was entirely devoted to an analysis of the function of costuming in the cinema.[117]

In terms of the exploration of language and cinema, however, perhaps the most incisive contributions to *L'univers filmique* came from Anne Souriau, daughter of Etienne. In her article, "Filmic Functions of Costumes and Decor," she examines not only the aesthetic values of the elements of costuming and set decoration, but also the ways in which they convey meaning. Citing examples from a variety of French and American films, she carefully explains how these elements function as "rules" of the diegesis, conveying information about plot and setting, psychological indications about characters, and the overall ambience of a scene.[118] These elements, she explains, are "attached to a system of signs, of images having an understood signification, and thus a true cinematic language."[119] Even more basically, she notes that

> The screenic [filmophanic] fact of the first degree (shadows and lights, forms, even colors) is interpreted by the viewer as having a signification, the second degree screenic fact. I see not only a white mass or a green rectangle; I see a sheet of paper or a door. The visual image has a meaning, just like the word-image in the spoken language.[120]

Pursuing her analogy between film and language, Anne Souriau suggests similarities between filmic signification and certain figures of speech. Referring to the figure of metonymy, "a word, and thus an image, used in place of another," she observes that "at base, the cinema is nothing but a continual metonymy" since it constantly shows us effects to suggest causes: "accumulated cigarette butts to express the passage of time, a blossoming branch or falling leaves to suggest spring or fall, a broken object to signify anger."[121] She cites similar cinematic conventions related to synecdoche (a part substituted for the whole), as when a single incident is shown to suggest a wide-spread occurence; and metaphor, when, for example, an object, a costume or a set is used to represent a character.[122] Anne Souriau's article represents one of the strictest applications of her father's aesthetics of correspondence to the film and one of filmology's most provocative texts on filmic signification. Agel's articles on filmic syntax are mere notations of isolated correspondences between literary and filmic techniques in comparison with Anne Souriau's treatment of these correspondences as a system of meanings constantly at work in a signifying process.

In another article in *L'univers filmique* entitled "Succession and Simultaneity in Film," Anne Souriau applies the same rigor to an exploration of the arrangement of shots and sequences. Noting that, on the filmophanic or screenic level, the film unfurls in a sequential fashion, she discusses the means by which the distinction is made on the diegetic level between actions which succeed one another in the fiction and those which are supposed to occur simultaneously.[123] Using a variety of films to illustrate her point, she concentrates mostly on a Tarzan film, which she selects almost at random and defends in a note, saying

> Is *Tarzan* not serious enough as a filmological example? Fine. And that is why we have chosen it. . . . In studying the films for the Thursday afternoon (or Saturday night) audience, we cannot separate ourselves from the world and the mass audience in order to enclose ourselves in an ivory tower . . . without losing sight of the ensemble of filmic facts.[124]

Pursuing her analysis, she distinguishes between certain arrangements of shots cut together to indicate a flashback, to develop a visual theme, to parallel certain types of occurrences, or to suggest an action which is repeated many times.[125] To a large extent, she adds, these different meanings arise from the sequential linking of shots by means of certain transitional "artifices."[126]

> Thus the filmmaker groups, separates and unites, on the celluloid and in the projection, events which are already ordered in the story we are being told; and he disposes of them in another order, corresponding to the requirements of filmic elaboration.[127]

This discussion of filmic syntax provides a direct filmological precursor to Metz's *grande syntagmatique,* a model for the various types of autonomous segments in the classical film, which he elaborated in articles published a decade and a half later.[128]

Only a handful of other filmological studies were devoted specifically to the exploration of filmic syntax. One of the earliest was Georges Sadoul's "Georges Méliès and the First Elaboration of Cinematic Language," an excerpt from his multivolume history of the cinema appearing in the first issue of the *Revue.*[129] But outside of Souriau's brief discussion of the filmic techniques of transition and the use of sound as punctuation, the only rigorous treatment of filmic syntax occurs in issue 2 in Lucien Sève's "Cinema and Method (II)." Here Sève examines the various ways in which shots are linked, in such a way as to compare "cinematic processes" and the "logical processes of discourse."[130] That is to say that if film is not a language in the strictest sense, it does communicate information in a discursive form. Pursuing this comparison, Sève provides five correspondences between discursive figures and filmic techniques.

Succession, enumeration: sequence, dolly shot, dissolve

Alternating opposition: shot/reverse shot, asyndeton

Introduction of a new idea: fade

Exposition, conclusion: long shot, pan

Consequence, concession: dolly-in on detail[131]

In these cases, the cinema has developed it own techniques corresponding to elements of discourse. Nevertheless, Sève observes, the cinema is restricted to the extent that "it cannot translate conjunctions which are not linked logically to successive action."[132] With Anne Souriau, he observes that the cinema is restricted to showing effects rather than causes, and therefore "the cinematic possibilities do not exactly correspond to those of discourse."[133]

In another article in the same issue, Maurice Mouillard elaborates on the absence of causality in the film, using this observation to examine the difference between the presentation of narrative literature and the presentation of film to an audience. In the written story, Mouillard observes, causes represent the "understanding of the universe by the one who speaks of it (the story-teller). . . . The world created by the word is inevitably a world 'in-itself,'" since it exists entirely in language. With the cinema, however, everything is different:

> Once I write 'he loved,' I pretend to give at once a thing and a past. The film has no past. The past does not exist except in the story. The past of the film unfolds in the present, or it does not exist at all.[134]

Despite the variety of correspondences and differences observed between film and language, the persistent fact remains that films do express, do communicate and do signify. As Cohen-Séat wrote in 1948,

> All filmic reality is normally found elaborated and presented in function of a signification, and thus *means* something. On the other hand, it is incontestible that this signification gives the viewer a feeling of understanding.[135]

Given the fact that the film has a meaning which is understood, linguistics poses the question of how that meaning is articulated. This is a question touched upon in the first issue of the *Revue* by Jacques Guicharnaud when he observes, "The cinema is undoubtedly the only art where the equivalence between the sign and the object signified is almost absolute." In contrast to the "abyss" (de Saussure's "arbitrariness") separating the word and the object to which it refers, the cinema involves a type of signification in which "the object is present in the image"; it appears "totally, as if by magic."[136]

For Cohen-Séat, it is this "initial identity between the representative life of human beings" and the filmic image which makes film "capable of being understood by all men."[137] He denies that these images are to be considered signs at all. They are, he writes,

> neither natural signs (it is not the *relationship* to the thing signified which results here from the laws of nature), nor expressive signs, nor even less 'artificial' signs in the sense of a voluntary decision which is more or less collective. These systems of images contain signs of one type or another; they are used, from a particular point of view, as one uses signs; but they are still real images, which a direct and immediate view transforms into an object of thought immediately present to the mind, and apprehended in its individual reality.[138]

It is not the image which is a sign for the object photographed, Cohen-Séat asserts; it is instead a matter of the use of those objects in a systematic way to signify specific things. His position does not contradict Roques's notion of the cinema's use of the languages of gesture and mime, nor does it refute Anne Souriau's understanding of costume, decor and set decoration as systems of signification employed by the cinema. Cohen-Séat simply denies that the image itself is a sign in linguistic terms. Adopting a solidly phenomenological position, he argues that the image is perceived as an image and apprehended as such. Cohen-Séat's understanding of the viewer's self-consciousness regarding the perceptual state is quite in keeping with the phenomenology of Mikel Dufrenne, who was himself influenced by Souriau:[139]

> Phenomenology is applicable primarily to the human sphere because in it consciousness is self-conscious; and that is the very model of our conception of phenomenal existence: the appearance as an appearance to consciousness of a meaning.[140]

In his article "Dialectic of the Concept of Cinema," from the first issue of the *Revue,* Maurice Caveing carefully outlines the phenomenological viewpoint regarding film language. The cinema, he admits,

> never offers us brute reality, but reality already in the process of interpretation; it doesn't present the world as objective Reality, but already as it has become Mind. What we mean when we say that the cinema is a language is simply that it is a form of development, of the life of the mind. But the Mind here immediately apprehends itself, that is to say that it is by itself the signification of the world. It is neither discourse nor mediated thought. Signification implies neither concept, nor word, nor language. Thus there does not exist in the cinema the original process of the formation of ideas, that is of concepts, and its 'system of images' is neither semiology, nor alphabet, nor algorithm. Indeed what language does is mediate the signification in a being which is different from the thing signified. In the cinema, on the contrary, the signification and the thing signified are nothing but the same: it is significant by itself, that is, immediately. . . . in saying that [film] is a language, we have said nothing which cannot be said of any art whatsoever.[141]

Caveing in no way denies the fact of filmic expression; he simply asserts that it is no different from the expression of any art—that is, immediately apprehended, and not reducible to a logical system, an idea considered repugnant by phenomenology.

It was Cohen-Séat himself who provided the most thorough examination of "the filmic discourse" in a series of lectures delivered at the Institut de Filmologie and reprinted in the *Revue* in 1949. In his introduction he outlined the central problem posed by the notion of film as discourse:

> With the filmic discourse it is a question of a dual problem. There are, in the *discourse,* those elements which arise from the analytic method and positive research: concrete elements, materials for experimentation, a realm of precise inquiry belonging to the laboratory. But

this very research brings us to another aspect of the question. The *filmic* discourse reveals its own traits and unique characteristics. These characteristics bring to light the reverse of that discourse we call *logical*, or *logos*, or any other name which is used to designate the foundations of thought. It then becomes a question of a much larger concern, which philosophy must examine.[142]

Discourse, Cohen-Séat notes, has evolved over thousands of years, encompassing many types of expression in all languages. But according to Leibnitz, discourse is more than the simple stringing together of words and phrases; it is the "passage of the thinking mind from one judgment to another, following an order which may be that of cause-and-effect, or may be something else."[143] Thus, Cohen-Séat observes, the *meaning* of discourse and reason itself are created by thought, within the mind and yet outside of it, by means of the elaboration and enunciation of discourse: "*Discursive thought, discursive faculty* are synonyms for *understanding* [*entendement*: judgment]; and this, in the final analysis, is what is in question."[144]

If film is discursive, however, it is not so in the same sense that language is. "Filmic images," Cohen-Séat contends, are not signs, and even less "conventions." "They are presented, by their very nature, as completely opposed to *a* system, and cannot be conceived of otherwise."[145] Communication, he continues, is always considered "*secondary* to a common technique: of writing, of spoken words, of whatever relationship to the convention of the sign or the verbal image."

> Our own images, for the viewer, are essentially secondary to nothing.... They are a reality, different undoubtedly from ordinary affective reality, but reality none the less; representative, certainly, but subjectively real. It is the mutual immanence of the act of reading and of signification which essentially characterizes comprehension.... That which produces and that which is produced are identical. Thus, the viewer is never informed *of* something, but *by* something.[146]

Reprising the phenomenological stance concerning the immediacy of art, Cohen-Séat asserts, "The cinema is an art precisely because it is not a language."[147]

It is the phenomenological view of art, elaborated by Merleau-Ponty and filtered through the aesthetics of Souriau, which determined the course of the aesthetic and discursive approaches of filmology to the filmic fact. Despite the scientific mission of the movement—the need to categorize, quantify, and compare the elements of the film—the pursuit of a strictly linguistic analysis of film remained theoretically unsound in the views of the large number of filmologists who demanded that the film be taken as a complete whole, as a work of art.

6

The Cinematic Fact: The Socio-Anthropology of the Cinema

Cohen-Séat's distinction between the filmic fact and the cinematic fact was conceived as the first great taxonomical distinction in the science of film. As defined in his *Essai,* the cinematic fact consists of "the circulation within human groups of an array of documents, sensations, ideas, feelings and materials offered by life and put into form by film in its manner."[1] Thus Cohen-Séat distinguishes between the filmic fact as "expression" and the cinematic fact as "circulation." To this extent, the cinematic fact more closely resembles Durkheim's social fact than does the filmic fact, insofar as it defines the cinema as a social phenomenon.

It is curious that, despite the sociological bent of Cohen-Séat's *Essai,* filmology placed the larger part of its emphasis on what was defined as the filmic fact, the study of film itself. But, as Christian Metz notes, following Cohen-Séat's definition,

> ...film is only a small part of the cinema, for the latter represents a vast ensemble of phenomena some of which intervene *before* the film (the economic infrastructure of production, studios, bank or other financing, national laws, sociology of the contexts of decision-making, technological equipment and emulsions, biography of film producers, etc.), others *after* the film (the social, political, and ideological impact of the film on different publics, "patterns" of behavior or of sentiments induced by the viewing of films, audience responses, audience surveys, mythology of stars, etc.), and finally, others *during* the film but *aside from and outside of it* (the social ritual of the projection of the film—less formal than in the classic theatre, but retaining its sobriety even in everyday sociocultural situations—the furnishing and decoration of the theatre, the technical methods of operation of the projectionist, the role of theatre attendants—that is to say their function in various economic or symbolic systems, which does not detract from their practical utility, etc.).[2]

Therefore, the cinematic fact is everything which is "extra-filmic," but which is nevertheless related to the phenomenon of the cinema. For this reason, the cinematic fact covers an extremely broad field, corresponding to several equally broad-based disciplines: sociology, history, anthropology, epistemology, etc. In this sense, as Metz notes, "for the 'fieldworker'... the cinema is not a unitary object."[3]

In filmological practice, it proved far easier to study the film itself than to analyze the historical, social and anthropological phenomena surrounding it. Filmic facts could be isolated more precisely, and submitted to the kind of scientific testing so central to the empirical bent of filmology. The problem of the psychological effects of the filmic fact could be posed within the framework of an experiment. Psychologically, the cinematic fact involved, as Soriano notes, "collective thought"[4]—a far more difficult phenomenon to isolate.

Perhaps this explains the difficulty for filmology of organizing and pursuing the study of the cinematic fact, and the degree to which its study lagged behind the theory and experimentation with filmic phenomena. Those cinematic phenomena defined by Metz as intervening prior to the film, such as industrial and technological factors, received only the most cursory treatment by filmology in its formative stage. Following a brief article by producer André des Fontaines on the position of the film industry with respect to filmology, which appeared in the first issue, the *Revue* never again turned its attention to the economic-industrial factors of the cinema. Preceded by an introduction which asserts the "essential fact... that the material of the cinema, conceived by filmology as an *institutional fact,* includes all the circumstances and interventions which determine this fact," des Fontaines's article provides a succinct economic and historical assessment of the problems of the French film industry.[5] Yet despite the economic determinism implicit in Cohen-Séat's analysis of the evolution of film history, these factors never played an important role in the work of filmology.

Similarly, filmological studies of cinematic technology are largely studies in perceptual psychology. In a substantial article appearing in issue 3/4 of the *Revue,* for example, R.C. Oldfield of Oxford University undertakes a rigorous study of the cinematic apparatus, but exclusively in regard to its capacity to create a perceptual illusion in the spectator.[6] A much later study by René Zazzo devoted to the new wide-screen techniques once again examines technology in terms of viewer perception.[7]

It is in the study of the cinematic fact that the structuring influence of the established academic disciplines on filmology is most evident. On one hand, the question of the social effects of the medium on its audience was posed within the framework of experimental psychology. On the other, the institutional fact of the cinema was relegated to the existing social sciences of sociology, anthropology and history. Questions regarding the industry and technology, unless they fell within the provinces of these fields, not only remained unanswered, but unposed.

Questions of History, Culture and Society

Writing in the first issue of the *Revue,* Raymond Bayer, professor of aesthetics at the Sorbonne and member of the board of the Institut de Filmologie, notes the "tendency of contemporary aesthetics to be a socioaesthetics,"[8] citing recent developments in the field of the sociology of literature. This, he argues, is precisely the direction in which filmology should take aesthetics, since "film, more than any other art, is inherently sociological."[9]

Certainly, most of the filmological studies emerging from such diverse disciplines as philosophy, perceptual and experimental psychology, and aesthetics were grounded in a common interest sparked by a new social phenomenon: the mass medium of the cinema. This was, in fact, the impetus behind the sociological framework of Cohen-Séat's *Essai,* which played so important a part in establishing the problematic of filmology. Yet, no direct application of sociology in relation to filmology appeared in the *Revue* before 1952, when Edgar Morin and Georges Friedmann published their manifesto "Sociology of the Cinema," in issue 10.[10]

Prior to this time, a handful of articles had appeared in the *Revue* which touched upon socio-historical, socio-cultural and socio-anthropological questions raised by the cinema. Most of these, however, represented translations and excerpts of works already published in English. Most notable among these were two articles by Siegfried Kracauer treating films in relation to their social, historical and cultural contexts. The first article, appearing in issue 3/4 of the *Revue* (October 1948),[11] was excerpted from his book *From Caligari to Hitler,* published in English in 1947.[12] Formerly an influential writer for the leading German newspaper the *Frankfurter Zeitung,* Kracauer spent World War II in the United States, where during the immediate postwar period he prepared this landmark analysis of the pre-Nazi German cinema. Subtitled "A Psychological History of the German Film," Kracauer's book contends "that through an analysis of the German films, deep psychological dispositions dominant in Germany from 1918 to 1933 can be exposed— dispositions which influenced the course of events during that time and which will have to be reckoned with in the post-Hitler era."[13]

Despite Kracauer's emphasis on the word "psychological," *From Caligari to Hitler* is a socio-cultural analysis of a group of films treated as artifacts of a specific historical period. Its goal is the definition of a mass psychology, an inherently sociological phenomenon. Asserting that "the films of a nation reflect its mentality," Kracauer supports his idea by citing two specific social facts:

> First, they are never the product of an individual. . . . Since any film production unit embodies a mixture of heterogeneous interests and inclinations, teamwork in this field tends

to exclude arbitrary handling of screen material, suppressing individual peculiarities in favor of traits common to many people.

Second, films address themselves, and appeal, to the anonymous multitude. Popular films—or, to be more precise, popular screen motifs—can therefore be supposed to satisfy existing mass desires. . . . even the official Nazi war films, pure propaganda products as they were, mirrored certain national characteristics which could not be fabricated. What holds true of them applies all the more to the films of a competitive society. General discontent becomes apparent in waning box-office receipts, and the film industry, vitally interested in profit, is bound to adjust itself, so far as it possible, to the change of mental climate. To be sure, American audiences receive what Hollywood wants them to want; but in the long run public desires determine the nature of Hollywood films.[14]

Thus, Kracauer's method of analyzing the mass psychology of prewar Germany is founded on the Durkheimian notion of a *conscience collective*, supported by a materialist assessment of a historically specific type of production grounded in the capitalist principle of supply and demand. It would be four years before Morin and Friedmann would offer so synthetic a theory of the sociology of the cinema in the pages of the *Revue*.

Further, Kracauer situates his study in the context of a social mission quite in keeping with the goals of filmology. First, he asserts that the methodology employed in *From Caligari to Hitler* "can profitably be extended to studies of current mass behavior in the United States and elsewhere." Second, he notes that such studies as this "may help in the planning of films—not to mention other media of communication—which will effectively implement the cultural aims of the United Nations."[15]

Kracauer's second article, which appeared in the *Revue* in 1950, was in fact a study undertaken for UNESCO[16] published in English in 1949.[17] Entitled "National Types as Hollywood Presents Them," the article analyzes the stereotyping of British and Russian characters in particular as depicted in American films between 1933 and 1949, a period beginning with the stirrings of World War II and culminating several years after its end. Kracauer directs his arguments toward film producers, whom he suggests may "find a more objective approach to foreign characters to be in their own interest." Noting the success of such semi-documentary dramas as Elia Kazan's *Boomerang* (1947), he asks

why Hollywood should not explore this success and try its hand at films, semi-documentaries or not, which serve in the cause of one world. U.S. audiences may even welcome a comprehensive rendering of Russian problems, or of life in Labor-governed Britain.

Or, of course, they may not. And Hollywood (any national film industry, for that matter) has some reason to believe that in the long run it knows best what spectators look out for in the movie houses. . . . This accounts for the primary importance of mass education. Unless organizations such as UNESCO can stir up a mass desire for international understanding, prospects for the cooperation of film producers are slim.[18]

Thus, Kracauer views the cinema as a powerful social instrument; but his notion of economic determinism leads him to the conclusion that society must change if the cinema is to change.

In the same issue of the *Revue* in which Kracauer's article on national types appeared, Professor Mario Ponzo of the University of Rome published a study of the cinema and collective images. Ponzo was also interested in character types, but from the perspective of mass psychology, with an emphasis on psychoanalytic theory. Asserting that human symbolic thought consists of "a succession and organization of visual images," he emphasizes the power of film in assuming an analogous form "which tends toward a meaningful conclusion," and which facilitates the viewer's "return to a primary state of thought."[19] Therefore, he observes, the film viewer "can maintain an attitude of receptiveness far more passive than in following graphic or phonetic expression when reading or listening to discourse."[20]

In addition, he notes, "visual images generally seem to possess a greater and more immediate affective power than abstract forms of thought."[21] Clearly, Ponzo refers only to the visual aspect of the film, since speech and sometimes reading also play significant roles in filmic communication. Yet his observations on the psychological aspects of film's visual element offer some insight into the power of the cinema, and represent one of the primary approaches psychoanalysis would offer to the study of film.

Carrying these observations to the level of mass psychology, however, Ponzo emphasizes the sociological ramifications of the power of the filmic image.

> Filmic language, which is above all affective-visual, can thus become a powerful means for modifying our social conduct. The success of this enterprise depends on a larger, more complete understanding of the principal forms of collective images and the psychological principles which determine their formation and reconstruction.[22]

Thus, Ponzo's analysis of the sociological effects of the cinema points toward the study of spectator psychology, while Kracauer seems more concerned with the way in which this social psychology finds expression through the capitalist structure of the film industry. Kracauer's approach is therefore more socio-historical, while Ponzo's is more socio-anthropological, suggesting the power of certain image-types throughout human civilization. Other images, he notes, correspond to more specific groups linked by such factors as "location, historical period, religion, profession, etc."[23]

The only elaboration of this socio-anthropological perspective in the *Revue* prior to the articles of Morin occurred in two brief pieces on the reactions of African "primitives" to film. The first, by John Maddison of the British Central Office of Information, presents the observations of the British

Colonial Film Unit in Nigeria. Based on the inability of African natives to interpret films, Maddison observes the cultural differences in the perception of film. While the Western viewer is accustomed to the two-dimensionality of the screen and its 30° periphery (as opposed to the 90° periphery of human vision), therefore compensating for these factors, the African who has never seen a film is unfamiliar with these conventions and cannot "read" the film properly. Maddison writes,

> Our mind, wanting to know the unknown, completes the image. We imagine what is lacking to us. For the Africans, the known is a very different notion from ours and often very limited. That is why we can easily understand that he judges films according to a whole set of familiar notions and within an African framework.[24]

In illustration, Maddison cites an incident wherein a native African audience, watching a film in which a chicken in the background of the frame walked off-screen, asked excitedly where it had gone. In another case he observes that the image of a pregnant woman on the screen provoked neither embarassment nor laughter in the African audience, which would apparently have been the case with a British audience of the time.[25] Thus, Maddison concludes that both film perception and film content are affected by the cultural orientation of the viewer.

For the Colonial Film Unit, this meant that films produced for African viewers had to employ specialized techniques, such as simplified editing and "slower" narration. "The use of these techniques," Maddison writes, "is based, not on the belief that [the African] mentality is different from ours, but on the conviction that they have not yet arrived at the same stage of development."[26] Such a statement, lacking in the cultural relativism which would soon characterize anthropological study, betrays a definite ethnocentrism and a positivist sense of the evolution of civilization quite compatible with Cohen-Séat's belief in the universality of the cinema. Still, Maddison's observations caused a great deal of discussion at the First International Congress of Filmology in 1947,[27] for the very acknowledgment of cultural differences seemed a contradiction of the notion of cinema's universality and the positivism underlying it.

An update of this study, appearing in the *Revue* in 1951, marks a certain change of position, based on the studies of M. L. Van Bever, chief of the government Bureau of Cinematography and Photography of the Belgian Congo. Citing Van Bever's observation that current films suitable for Western audiences were not suitable for "so-called primitive societies," the article notes,

> It is the African's incomprehension of film which raises the question of a fundamental difference of mentality, of civilization, or simply of a handicap or displacement in relation to a "civilized" audience whose education has gone on for half a century.[28]

Acknowledging that such cultural differences are fundamental, and that the relationship of cinema to Western and African cultures is radically different, this brief article clearly presents the institution of the cinema as "the product of a determined civilization—the West in the 20th century."[29] Here the notion of the cinema's historical and cultural specificity places the idea of its universality in question and opens the way to the questions of film and ideology which would soon be raised by Morin.

Prior to 1952, however, the only French contributor to the *Revue* to devote much attention to situating the cinema in a historical context was Marcel Cohen in his 1947 article, "Writing and Cinema." A Marxist professor of Oriental Languages at the Sorbonne since 1939 and one of the foremost linguists in France during this period, Cohen believed that language was a social mechanism related to, but not determined by what Marx defined as the economic base.[30] His analysis of the development of the cinema as a means of communication demonstrates its relationship, on one hand, to the historical development of the techniques of production, and on the other, to the relatively independent facts of language and expression. "The great inventions in expression and communication which have appeared in different epochs of history," Cohen writes, "should be situated in relation to facts of civilization, and both of these in relation to the intellectual and artistic life."[31] Thus, he examines the cinema as a part of a historical context which produced both rapid transportation and rapid communication (telegraph, telephone, radio). Tracing the beginnings of writing from approximately 4000 B.C., Cohen notes the correspondence of the invention of printing to the development of modern capitalism and of a middle class, a period in which individual literacy increased and art was brought into the home. The telephone and telegraph represent the capacity to transmit information instantaneously; and the phonograph added the capacity to record not only a message, but a performance as well.[32] The development of the cinema must be seen in this context, Cohen asserts, although it is still

> not easily situated in relation to other means of expression, of recording and of transmission. From its birth it has stood apart: not created for immediate needs, like writing or the telephone, it arose from the experiments of a scientist who wanted to study motion, Marey;[33] it came into its own as a *deluxe* entertainment with presentations in the Grand Café in Paris, and then at the Robert Houdin theatre of illusions.[34] Its unique characteristics have always been linked to practical documentary reproduction, to intellectual choice and to artistic expression. Not that these elements are absent from spoken language or writing: every voice is harmonious or discordant, every manner of speaking conveys a measure of elegance and emotion, as all writing is more or less aesthetic, and all photographs more or less decorative. But the cinema is new and superior in its particular synthesis.[35]

Ultimately, then, Cohen is less interested in situating the cinema within a Marxist historical context than in defining its position within the history of expression, both communicative and artistic, and in speculating on the implications of its unique characteristics within this context. In this respect, he notes that the function of verbal language in communication, persuasion and thought has remained largely unaffected by the cinema; while writing, on the other hand,

> has already lost, and will undoubtedly continue to lose, certain of its practical uses, since it is no longer as indispensable as when it was the most refined means of conserving and transmitting thought....[36]

Thus, cinema is not simply determined by its historical context; it also affects the context by altering the roles of other means of expression. Cohen does not speculate upon the immediate socio-historical ramifications of such a change.

Edgar Morin and the Socio-Anthropology of the Cinema

No comprehensive attempt to apply sociology in the context of filmology was made by French scholars until Edgar Morin's and Georges Friedmann's article "Sociology of the Cinema" appeared in a 1952 issue of the *Revue*. One of the key figures in French sociology during the 1950s, Morin had not been among the founders of filmology, nor would he affiliate himself with the movement for more than a few years during the 1950s. Nevertheless, his work in the socio-anthropology of the cinema was the most influential in that field during the decade, and the *Revue* provided him an important forum prior to the publication of his two books on the subject, *Le cinéma ou l'homme imaginaire* (1956) and *Les Stars* (1957).

Both Edgar Morin and Georges Friedmann were Marxists, though neither was affiliated with the Communist Party in the 1950s. Along with Georges Politzer and Henri Lefebvre, Friedmann was among the first group of French intellectuals to begin studying and propagating Marxism in the late 1920s and early 1930s.[37] His criticisms of Stalinism during the 1930s had offended the French Communist Party, always pro-Soviet in its orientation; but during the Occupation of France, Friedmann had played a key role in the Comité National des Ecrivains, a Communist front group.[38] After the war, he became a professor at the Conservatoire des Arts et Métiers, and later the Director of the Centre d'Etudes des Communications de Masse in Paris. Mark Poster refers to Friedmann as "an independent Marxist sociologist of work," who was interested in the effects of mechanization on society. Friedmann distinguished between a "natural milieu" and a "technical milieu," the latter characterizing modern, mechanized society, where machines dominate "rhythm, time, sensibilities, values."[39] Friedmann's interest in the cinema was secondary, but it arose from this concern with the technical milieu. Further, in visits to America, he had observed a shifting of the "center of gravity" of workers from work activities to non-work activities,[40] which suggested an increased importance for the study of leisure activities, and an impetus for exploring the mechanized recreation of the cinema.

Morin was of a younger generation than Friedmann, and had joined the Communist Party in the spring of 1942, during the Occupation. As with many French intellectuals tending toward Marxism during the 1930s, Morin had been critical of Stalinism and the dogmatism of the French Communist Party, until the beginning of World War II. More than two decades later, he explained the influence of the Soviet sacrifices in the fight against the Nazis in shaping his own decision to join the party: "Stalingrad washed away all the crimes of the past when it did not justify them. The cruelty, the trials, the liquidations found their finality in Stalingrad."[41] Following a renewal of Stalinist persecutions in the postwar period, however, Morin failed to renew his party membership in 1950;[42] and after publishing an article in the Trotskyist *L'Observateur*, he was officially expelled in 1951.[43]

During this same period, Morin became a researcher in the sociology section of the Centre National de Recherche Scientifique, under the tutelage of Georges Friedmann. Explaining later how he became involved in research on the cinema, Morin noted his isolation at this point from both the "bourgeois world" and the "Stalinist world." Examining his personal history in the popular Marxist mode of the self-critique, he confesses that he lacked "the courage to approach a virulent subject, directly politicizable, that is to attack academicism, mindless empiricism, arrogant dogmatism."[44] Thus, the study of the cinema represented a "refuge," as well as

> a subject which would please my mentor, Georges Friedmann, whose influence had played a decisive role in my admission to the C.N.R.S. Friedmann saw and thought "machine." I thought primarily of the aesthetics (a politically disreputable subject) of the machine in contemporary society. Friedmann liked the subject; but very quickly, even before beginning, it bored me. I chose the cinema. Certainly, the cinema is a machine, a machine-art, an art-industry. Certainly, I was inspired by the idea, already complex and recursive, of understanding society with the help of the cinema, as well as cinema with the help of society. . . .[45]

An "existential Marxist" highly influenced by Sartre's concept of "play," Morin argued for the role of culture in Marxist theory throughout his career.[46] His concern with art and with the machine made him one of the first sociologists in France to devote serious attention to the cinema.

Morin's and Friedmann's 1952 article "Sociology of the Cinema" was a brief but comprehensive attempt to divide and categorize Cohen-Séat's cinematic fact amongst the various branches of the social sciences. Therefore, in their introduction, they forward a view of the cinema as *technique, institution* and *reflection* of a human universe."[47] Echoing Cohen's observations on the socio-historical position of the cinema, Morin and Friedman observe that cinema is "a fact of a technical and mechanical civilization." In terms of Friedmann's conception of mechanized, modern society, this places the cinema in the precise context of

> a civilization in movement and obsessed by the problem of movement: it is not by chance that, synchronically, technology, the arts, scientific theory and philosophy are forced to confront, each in its own way, the movement of things.[48]

The technique of cinema is a fact of a technological civilization; but cinema is more than technology, for "from cinematic techniques are born industries, commerce and cinematic spectacles."[49] Therefore, the cinema is also an institution. Finally, the cinema is a reflection of society, not only in the fact that it records what is before it, but also in its expression of collective desires and psychology.

> True recording eye, not only does it seize objects and people in their visible reality; but also, through the stories it invents, the imaginary situations it dreams, it corresponds to subjective realities (psychological and dream-like) of the collective character.[50]

In this sense, Morin and Friedmann can assert that all film is "documentary, a social document."[51]

Emphasizing that the problems of the cinema as technique, as institution and as social psychology are closely, and in a Marxist sense, dialectically linked, Morin and Friedmann assert the importance of approaching the cinematic fact through the interconnected disciplines of sociology and anthropology. In pursuing their argument, they divide their discussion into two broad categories: first, the "socio-filmological given" of the cinematic institution as industry; and second, "the reflection of society on the level of filmic content."[52]

In terms of their first category, the institution of the cinema is presented in the dialectical relationship of art and industry, of standardization and individuality. Tracing the development of the film industry from the beginnings of (horizontal) monopolization and vertical integration of production, distribution and exhibition, and observing the division of labor inherent in the studio system, Morin and Friedmann demonstrate the tendencies of the cinematic institution toward the mass production of standardized commodities characteristic of advanced capitalism.

> Industrialization, concentration, rationalization, division and parcelization of labor tend to produce *standardized* objects, that is, films in a repetitive series, endlessly offering the same situations, the same loves, the same humor.[53]

On the other hand, there is a characteristic of individualization within the film industry, an opposite pressure to "break down concentration, to compensate for rationalization, to fight against standardization," which grows out of two other facts: the box-office risks of the cinematic enterprise and the need for individuality in each film product.[54] The cinematic marketplace demands a certain uniqueness of each film if the monetary risk taken by the industry is to pay off at the box-office; thus, the role of the director and the industry's search for the new and the original—a search "always counterbalanced by the standardized machine; the producers both endlessly decrying the lack of good scripts and cursing when they are presented one."[55]

This opposition between standardization and individualization is "tied dialectically to the industrial conditions of film," which are linked to the "masses" that create and satisfy the industry. In terms of the creative talents involved, this dialectic demands an individuality of actors "even as it depersonalizes them by making them myths (stars)," and "snares original literary talent, but encloses it in the mold of standardized cinema."[56] Thus, it is the Marxist dialectic which provides Morin and Friedmann a means of exploring the seeming paradox of the cinematic institution.

> The dialectic of individualization and standardization permits us to understand that there is not, on one hand, cinematic art and, on the other, the film industry; but that the objective condition of this mass industry contains within itself all the truths—of vulgarity and refinement, of novelty and cliché, of aesthetic and anti-aesthetic—which express themselves, confront one another and become entangled in the film.[57]

Within this dialectic, something of the cinema's power may be observed: standardization opens the film to the masses, while individualization brings with it the persuasive power of art.

In this sense, the cinema resembles myth: its archetypes maintain the same "latent" content while remaining diverse "in the infinite richness of their imaginary superstructures."[58] These mythic ramifications can also be observed economically, politically and socially. From an economic standpoint, the cinema brings with it a number of "para-cinematic industrial activities"; in illustration, Morin and Friedmann cite the fact that *Snow White* generated 117 licenses to market 2138 products related to the film. From a political standpoint, they note that the cinema is supervised and frequently utilized by the State as a result of its mass appeal. Finally, on a social level, the cinema determines a certain imitative conduct in daily life, and contributes to changes in public opinion.[59]

Exploring their second category of filmic content, Morin and Friedmann note that "a single film has diverse, sometimes contradictory contents" which are not only the expressions of a given culture, but also of a precise historical moment in that culture.[60] Therefore, they divide their analysis of film content into three categories: social, historical and anthropological.

In an observation very close to the thesis of Kracauer's *From Caligari to Hitler,* Morin and Friedmann write that "film translates and betrays, in its way, the ensemble of a society's realities." These realities are rarely clear-cut or abstract, but "a confusion of relations and social factors." Primary among these, they note, are those factors relating to "the authority of established institutions." This applies to apolitical films as much as to political ones; and for Morin and Friedmann, it is not a question of propaganda, but one of ideology in a broader sense. Therefore, they are interested in "the conformity of films to norms of legal morality; where good is confused with the moral, and bad with the illegal." These factors are present in apolitical, entertainment films, for "their entertaining characteristic is manifest precisely within the framework of these values." What is left unsaid is as significant as what is made explicit; and this is especially clear in terms of filmic taboos, whether they are dictated by official censorship or internal agreement. "Unspoken" dictates (e.g., the length of a screen kiss) are spoken quite strongly.[61]

> It is a matter of "collective representations," mentalities or ideologies reigning within a society. These correspond to an ensemble of values, attitudes, prejudices and knowledge of current mores in a sort of daily, collective "praxis."... The standard film not only avoids going against collective representations, but attempts to adapt itself to them.[62]

This standardized adaptation to collective ideology represents a tendency toward a lowest social common denominator, toward stereotyping and cliché. Citing Béla Balázs's observation that the standardized cinema is "petit bourgeois," Morin and Friedmann refer to its "shopgirl mentality."[63] Further, they cite a *Hollywood Quarterly* article by Lester Asheim, "From Book to Film: Simplification," in which the author examines the adaptation of 24 classic novels for the screen and their simplification to appeal to a viewer with a mental age of 14 years.[64]

Vastly simplifying social complexities, the standardized film "relates a story whose conflicts of action dynamically pose conflicts of values which translate collective ideas." For the most part, such films emphasize "ideal conduct and the moral 'pattern' proposed by social authority, which lead to an exemplary solution."[65] Most often, films which place social values in opposition to the law are set in a time and place removed from the social circumstances of the film's production, as is the case with films about heroes like Robin Hood or Zorro. Morin and Friedmann trace the filmic presentation of ideal types not only in Hollywood films, but in films from Britain and the Soviet Union as well. Once again, they observe a dialectical interchange in the function of filmic content, for "at the same time it manifests problems or conflicts in society, film presents ideal types—good or bad—in relation to these problems or conflicts."[66]

In terms of the cinema's historical contents, Morin and Friedmann observe that

> film conceals a content rather strictly determined by the moment in which it is produced. In the extreme, the historical contents and social contents are confused to the extent that the latter cannot be disassociated from a phase of social history, and the former cannot be abstracted from social problems.[67]

In this respect, a historical distance on war films produced during the Second World War provides an important perspective for understanding the social ramifications of their contents. Citing Kracauer's analysis of the prewar German cinema, Morin and Friedmann propose "a sort of social psychoanalysis" which would demonstrate how

> certain films, apparently detached from a precise social reference, can have an allegorical content much richer, sociologically and historically, than a realist film, limited by the taboos of censorship or production.[68]

Thus, they observe that certain "semi-psychoanalytic" American films, such as *Give Us This Day* (1950), *14 Hours* (1951), *Rope* (1948) and *The Thing* (1951), demonstrate a deep common anxiety, and are therefore as revelatory about the Cold War mentality of the United States as are the overtly "anti-Communist" films, especially since these entertainment films are not a direct product of the state's propaganda machinery.[69] Citing the examples of Carné's films *Quai des brumes* and *Les Visiteurs du soir,* made under the Vichy government, Morin and Friedmann observe that "the more stringent the censorship, the more film, which cannot approach concrete problems, takes refuge in fantasy and mysticism."[70] It is not so much a matter of circumventing official censorship as it is of finding a means to express certain collective longings. For example, they note, Tarzan films are "in reality strictly tied to the myths of a mechanist society about the natural state, and Westerns express the aspirations of this same society toward a free life of riding and adventure."[71]

From the observations of mythic contents in popular films, Morin and Friedmann make an easy transition into their exploration of the cinema's anthropological and psychological contents. It is in this area that they note the cinema's penchant toward universality.

> Psychological, or better anthropological contents are by themselves common to all men. They permit us to understand that *homo cinematographicus* is not merely an abstraction of the box-office, but a basic reality. The same Western, the same Tarzan movie finds an audience in Europe, Japan and black Africa. Its form is universal—that is, simplified in the

extreme. Its contents are especially universal. They express profound feelings of infantile or archaic familiarity regarding animals (the faithful horse, Rin-Tin-Tin, apes, elephants—all anthropomorphized), the brute participation of man in nature, elementary themes of aggression and defense, and those no less elementary themes of the struggle between good and evil.[72]

Thus, Morin and Friedmann argue that certain psychological proclivities common to mankind, despite cultural differences, are found in film, much as they are in myths. Instead of challenging the notion of universality, as did the reports on the cinema and African natives, the anthropological perspective offered in "Sociology of the Cinema" seems to lend support to Cohen-Séat's notion of film as a universal language. But Morin and Friedmann are careful to note that certain films are more "universal" than others: "Films that emphasize the national characteristics of the country from which they come, or characteristics proper to a specific historical moment, run the risk of losing psychological contact with universal audiences."[73] Thus the more realistic and topical a film, the less universal appeal it tends to have.

Without drawing any organic conclusions or discussing methodologies, Morin and Friedmann are satisfied to pose their socio-anthropological approach to the field as a challenge to filmology "to incite us as a group, and beyond our more or less artificial specializations, to roll up our sleeves and get to work." It is the synthetic quality of filmology which they view as its strength, for film is "a *human* fact, whose unity and profound realities cannot be understood or explained except in the converging light of all the disciplines which take man as their subject."[74]

The only other significant article by Morin to appear in the *Revue* was a tentative examination of the cinematic audience published a year later, and based on a variety of secondary source studies. Although audience research had become common during the postwar years in America and England, no real tradition of such research had been developed in France by 1953. Therefore, Morin's "Research on the Cinematic Public" is an attempt to establish a framework for the analysis of the moviegoing public, which he does by gleaning what he can from existing statistics and posing questions he feels are central to a sociology of the cinema.

Referring to audience studies already conducted in the United States and Britain,[75] Morin notes their focus on specific publics as opposed to the filmgoing public in general. It is therefore difficult, he notes, to integrate cinematic phenomena as a whole into a proper historical, demographic and economic context. Further, the demographics provided by such studies do little to account for "tastes, motivations or even regularity of attendance."[76] Finally, he adds, the methods of research—primarily the interview and the questionnaire—provide little hope of accurate data, since they make little compensation for either the sincerity of the subject questioned or the lucidity of his memory in recalling patterns of behavior.[77]

For these reasons, Morin begins by posing the most basic questions: what is the cinematic public? how many people go to the movies? does the number vary, increase, decrease, remain stable? what proportion of the population is touched by the cinema? how does this vary from country to country? within different social milieux?[78] These questions raise other questions touching on audience psychology and the "need" for cinema, the reaction of that need "to social and monetary difficulties compared to the reactions not only of other leisure demands (theatre, sports) but to the complex of economic needs as well."[79] In sociological terms, Morin poses the question of the demand for cinema in terms of its relationship to historical developments, crises and wars, and in comparison with the effects of such historical factors on economics, social life and religion.

To begin posing these questions in terms of the information available, Morin constructs several charts, the most significant of which provides a comparison between yearly attendance figures from 1927 through 1950 for 10 countries: the United States, France, England, Germany, Italy, Canada, Holland, the USSR, Norway and Brazil. Compiled from available sources for each nation, the chart is filled with gaps, and no single country exhibits figures for every year.[80] A second chart compares the attendance figures for the United States, England, Canada, Italy, France and Holland to the population figures of each country as a whole and to that part of the population Morin refers to as "cinematic"—that is, the population from age 10 to 59, considered to make up most filmgoers. Calculating in this way an average yearly attendance for each country during one or two years in the late 1940s, Morin is able to observe, for example, that the average attendance in England is at least equal to that of the United States, while France is only about one-third of that. He further divides the countries into categories of high yearly attendance (over 20 times per person = U.S., England, Canada), medium attendance (10-20 times per person = Italy, France) and low attendance (less than 5 times per person = Holland).[81]

In mapping the development of movie attendance, Morin employs his first table to observe that the great leap in American attendance occurred between 1922 and 1929, when the figures doubled; that British attendance doubled between 1936 and 1947, French attendance doubled between 1930 and 1945, Italian attendance tripled between 1936 and 1950, and Soviet attendance quadrupled between 1938 and 1950. This unequal development from country to country, Morin observes, is a result of diverse economic and cultural factors. Nevertheless, "it always translates a capital fact which is the development of a public toward *universality.*"[82] Observing that this development continues in the underdeveloped countries, he also notes that, while "attendance tends towards *universality,* it seems that, in the U.S. since 1930, and since 1947 in the Western countries (e.g., France, Germany) it tends towards *stagnation.*"[83] For Morin, it is the cinema's tendency to be universal, as Cohen-Séat supposed, that suggests a unitary analysis of the cinematic public as a whole. The notion of a saturation point suggests a limit to this universality which he feels should also be defined. Finally, the differences in development from country to country emphasize the necessity of understanding the socio-historical contexts in each case.[84]

Morin begins his analysis of this universality by attempting to examine the filmgoing public from different perspectives. First, he suggests a correlation between attendance and social class, "socio-economic level" and/or "level of education." In examining demographic figures, he finds no significant correlation in this field. To support this, he compares an American audience study by Leo Handel for the Motion Picture Research Bureau, which found more frequent attendance by the wealthier and better educated, with a British study by Moss and Box which found precisely the opposite. The variations in Handel's study, Morin observes, are in fact very slight, and not really significant.[85] On the other hand, a 1947 study by Paul Lazarsfeld concludes that the level of education has virtually no effect on the movie attendance of people under the age of 45.[86] The only real correlation between attendance and social class seems to be a very slight dominance of the "lower-middle, upper-lower classes," which, as Morin observes, corresponds to the latent ideology of films in capitalist countries.[87]

Similarly, the sex of the viewer seems to have little to do with attendance (except with regard to women in cultures where their roles restrict attendance; e.g., India, the Arab countries).[88] Nor is climate a factor which seems to have any effect at all on moviegoing (although weather, of course, does).[89] Attendance does seem to vary according to the size of the population concentration, as urban attendance in France, for example, exceeds attendance in rural areas. This, however, according to Morin, might be due to "*geographical* not *sociological* causes." There is no evidence that the cinema is an exclusively urban need or product, for "where the means of communication exists there are no differences between attendance and urban or rural residence." Nor is there any support for a correlation between high attendance and what Friedmann refers to as a "technical milieu."[90] Dividing population centers into four categories according to size, Morin compares the figures for the percentage of the total population represented by each category with those of the percentage of total admissions for each category. For cities over 100,000, the ratio is 1.34; while cities from 50,000 to 100,000 and from 20,000 to 50,000 are virtually identical to each other, with ratios of .74 and .75, respectively. Curiously, for population centers from 2,000 to 20,000 inhabitants, the ratio rises again to .92.[91] Based on the figures, Morin observes that the cinema

is currently a fundamental element of urban life, whatever the industrial, mechanist, commercial, administrative or morphological character of the city. This said, the factor of urban concentration, predominant in the great population centers or regional capitals, statistically determines the greatest attendance. But these factors cease to work, or work differently (perhaps small towns have a more centralized life than medium-sized towns) in towns of less than 100,000. Factors *still unknown* strongly influence attendance.[92]

The single factor Morin observes which does seem to affect attendance is that of age. Citing a 1933 American study by Edgar Dale which situates peak attendance at age 20, and a 1949 *Film Daily Yearbook* report that 41 percent of filmgoers are between 15 and 24 years of age, while 66.75 percent are under 35, Morin observes that "age is the determining factor for frequency of attendance."[93]

Having examined a variety of differential sociological criteria for attendance, Morin once again asserts the notion of the cinema's universality.

This returns us to an anthropology of the cinema, a primary notion posed at the beginnings of filmology by M. Cohen-Séat.
The anthropological notion never eliminates the sociological problems.... On one hand, the cinema is potentially universal; in fact, it is not. There are currently unequal factors in the development of attendance.[94]

Based largely on studies of the American and British publics, he reiterates the slight dominance of the middle class among moviegoers, of urban residents and of inhabitants of small towns, and most significantly, of the adolescent age group. "Since these studies never cover France," he suggests, "it would be interesting to see if the frequency of attendance of the young and the fall in attendance after 30 and 40 is the same in this country as in the rest of the world."[95] Given the determining factor of adolescence, however, Morin is willing to suggest a connection to the common filmic themes of sex and love, crime and aggression, which correspond to "adolescent crises." Yet, he also notes the predominance of the same themes in literature and the theatre. Perhaps, he suggests, this reflects the fact that adolescence is the time in which a person's problems are posed most vitally and violently; and perhaps this, too, goes to explain something of the universality of filmic content.[96]

Morin himself would not pursue the amassing of data required to fill the gaps in available information. His article serves more as a methodological model employing readily available figures and studies both to point out the gaps and to suggest certain general observations which can already be made. His central concern seems to be to provide a modicum of empirical support for the idea of the cinema's universality, a key concept for his further explorations of an anthropology of the cinema.

Morin's next major work on the cinema, a 1956 book entitled *Le cinéma ou l'homme imaginaire,* was subtitled "Essay in Sociological Anthropology," and indeed it examines the cinema as an anthropological phenomenon of a technological culture. In a 1977 preface to a subsequent edition of this book,

Morin emphasizes that his study was completed in the wake of his previous socio-anthropological examination of the human treatment of death, *L'homme et la mort*,[97] in which he had discovered a

> formidable imaginary universe of myths, gods and spirits, a universe not merely superimposed on real life, but making up a real part of anthroposocial life. It was finally quite surprising that the imaginary played so constitutive a role in human reality. For, in its fashion, the formidable feeling of reality emanating from the images artificially reproduced and produced on the screen posed, inversely, the same question.[98]

In *L'homme et la mort*, Morin had identified two basic types of universal beliefs in an afterlife.

> one being the belief, or better, the experience of the *double*, the *alter ego* or other self, recognized in the mirror, the shadow, and liberated in thought; the other being the belief in the metamorphosis of one form of life into another.[99]

In *Le cinéma ou l'homme imaginaire*, he departs specifically from the question,

> in what sense and in what new ways does the modern cinematic universe revive the archaic universe of doubles? Why has the *cinématographe*, at its beginning a technique of reproducing movement, with a practical, even scientific usage, from its earliest days produced cinema, that is, imaginary spectacle, and with the films of Méliès, the magic spectacle of metamorphosis.[100]

Thus, Morin perceives an essential link between "the realm of the dead" and that of cinema, suggesting an anthropological factor "tied to something very fundamental and archaic in the human mind."[101]

This orientation carries over very strongly in Morin's observations on what he calls *le génie de la photo*.[102]

> In photography, it is precisely the *presence* which gives life. The primary and strange quality of photography is the essence of the person or thing which is nevertheless absent.[103]

As the "presence of an absence," the photograph serves a function almost identical to the relics of the dead, becoming the contemporary fetish for the "familial cult," preserving moments of joy (Morin emphasizes the stereotypical command, "Smile"), and functioning as *souvenirs* (in French, literally, "memories").[104] Morin's observations are very close to those made by André Bazin in his article, "The Ontology of the Photographic Image," where Bazin writes that the photograph "embalms time, rescuing it simply from its proper corruption," and that it possesses an "irrational power ... to bear away our faith."[105] Citing Bazin, Morin elaborates that the photograph encompasses the entire anthropological field, beginning with the memory and ending with the phantom, because it accomplishes the conjunction of qualities which are both parent to, yet different from the mental image, the reflection and the shadow. [106]

This projection of the double is essential to Morin's anthropology of the cinema, and he relates it to Sartre's observation that "the essential characteristic of the mental image is the way in which the object is absent within its very presence."[107] The "ghostly" quality of the image arises from the intensity of the presence it conveys in the object's absence. "The subjective amplification," Morin observes,

is a function of the objectivity of the image, that is, of its apparent material exteriority. A single deluded movement correlates the subjective value and the objective truth of the image until they reach an extreme "objectivity/subjectivity" or hallucination. [108]

It is this projection of a double which enables a belief in its immortality, and therefore, of an afterlife. Furthermore, Morin observes, "The *double* is effectively universal in ancient man. It is, perhaps, the only great universal human myth."[109]

Anthropologically, then, it is the connection of photography with this universal myth which provides a possible basis for arguing the universality of cinema. Nevertheless, Morin carefully distinguishes between photography and cinema. First, the cinematic image projected on the screen is liberated from the material support (the plate, paper) required by the photo. And while the photo is enjoyed privately, the cinema is presented as spectacle. Therefore, the cinema, unlike the photo, does not crystalize the image, allowing it to become an object of fetishism.[110] Citing Michotte van den Berck to the effect that it is the cinema's movement which lends a large portion of the illusion of reality, Morin points out that the cinema is the ultimate realization of the image as "shadow-reflection," with a life of its own.[111] Noting the very early cinematic proclivities toward the fantastic, he emphasizes the transformation of objects as a quality which seems to lend them life.[112]

Although not strictly a part of the work of filmology, Morin's *Le cinéma ou l'homme imaginaire* quite clearly emerges from the problematic posed by the filmologists. First, it represents one of the only serious attempts of the period to treat the cinema as an anthropological phenomenon, with relationships to myth, ritual and religion. Thus Morin's study is a direct application of an established discipline, almost ignored in the pages of the *Revue,* to the subject of film. Further, Morin draws liberally from the work of filmology in his examination of his subject, quoting Souriau, Agel, Cohen-Séat and Maddison, and synthesizing a variety of points of view in a way that filmology rarely achieved.

Morin's eclectic though synthetic sensibility is even more evident in his second book on the cinema, *Les Stars*, published in 1957. Here he examines the phenomenon of the movie star as a product of films, of an industry, of capitalism and commercialism, and of culture. Elaborating on the observations made in his earlier article with Friedmann, he explores the dialectic of the standardization and individualization of stars through a history of the star system and analyses of the careers and images of James Dean, Charlie Chaplin, Marilyn Monroe and Ava Gardner. In the process, Morin provides a number of fascinating observations on the psychological, sociological, economic and mythological "meanings" of stars. Writing of the star as a product of a specific time, place, culture, medium and mode of production, Morin observes,

> The star-object (merchandise) and the star-goddess (myth) are possible because the techniques of the movies excite and exalt a system of participations which affect the actor both in his performance and personality.
>
> Of course the star was—and is—only one of the possibilities of the movies. She was not, as we have pointed out, a necessary condition of the basic nature of cinematic expression. But the latter has made her possible. Another cinema, one founded on "non-actors," might have taken hold equally well. But the capitalist economy and the mythology of the modern world, and essentially the mythology of love, have determined this hypertrophy, this hydrocephalism, this sacred monster: the star.[113]

Written as a popular book, *Les Stars* is well-researched and learned without being dry, cleverly crafted without sacrificing the complexity of scholarly synthesis. In both his global view of the cinema and his desire to reach a broader audience, Morin stood virtually alone among the filmologists. He was also one of the only such researchers whose academic interest in film led him into filmmaking.

In December 1959, Morin sat on the jury along with ethnographic documentarist Jean Rouch at the First International Festival of Ethnographic Film held in Florence. Afterwards, he wrote an article for *France-Observateur* proposing a new type of documentary which he termed *cinéma-vérité*.[114] He also proposed to Rouch that they make such a film together—an ethnographic film set, not in Africa, but in Paris, in which a number of inhabitants would be asked to express their feelings about their lives.[115] In his synopsis submitted to request a shooting permit from the Centre National de la Cinématographie Française, Morin described the project as a "research film." "It is not a sociological film, properly speaking," he writes. "It is an ethnographic film in the strongest sense: it examines man."[116]

The outcome of this project was *Chronique d'un été*, shot in the summer of 1960, which became one of Rouch's best-known films and marked the inauguration of what was soon known widely as *cinéma-vérité*. In it, a variety of Parisians of different social classes and background are interviewed by Morin and Rouch, introduced to one another, and finally shown the footage already shot. Centered around two basic questions, "How do you live?" and "Are you happy?," *Chronique d'un été* offered, according to Morin, "the possibility of a confessional without a confessor, the possibility of confessing to all and to no one, the possibility of being a little bit *oneself.*"[117] In this project, Morin combined both his interests in anthropology and in popular culture to create a contemporary ethnographic document of the society he knew best in one of the most popular media available.

Morin's work in the socio-anthropology of the cinema accounts for most of filmology's contribution to the field. His two articles in the *Revue* provide a strong analytic basis for future work, and his two books on film apply these methods to specific subjects with some insight. On one hand, Morin points forward to the psychological and psychoanalytic questions directly related to a social anthropology of the cinema, especially in his examination of the primal and mythic functions of film in *Le cinéma ou l'homme imaginaire;* on the other hand, his research points back toward Cohen-Séat's positivist hope for a universal film language.

Curiously, however, the Durkheimian framework established by Cohen-Séat's *Essai* never assumed a primary role in filmology's forays into cinema and sociology. Cohen-Séat was himself led by his scientific interest in the cinema toward specifically psycho-physiological experimentation. It was not until the early 1960s that he would once again demonstrate a primary concern for sociological questions in two books, *Problèmes du cinéma et de l'information visuelle* and *L'action sur l'homme: Cinéma et télévision,* both published in 1961. In the former book, Cohen-Séat divides his concerns about the mass media, now including television, between social and psychological problems. Apparently influenced by Morin and his work in the field, Cohen-Séat asserts the primacy of anthropological study in providing answers to the sociological crisis of the media. His treatment of psychological issues includes a variety of information amassed from the studies of filmology, as well as an exploration of *photogénie* owing much to Morin.[118]

L'action sur l'homme was co-written with Marxist theorist and professor of philosophy Pierre Fougeyrollas, who, with Morin, Henri Lefebvre and Roland Barthes, was among the group which founded the non-sectarian Marxist journal *Arguments* in 1956.[119] Writing in his book *La philosophie en question* (1960), "Without doubt, the anguish of contemporary man resides in the technification of his existence,"[120] Fougeyrollas contributes to his work with Cohen-Séat a sense of urgency just as acute as that of Cohen-Séat's *Essai.*

> The profound transformations of our social existence, the disorders of individual adaptations which characterize our times cannot be solely the signs of an evolution we can gladly admit has occurred too quickly. The multiple changes which have intervened on diverse levels of the human condition could end tomorrow in a radical and global variation of such a major sort that it could only be called a *mutation.*

Everything goes on as though the crisis we are going through has not become acute enough to cause alarm.... Nevertheless, what will happen if we are one day forced to admit that an irreversible transformation has taken place, and that the human being has become something *other*, so to speak, without knowing it?[121]

According to Mark Poster, *L'action sur l'homme* "reached what was, for a Marxist viewpoint, the worst possible diagnosis that the primary mutilation of men occurred no longer at work, but in leisure activities."[122] Although perhaps colored by the pessimism of a decade and a half in which the filmologists had been unable to affect the face of the film medium in any meaningful way, the basic assessment of the crisis posed by the media had progressed very little from that observed by Cohen-Séat 15 years earlier.

Questions of Censorship

Although a sense of social mission was explicit in Cohen-Séat's original conception of filmology, the thrust of the new discipline remained primarily theoretical. In practical terms, in fact, filmology's major achievement was the legitimation of film study within the French academic institution. Shaping the cinema as social practice proved to be a far more difficult goal, and the results were far less immediate.

Almost from the beginning of the cinema as an institution, social critics had posited the possibility of its dangerous effects. Since at least 1909 in the United States and 1912 in England and France, reformers had made attempts to regulate or censor the cinema in order to protect viewers in general and children in particular.[123] To a significant extent, the social mission of filmology descends from this very early concern about the social effects of film; and a concern for the cinema's effects on children remains a central focus throughout filmological studies, be they sociological or psychological. As early as issue 2, the *Revue* had reported British audience studies which emphasized the widespread influence of film on the behavior of children and adolescents.[124] In issue 6, another British study involving 5000 subjects between the ages of 13 and 17 pinpointed certain factors of concern: the effects of films on the vocabulary and choice of reading material of the young; the capacity of underage viewers to gain entrance to "adults only" screenings; and the dramatic increase of adolescent movie attendance during the early 1940s.[125]

In 1952, the International Congress of the Press, Cinema and Radio for Children, held in Milan, and the International Conference on Infancy, held in Vienna, both devoted their attention to questions of the deleterious effects of the media on children. Reporting on these international gatherings. Hélène Gratiot-Alphandéry writes,

The interest and emotion with which these questions were posed in different countries was confirmed by the fact that, barely several weeks after the Congress in Milan, the International Conference on Infancy, which brought together the representatives of 64 countries in Vienna, voted a resolution asking parents, educators and specialists to unite in "undertaking a campaign to boycott and limit the influence of injurious books and magazines and pernicious films and to demand an effective regulation of publication, projection and sale of such books and films within the limits of the freedom of the press."[126]

Therefore, far from representing the only group concerned with questions of the cinema's effects on children, filmology simply provided a forum for a discussion of widespread concern, offering a certain empirical orientation for the questions posed.

Questions of regulation, censorship and social control of the cinema provided an important subtext to many of the psychological studies undertaken by filmology; but these questions were never posed in a methodical way by the *Revue* until issue 14/15 (July-December 1953), which was devoted entirely to the question of social control. In his introduction to the issue, Cohen-Séat situates the question of censorship in terms of a social defense mechanism similar to the defenses and repressions of the individual ego. "Every censorship apparatus," he writes,

> is the response of a group to the precise dangers by which it feels threatened, and to the vague idea it has of the risks concerning its equilibrium. As badly formulated as these risks may be, the mechanism corresponding to the defenses of social groups is expressed quite clearly in the organs and apparatus charged with exercising censorship. In brief, whether it be a matter of superstitions or taboos, of political or religious prohibitions, or of educational principles and theories, human groups demonstrate, in their collective conduct, systems of auto-defense pushed to the limits by censorship.[127]

For Cohen-Séat, such defense mechanisms present themselves as a necessity of the social organization; but his positivist stance demands that, in a scientific society, such defenses should be determined in the most rational way possible.

> ... if censorship has the mission of protecting individuals in the group and the group itself, it supposes that we consider the dangers to which the absence of censorship would expose the individual and the group. This is the central issue: that the nature of these dangers remains, most of the time, poorly defined.[128]

It is from this perspective that Cohen-Séat asks precisely what are the cinematic phenomena which menace the equilibrium of the individual and the society. The cinema's relationship to delinquency, he notes, has been posed again and again without conclusive evidence.

> Notably, for the past two years, study conferences, international congresses and lectures have attempted repeatedly to provide an agreeable base for measures of control regarding

the modern techniques of communication in general and the cinema in particular. This work, which has generally resulted in more or less formal conclusions, important in themselves, still does not seem to have led to positive solutions, nor has it resolved the discrepancies in practice.[129]

Therefore, Cohen-Séat views the mission of filmology as posing the question of censorship rationally and scientifically, and providing the data by which the determinations of social control can be made.

The articles following Cohen-Séat's introduction, however, did less to provide hard data than to indicate the areas in which such data was desperately needed. For the most part, they were position papers on the subject of censorship. Professor Mergen of the University of Mayence and Director of the Luxemburg Institute of Social Defense, for example, offers the opinion that "a film can perfectly well be a work of art while having bad repercussions on the collective or individual psyche."[130] Thus, Mergen argues, there can be no confusion between aesthetic value and social effects when it comes to social control. The cinema does have effects on mental hygiene, he continues, but they are neither immediate nor spectacular: "They are slow, but consequential; for good or bad; for health or sickness." Nevertheless, he adds, any action taken toward censorship "should be grounded in scientific considerations to the exclusion of all others (above all, political)."[131] Mergen's ideal of separating scientific and political considerations, much like the separation of aesthetic and social considerations, came under attack in another article in the same issue written by Edgar Morin.

Morin's piece, "The Problem of the Cinema's Dangerous Effects," is largely a refutation of simplistic correlations between film content and social behavior. Tracing social reactions to the cinema from the early part of the century, and touching upon the American studies of film and delinquency in the 1930s, he places the current concern with social control in the perspective of "dogmas more or less consciously arising from an 'anti-cinematic psychosis.'" All such equations between film and imitative social behavior, Morin argues, are the result of forgetting that "the situation of the viewer is essentially an aesthetic situation."[132] He admits that studies indicate certain secondary influences in social and sexual behavior; but essentially, he asserts, "the drama represented on the screen—crime, murder, violence—is resolved in catharsis."[133]

In the same issue, an article by Gertrude Keir of the Psychology Department of the University College of London, entitled "The Role, Necessity and Value of Censorship," argues exactly the opposite. Defending the British ratings system which restricts attendance by age, she asserts that "fear provoked by the cinema cannot have so great a cathartic effect as some pretend if it provokes nightmares or similar troubles."[134] Morin, on the other hand, asserts the equally supportable conjecture that film plays "a beneficial role as an escape valve for aggressive impulses."[135] Arguing that the belief in the cinema's dangerous effects ignores the fact of the aesthetic situation of the viewer and subscribes erroneously to an assumption of a dangerous susceptibility in youth, Morin writes,

> An examination of the problem of the pernicious influence of the cinema brings us to reject all justifications of censorship in this area. The true sociological foundations of censorship run far deeper than all the secondary justifications and pretexts put forward. Their realm is that of the political taboos of the established order and of magical taboos which reject the horror of the decomposition of bodies and the frenzy of lovemaking, the nudity of death and sexuality.[136]

Thus, Morin situates the question of censorship within the context of ideology.

It is the article by Dr. Serge Lebovici, an important contributor to filmological research in psychology and psychoanalysis who instructed a course in criminology during 1952-53, which offers the most thorough presentation of the filmological question regarding the cinema and criminal behavior. He begins by noting that virtually no conclusive research on the subject is available, but that the questions posed have generally fallen into two categories:

1. Are there precise cases where film can be invoked as the cause—if not uniquely, then at least primarily—of criminal conduct?
2. By what means is film capable of affecting the anti-social behavior of the delinquent?[137]

Agreeing with Morin's position that current assumptions correlating the cinema and crime are hasty and ill-founded, Lebovici nevertheless offers certain data gained from empirical study. Delinquency, he notes, is not an isolated act provoked by any single factor. Yet, in terms of social observation, "maladjustment can begin to express itself in the abusive frequentation of the cinema, which may lead to truancy, brawls, familial thefts, venal homosexuality, prostitution, etc."[138] While the cinema cannot be considered "a specific factor of criminality," Lebovici continues, it plays a certain role simply by the importance it holds in contemporary society; therefore, criminology cannot ignore it as an influence on "certain individuals predisposed toward delinquency or on habitual delinquents."[139] Acknowledging the difficulties involved in keeping children away from films, even when those films are restricted, Lebovici concludes by observing that the legal question is "delicate," without proposing any practical solutions.[140]

The speculations on censorship in issue 14/15 represent something of the breadth of filmology's concerns with social praxis. In practical terms, the debate on censorship would never produce a unified position or course of action. Nevertheless, the concern with social control informed much of the research undertaken by the filmologists, especially with regard to psychological studies, which focused mostly on children and adolescents.

Psychological Considerations:
Theoretical Studies

From the very inception of filmology, psychology played a key role in its approach to film. At the first assembly of the Association pour la Recherche Filmologique, President Mario Roques stated quite clearly that he considered filmology to be of "most interest" to psychologists.[1] Writing in *La Pensée* in 1947, Henri Wallon, one of France's most outstanding child psychologists, who had operated his own laboratory in experimental psychology since 1922,[2] forwards the opinion that psychology is the very basis of filmological study. "In all the problems raised by the cinema in the applications of art or philosophy," he writes, "there is a psychical and technical subfoundation which must be explored in order to pose them correctly."[3]

Assessing the historical foundations of the movement ten years later, Ernesto Valentini writes,

> It can be said that, at the beginning of filmology, Cohen-Séat's book did not particularly emphasize the psychological aspect. He chose the nature of the film/viewer relationship as the basis of his conception, drawing attention to the way the viewer participates in the film, reliving it more than simply watching it. I would like to point out that, for this man who was not a psychologist but a man of culture and a careful researcher, the relationships between the film and the viewer pointed precisely to the filmic themes of other disciplines (for example, aesthetics, sociology, ethics and teaching) because the psychological foundation underlies them all.[4]

Thus, Valentini sees psychology as the implicit foundation of filmology, even in Cohen-Séat's first posing of the problematic. Certainly, Souriau located his filmological considerations in relation to psychology, despite his primary concerns with philosophical questions of art and the scientific analysis of the art work.[5] For the sociologist as well, the study of the film's effects upon society found a basis in the study of its effects on the individual viewer and touched upon questions of mass psychology.

Henri Wallon was nevertheless the primary spokesman for the psychological considerations of filmology during its early years. In his first article for the *Revue*, "On Several Psycho-Physiological Problems Posed by the Cinema," he outlines the way in which psychological questions organize the filmological question. Proceeding from an assumption similar to Cohen-Séat's with regard to the changes in society and in the individual wrought by the cinema, he poses the questions of its effects specifically in terms of psychological and physiological dependencies:

> We must not avoid the fact that the cinema has become for certain people a need whose deprivation causes a kind of anxiety. The cinema for the cinema, and not for a good film or a nice story, has become a requirement which has considerably expanded the number of its faithful. Is this not proof that it creates reactions independent of anything but itself, reactions by which it touches certain profound and elementary sources of the feelings, as do mountain climbing and the use of toxic chemicals?[6]

Mentioning a variety of changes in people's perception brought about by film, he notes the similarity of the cinema to "what Lévy-Bruhl called 'the primitive mentality,' [in which] strange coexistences and inexplicable correspondences play a part in common beliefs."[7] In terms of the viewer's psychological relationship to the film itself, Wallon notes that the cinema "operates in the place of the spectator. It presents the object from successively different angles; it chooses details for closeups. It substitutes its investigation for our own."[8] Here Wallon raises questions not only of the viewer's thought processes in front of the movie screen, but of the necessity of comprehending the manner in which events are related. Therefore, he observes, filmology must attempt to discover at what age and mental level a person is capable of understanding the film story. Finally, Wallon raises the question of the viewer's psycho-physiological reactions to the film, asking what effects the accommodation of the eye to the perception of the luminous image must have, including perhaps "fatigue, a vague hypnotic influence, a feeling of effort."[9] Thus, in this fundamental article, he surveys the breadth of filmology's psychological considerations, from those questions which must be answered by psycho-physiological experimentation to those psychoanalytic questions implied by the film/viewer relationship.

Experimental psychology, of course, provided filmology with its most precise empirical data; but this data was quite limited in its application when isolated from the thrust of the other considerations of the movement. Prior to the publication of experimental data in the *Revue* in issue 3/4 (1948), psychological questions tended to be posed in psychoanalytic and pedagogical terms. Simultaneous to the publication of this empirical research, the *Revue* also published studies on filmic perception philosophically grounded in phenomenology. The duality of these approaches was never fully resolved in a single filmological position. Instead filmology served to establish a problematic which requires scientific precision, while encompassing a philosophical stance that denied the primacy of science.

For the purpose of this study, the psychological considerations of filmology will be divided into two major groups: theoretical and empirical. Here I will treat the theoretical and philosophical studies concerning the psychological aspects of film, which may be grouped into two major categories: (1) the application of perceptual psychology, with its existential phenomenological bases, to the filmic fact, a combination which many filmologists found well suited to explain the way in which the viewer perceives the screen; and (2) the application of psychoanalytic theory, a relatively minor consideration for filmology, but one which offers an interesting and ultimately fundamental position. The following chapter will examine the empirical psychological studies by which filmology asserted its scientific basis, its attempts to apply this research in pedagogical practice, and the position of such research at the time of the Second International Congress of Filmology in 1955.

Perceptual Psychology and Film

The key text for situating the perceptual studies of filmology was written immediately prior to the actual foundation of the movement. Originally delivered as a lecture at IDHEC in 1945 by the influential phenomenologist Maurice Merleau-Ponty, the article demonstrates a clear application of phenomenological studies to the study of film. According to Merleau-Ponty, the "new psychology," which is perceptual, demonstrates that "the perception of forms, understood very broadly as structure, grouping or configuration should be considered our spontaneous way of seeing."[10] He refers here to something more than the registration of light on the retina and the transmission of that data to the brain via the optic nerve. "I perceive in a total way with my whole being," Merleau-Ponty continues, "I grasp a unique structure of the thing, a unique way of being, which speaks to all my senses at once."[11]

Beginning with this model of perception, and its emphasis on structuring and the gestalt of the subject, Merleau-Ponty demonstrates its direct applicability to film.

> If we now consider the film as a perceptual object, we can apply what we have just said about perception in general to the perception of a film. We will see that this point of view illuminates the nature and significance of the movies and that the new psychology leads us straight to the best observations of the aestheticians of the cinema.
>
> Let us say right off that a film is not a sum total of images, but a temporal gestalt.[12]

To demonstrate this claim, Merleau-Ponty cites the famous "Pudovkin experiment" (more often referred to as the "Kuleshov experiment") in which the same shot of an actor's face was perceived differently by an audience in each instance that it was edited together with images of various objects. The varying perception of the same object according to its context supports Merleau-Ponty's conclusion that "the meaning of a shot therefore depends on what precedes it in the movie, and this succession of scenes creates a new reality which is not merely the sum of its parts."[13] Thus Merleau-Ponty offers an explanation of the operation of the cinema which resembles the Soviet theorists' understanding of the function of montage, and which again raises the question of film language in its concern with "structuring" or syntax.

Yet Merleau-Ponty is less concerned with the film's construction of meaning than he is with the links between the "new psychology" and existential phenomenology, both of which present

> consciousness thrown into the world, subject to the gaze of others and learning from them what it is; [the new psychology] does not, in the manner of classical philosophies, present mind *and* world, each particular consciousness *and* others. Phenomenological or existential philosophy is largely an expression of surprise at this inherence of the self in the world and in others, a description of this paradox and permeation, and an attempt to make us *see* the bond between subject and world, between subject and others, rather than to *explain* it as the classical philosophies did by resorting to absolute spirit. Well, the movies are peculiarly suited to make manifest the union of mind and body, mind and world, and the expression of one in the other. That is why it is not surprising that a critic should evoke philosophy in connection with a film.[14]

It is finally in this philosophical context that Merleau-Ponty sees the question of film and psychology:

> ... If philosophy is in harmony with the cinema, if thought and technical effort are heading in the same direction, it is because the philosopher and the moviemaker share a certain way of being, a certain view of the world which belongs to a generation. It offers us yet another chance to confirm that modes of thought correspond to technical methods and that, to use Goethe's phrase, "What is inside is also outside."[15]

Merleau-Ponty's article provides the philosophical basis for the kinds of studies of filmic perception which appeared in issue 3/4 of the *Revue,* the most rigorous of which was prepared by Dr. R. C. Oldfield of Oxford University and entitled "Visual Perception of Images in the Cinema, in Television and in Radar." Like Merleau-Ponty, Oldfield maintains not only the usefulness of perceptual studies in examining the cinema, but the importance of cinema in providing "those who study visual perception a research tool whose power and flexibility surpass all those which have existed up to this point."[16] In his article, Oldfield carefully analyzes the changes which occur between the "original scene and the final impression made in the subject."[17] The (filmophanic/screenic) image itself is simply "composed of a certain spatial distribution of luminous intensities on the surface of the screen. In addition, 25 times a second [sic] the total brightness is briefly reduced to zero."[18]

Noting that the impression of the filmic image on the retina is therefore quite different from the impression made by the object represented by the image, Oldfield demonstrates that "visual perception is not simply a passive recording of an external stimulus, but...consists of an activity of the perceiving subject."[19] He then proceeds to discuss the devices which allow the viewer to reconstitute the light patterns on the screen as objects in motion: the phi phenomenon, which leads to the perceptual construction of apparent movement; the phenomenon by which figures in perspective are perceived in depth; the luminous quality of the screen, which focuses perception on the image as separate from the darkness of the theatre; and the notion of gestalt psychology that "the orientation and the position of objects in the visual field tend to remain constant despite incessant movements of the eyes, the rotation of the head and the changes in the attitude of the body," which accounts for the constancy of filmic perception despite changes from shot to shot.[20] All of these factors, Oldfield writes, contribute to the impression of reality given by the cinema, which depends less on a precision of detail than on psychological responses.

In the same issue of the *Revue,* Albert Michotte van den Berck, professor at the University of Louvain and Member of the Academy of Belgium, pursued the phenomenological question of the film's impression of reality with even further precision. Michotte begins with the following premise:

> It seems certain that cinematic representations give to the majority of viewers throughout most of a film a very lively impression of the *reality* of the things and the adventures which they perceive on the screen, and that this impression easily surpasses what the other plastic arts are able to achieve.[21]

Commenting on the viewer's tendency to identify the filmic image with the actual object it represents, he goes on to examine the possible perceptual factors which might encourage this equation of the "symbol" and the "symbolized,"[22] the most important of which is movement. According to Michotte, movement on the one hand "liberates the object from the plane in which it is integrated," while on the other it provides the single element of the film which "always possesses the character of reality," since the *movement* of the patterns of light on the screen is actual; that is, movement is a reality unlike the objects which are simply represented and constructed by the viewer from the various light impressions on the screen.[23]

In the following issue of the *Revue,* Pierre Francastel, later renowned as a pioneer in the sociology of art, took issue with Michotte in an article entitled "Space and Illusion":

> The affirmation sometimes made that movement is always exactly and faithfully perceived is misleading. Movement does not exist in itself, detached from objects and from different coordinates of plastic space. It does not possess a privileged character, it is not an essence. It is not perceived except as a quality abstractly detached from a more complex whole.[24]

For Francastel, the primary consideration is the film's representational quality.

> Whatever may be the role of movement or time or any other technical or psychological element in the mechanism of expression and filmic comprehension, we must never forget that film postulates space. It is for that reason above all that it is distinguished from literature and music, and that it is grouped, for obvious reasons, with the plastic arts.[25]

In this way, Francastel poses the problem of filmic movement as "an aspect of space/time conflict more alive than ever in our epoch. The analysis of different rhythms, different film times, on the screen and in our minds, constitutes one of the first objects of inquiry supposed by a methodically elaborated filmology of plastic space."[26]

Setting himself at odds with Oldfield and Michotte, Francastel turns his attention to the conventions of representation:

> The point of departure for all concrete speculation on filmic space is in the recognition of the psychological and social character of perspective. It is not a golden rule or a fixed law corresponding to a substantive law of nature; it is a function of the intellect, one of the frames which confers an order to the sensations in the mind.[27]

This approach to the filmic image corresponds closely to the views forwarded on the subject of painting in Francastel's *Peinture et société,* published at approximately the same time as his filmological study. In this book, he traces the historical correlations between cultures and their representations of plastic space, beginning with the development of perspective in the Renaissance to its breakdown in the modern movement of Cubism.[28] As does his book, Francastel's article on film emphasizes the socio-cultural determinations of representation:

> Each epoch, each society, each age of humanity, each profession, each human being has its attention attracted by a particular aspect of the exterior world; each has its space, its perspective. Film does not propose to us a plastic representation of space substantially different from those of the other arts. The introduction of movement has not introduced the problem of time into the plastic representation of the world, nor has it revealed a privileged system more definitive than others.[29]

Thus, perspective in film, as in the painting of the Renaissance, is a structuring of representation according to a specific, determined system. It is in this manner that Francastel moves the problem of perception back toward the question of signification:

> The great error which is constantly committed is to begin the study of film as if the cinematic spectacle placed us in the presence of reality's double. We must never forget that the film is constructed of images—fragmentary objects, limited and elusive, like all objects. What appears on the screen is neither real nor what was envisioned in the mind of the filmmaker, nor even the image which forms in our minds; it is a sign, in the strictest sense of the word.[30]

Albert Michotte van den Berck answered Francastel's rather direct critique of his article in the following issue of the *Revue,* taking Francastel to task for misunderstanding and even misquoting him. Without responding to any of Francastel's specific points, Michotte explains that he had never asserted that movement was responsible for the viewer's impression of volume or depth, but that it was simply one of the characteristics which contributed to producing the effect of reality. Obviously a bit angry, Michotte lamented a problem which had plagued filmology from the beginning:

> All this shows once again how difficult it can be for people of different backgrounds, practicing different disciplines, to comprehend the questions posed in the framework of their own science and the significance attached to the solution of those problems.[31]

The question of perception vs. signification would remain the subject of a continuing theoretical debate throughout the development of filmology. In issue 3/4 of the *Revue,* Marc Soriano had already begun to address this difficulty in a comparison between the reading of literature and the understanding of a film. As opposed to reading a text in a given language, where letters and words are indeed *signs,* Soriano argues, the film viewer

> does not move from image to image, from an image perceived on the screen to its signification, and from this signification to the following image; it is far more a case of him perceiving the signification in the image.... [Reading] appeals to the mediating power of meaning (our view delivers signs to us); the cinema, on the contrary, has an immediate power and, like reality, gives us a representation taken from possession. That is the reason that the pastime of reading assumes a "trained" culture, while the cinema became quickly accessible to a vast audience.[32]

For Soriano, the basis of the viewer's capacity to perceive "signification in the image" arises from a simple observation: "Like all other perceptions, that of the cinema is spatio-temporal. From the point of view of the viewer, it is quite close to perception itself."[33]

Jean-Jacques Riniéri elaborates this point more philosophically in his essay "The Impression of Reality in the Cinema: Phenomena of Belief," which appeared in Souriau's *L'univers filmique* in 1953. Reiterating Michotte's observation on the reality of screenic movement, Riniéri asserts that it is the viewer's apprehension of this reality which lends a sense of belief to what Souriau defined as the "second degree screenic phenomena, that level which determines the plane of immediate signification, where the first apprehension of the filmic object by the consciousness takes place."[34] This first degree reality, Riniéri admits, operates to a far smaller degree than in the theatre, where the actors and objects are actually perceived; yet the cinema makes up for this in two ways. First, it expands the possibilities of representation available to the stage, making a "compensatory investment" of imaginative energy on the level of the "second degree." Second, it increases this effect by encouraging a passive receptiveness in the viewer.[35]

Riniéri is nevertheless careful to distinguish between exterior reality and the first degree reality of the screen, which is the source of the viewer's "belief":

> the brute given of the screen, stripped of all signification in reference to the cosmic universe. This dimension is that of pure sensation with the affective values which that calls forth.... That is, the problems of reality in the cinema have an aesthetic and philosophical incidence which is singularly attached to the realm of perceptual psychology: the screenic realm is not only one determination among others in the field of perception; it is also and above all the promoter of a new type of reality and a new type of belief.... [36]

It was Henri Wallon, also writing in 1953, who most clearly defined psychological questions raised by this new type of reality. Observing that perception "first supposes exterior excitations, then that these excitations provoke a representation, and finally that this representation be placed in relation to other objects,"[37] he describes the way in which reading proceeds from the perception of the letters and words to the evocation of representations in the reader's mind. These representations may have nothing to do with the external world, and therefore have nothing to do with perception. Yet, in the cinema there is no distinction between the image in the mind and the image on the screen. Thus, Wallon distinguishes between the perceptual act and the filmic act. In the perceptual act, the object is separate from the subject; "two beings are posed, facing one another, my partner or the object and myself."[38] The filmic act departs from this duality:

> If the cinema produces its effect, it is because I identify with its images, because I forget myself more or less in favor of that which unfurls on the screen. I am no longer in my own life; I am in the film which is projected before me.[39]

Virtually every application of perceptual psychology by the filmologists attempted to define this "filmic act," to describe what Riniéri called "a new type of reality and a new type of belief." Theoretically, the superficial resemblances between the filmic image and the external world were not enough to justify the viewer's sense of "belief," the impression of reality engendered by the cinema. It was even more difficult to explain the way in which this art, whose images were apprehended in their full immediacy by the viewer, could also construct meaning in the viewer's mind. Thus, a problematic was posed by filmology which was not to be revived until the 1960s, when Christian Metz began once again to attempt a reconciliation between filmic perception and the question of film signification.

Psychoanalysis and Film

Although a number of significant articles applying psychoanalytic theory to film appeared in the first five issues of the *Revue,* psychoanalysis remained a relatively minor field for filmology. Its importance to the movement diminished as the filmologists became increasingly interested in empirical data; yet at the beginning, psychoanalysis seemed theoretically equipped to treat the central filmological question of the viewer's identification with the screen.

Like many of the articles appearing in the first issues of the *Revue,* the psychoanalytic studies remained somewhat unfocused. Cohen-Séat's *Essai* had left the filmological position of psychoanalysis rather vague, offering only a few questions which might be answered by the field. Even more indicative was filmology's grouping of psychoanalysis under the category of "Normative Studies," emphasizing the practical use which the field might be able to make of the cinema as an analytic tool, in opposition to the theoretical contributions it might make to the study of film.

It was not until issue 6 that Serge Lebovici, a clinical psychiatrist and teacher at the Faculté de Médecine in Paris, published an article in the *Revue* which attempted to group psychoanalytic concerns regarding the cinema. In this article, Lebovici observes two major applications of psychoanalysis to the study of film:

1. to the film itself, inasmuch as it is a human production and material for study;

2. to the spectator, his attitude and his reactions in front of the screen, and his action upon the film.[40]

This division of psychoanalytic concerns between the film text and the film viewer not only categorized previous studies, but also indicated the two major areas in which psychoanalysis would be applied to the cinema by later theorists in France during the 1970s.

Lebovici's own application of psychoanalysis involved the comparison of film and dream. Like the dream, he observes, "cinematic language is 'in images,'" and both film and dream utilize a "symbolic writing" in conveying meaning.[41] The narrative mobility of the film provides another point of comparison, since

the images of the dream are inverted; they succeed one another without causal lines; they are condensed, "overdetermined." In much the same way, the camera does not follow a character in all his movements. It shows him from different successive viewpoints. It goes from one character to another.... [42]

Finally, he notes, the film functions as wish-fulfillment for its audience, in much the same way Freud describes the function of the dream for the dreamer. Implicit in this comparison of film and dream is the suggestion that a film might be submitted to the same kind of analytic method applied to the dream by the psychoanalyst; and though Lebovici does not himself pursue such a "textual analysis," he proposes a theoretical basis for the work which such film analysts as Thierry Kuntzel would undertake more than 20 years later.[43]

Turning to the question of the viewer's relationship to the screen, Lebovici once again notes the similarities to the dream. The dream is perceived as a series of images seemingly exterior to the dreamer, he observes: "Thus the dream has the character of a spectacle and often the dreamer does not participate in his own dream...the dreamer watches [*assiste:* attends; witnesses] his own dream."[44] The situation of the dreamer therefore bears some significant similarities to that of the film viewer, which are emphasized by the filmgoer's passivity before the screen in the darkness of the theatre. The significant difference, Lebovici notes, is that, despite the passivity of both the dreamer and the film viewer, the dreamer is nevertheless the "author of his dream," which is not the case in the cinema.[45] Lebovici concludes his article with a justification of psychoanalysis in filmology which he claims must be based on the idea that "concrete interpretations exist between filmic facts and psychic facts."[46] Forwarding an observation which was made as early as 1916 by American psychologist Hugo Munsterberg (whose work on film was virtually unknown in the late 1940s),[47] Lebovici contends that "the film is constructed in the image of our psyche; and it is certainly not—given its importance—without some effect upon it."[48]

The most complex psychoanalytic analyses of the film/viewer relationship to arise from filmology, however, appeared in the *Revue* prior to Lebovici's article. Written by a young scholar named Jean Deprun, the articles "Cinema and Identification" and "Cinema and Transfer" involved a fairly technical theoretical comparison between the relationship of the film viewer and the movie screen and that of the patient and the psychoanalyst. In the former article, Deprun applies psychoanalytic terminology to that aspect of the film/viewer relationship which Wallon would summarize as "I am no longer in my own life." As Deprun put it, "I discharge myself of my ego."[49] Pursuing his examination of the viewer's identification with the screen, he observes that "the filmic image requires no perceptual effort. It is given to us already perceived, already centered."[50] Thus, to some extent, the film usurps the ego of the viewer, working in its place to choose and process what he sees.

Deprun is therefore careful to distinguish between the cinematic situation of the viewer and the often compared situations of the dream and the hallucination, where "the image remains my own work: I hold it at arm's length; I am its dupe and its accomplice.... The consciousness which dreams fascinates itself; in the cinema, I am fascinated from *without*."[51] For Deprun, the cinematic situation bears a stronger resemblance to hypnosis, in which (according to Freud) the hypnotist is substituted for the subject's ego ideal (the terrible father, the loved mother, etc.) and, on the strength of the fascination of the hypnotized subject and his/her fixation on a brilliant object (Deprun: "and how can we not think of the movie screen?"), is able to direct the subject's thoughts.[52] Deprun quotes Freud: "It is as though the hypnotist said to the subject: now that you no longer occupy yourself except in my person, the world has lost its interest."[53]

The comparison between the subject directed by the hypnotist or psychoanalyst and the viewer directed by the screen is pursued further in Deprun's second article, "Cinema and Transfer." Here the viewer's identification is compared to the psychoanalytic conception of "projection," where the subject attributes his/her own feelings and/or faults to others. As Deprun puts it, *"Projection changes timidity into hatred; it finally puts my own forces to work in the world."*[54] The psychoanalytic cure involves a process of stable projection, in which the patient transfers infantile reactions onto the analyst. If the cinema works in much the same way, Deprun asks, "can it, like the analyst, use its influence to render influence impossible? . . . Can the cinema in its present state assure the projection of [neurotic] complexes?" If so, he explains, it would require two conditions: first, that these complexes be raised from their depths and "figured" as manageable (*maniable:* controllable) objects; second, that, once projected, they be dissolved, ridding the subject of them altogether. The cinema accomplishes the former, Deprun writes, but not the latter. Nevertheless, the correlations between the two processes are striking.[55]

Two articles appearing in the early issues of the *Revue* undertake the comparison of the viewer/film relationship to specific psychoanalytic practices, implying a protential application of cinema to the analytic process. Psychiatrist Robert Desoille, in his article "The Daydream and Filmology," describes a personally developed therapeutic process known as the "directed daydream" (*le rêve éveillé dirigé*) in which he directed a resting patient through a reverie, describing scenes for him/her to imagine. Desoille notes several obvious analogies to the action of the film on the viewer, very much in keeping with Deprun's observations on the analogy of hypnosis.[56] The second article, "The Film Process of Projective Analysis," written by Agostino Gemelli, a Milanese university professor and President of the Pontifical Academy of Sciences, attempts to demonstrate that film can be utilized as an analytic tool similar to, but more effective than, for example, the Rorschach test or the psychodrama.[57]

Despite such provocative articles as those by Deprun and Lebovici, psychoanalysis remained outside the main theoretical thrust of filmology. Even aesthetic philosophy found a more central role in the movement, due to the compatibility of Souriau's aesthetics with the scientific empiricism underlying many of filmology's basic assumptions. The psychoanalytic study of the cinema therefore emerged as a relatively minor part of the problematic established by filmology, but it laid the groundwork in its field with such precision that, when the linguistic studies of film in France during the 1960s moved further into psychoanalytic considerations, they returned to the place where Deprun and Lebovici had begun.

8

Psychological Considerations: Empiricism and Social Application

In *Language and Cinema,* Christian Metz focuses his discussion of filmology on the empirical study of the film viewer, which was perhaps the movement's single most characteristic contribution. "Filmology, for the most part, concerned itself with the study of film with methods proper to psychology, experimental and social psychology in particular," he writes. "It is precisely in this area that it has achieved its most precise results."[1] In fact, this precision was limited to specific cases, since few of the studies published in the *Revue* corroborated one another in terms of actual data. Filmology's main difficulty with empirical studies, however, was more profound. Despite the organizational project of the First International Congress of Filmology, the direction of laboratory experimentation by the Institut de Filmologie, and numerous articles on the subject appearing in the *Revue,* no consensus of goals or procedures was ever established which might have synthesized the wide variety of empirical studies undertaken. Cohen-Séat's *Essai* had left the issue unresolved, assuming that a synthesis would arise in the course of practice; yet, even at the time of the Second International Congress of Filmology in 1955, where empirical research not only dominated the concerns of the gathering, but demonstrated itself to be the only vital enterprise remaining within the province of the movement, no consensus on the direction or methods of research could be reached.

Basically, the empirical research carried out by the filmologists can be divided into two broad categories: the first, involving the testing of the viewer's psycho-physiological responses to filmic stimuli, with an emphasis on the monitoring of brain waves by means of the electroencephalograph (EEG); the second, employing the methods of psychological testing to provide descriptive data for the evaluation of the film/viewer relationship in terms of the viewer's response, comprehension and memory.

Practical applications of these studies remained vague, despite the fact that practice was a great concern to filmology, given its social mission. The question of application is formulated as a debate running throughout a number of psychological studies published in the *Revue.* The question was whether filmology was to study film by means of psychological tests, or whether filmology was to demonstrate the potential of film as an instrument in the advancement of experimental psychology. Finally, the single concrete application of filmological testing seemed to be in the use of films for teaching. The pedagogical potential of film returned again and again as a theme in the *Revue,* probably because it was in this area that filmology could point toward its only practical effects upon the object of its study.

Psycho-Physiological Testing and Filmology

Given the scientific project of filmology and its central question regarding the effects of film on the viewer, the methodical testing of the film audience was given a high priority by the members of the movement. Cohen-Séat had emphasized the importance of hard empirical data; Wallon reiterated the importance of psycho-physiological testing; and even Souriau would attempt to apply the empirical method in proving his philosophical assertions.

It was not until issue 5 of the *Revue,* however, that the results of the first filmological tests were published. Once this was begun, however, the trend continued in full force throughout the 1950s. What is particularly interesting about this most "scientific" enterprise of filmology is the lack of any real theoretical focus in the experimentation. The main emphasis of the psycho-physiological testing centered on the examination of electroencephalograms of subjects submitted to certain stimuli—not all of which corresponded directly to film viewing.

When filmology embarked on its scientific study of film, psycho-physiological testing was given the highest priority among some of the movement's key figures, largely due to the fact that no such experiments had been carried out in any methodical way. Addressing a symposium on filmology at the Eighth International Congress of Psychology in Stockholm, July 1951, Henri Wallon once again asserted the importance of such tests:

> Physiology is the root of the cinema, since it is the persistence of the retinal image which renders possible the perception of movement from successive images projected on a screen at a proper cadence. A number of physiological questions can be posed: the limits of possible variation in this cadence and the optimum cadence; the accommodation of vision to the variable luminescence of the screen, much brighter in its relation to the darkness of the theatre; and even the possible consequences of asynchronization or hypersynchronization between the rhythm of the retinal images and the cerebral rhythms which electroencephalography today permits us to study experimentally.[2]

By the time of this Congress, several of the experiments suggested by Wallon had already been begun by filmological researchers.

Although it was issue 7/8 before the *Revue* published the results of the first electroencephalographic experiments, issue 5 ran the results of what the *Revue* called a "filmological experiment" which had taken place in 1920. This experiment, entitled "Respiratory Reactions in the Course of Cinematic Projection," was carried out by Dr. E. Toulousse, a former director of the Laboratory of Experimental Psychology at the Ecole des Hautes Etudes, and Dr. R. Mourgue, a physician of the public mental hospital. Stating the objectives of their experiment in 1920, they wrote, "We have limited our research to a single point: can we evaluate the reactions provoked by a film on its viewers, whatever its aesthetic value may be?"[3] Interestingly, Toulousse and Mourgue demonstrate a knowledge of Hugo Munsterberg's work regarding the effects of advertising on the public's selection of products, but seem to be unaware of his writings on the film. It is nevertheless Munsterberg whom they cite as an inspiration for their study, which involved monitoring the respiration of two female subjects, "one very emotional, the other expressing little feeling," in approximately 100 situations of film viewing. "We have not made a psychological study," they assert. "The single thing we wished to know was whether or not there was a reaction." Their conclusion was that a reaction did occur, but without any real consistency.[4]

In his introduction to the *Revue*'s reprinting of this 30-year-old study, Yves Galifret refers to Toulousse and Mourgue as "illustrious predecessors" of filmology, and discusses similar experiments recently undertaken by Enrico Fulchignoni, a professor at the University of Rome and a "distinguished filmologist," demonstrating that the reduction of projection speed from 24 to 16 frames per second provokes a slowing of the respiratory rhythm of the viewer, accompanied by an increase in the amplitude of respiratory movement.[5]

In an article from the previous issue of the *Revue*, "Cinema and the Physiology of Sensations," Galifret had posed another significant physiological question requiring experimental examination.

> The question is raised of the possibilities of interference between the autonomous alpha rhythm and the rhythm of the cinematic projection. Should we search in such a mechanism for the cause of migraines, which we know were once provoked in the devotees of the *théâtre cinématographique* by the rhythm of 16 frames per second?
>
> Can we not ask if this captivation of the brain's autonomous rhythm by a rhythmic stimulation is capable of provoking states close to hypnosis?[6]

Providing an answer to these questions required the study of the viewer's brain waves during the course of projection; and, as Wallon had suggested, the key to such a study was the relatively new technique of electroencephalography.

The first results of such a study to appear in the *Revue* (issue 7/8) came from an experiment by Henri Gastaut, of the Neuro-Biological Laboratory of the Faculté de Médecine at Marseilles, in collaboration with Annette Roger. The object of their test was to determine the psychological, somatic and electroencephalographic responses of subjects submitted to an "intermittent rhythmic luminous stimulus." Cohen-Séat had himself posed the question to the Faculté de Médecine of Marseilles as to whether such stimulus could account for psychological and somatic changes in the viewing public. Gastaut and Roger attempted to provide at least a partial answer.[7]

The experiment did not involve the actual projection of film, but the rhythmic flashing of a light placed close to the face of the subject, whose eyes remained closed. The psychological effects on a group of "normal subjects" involved a visual impression of geometrical patterns, accompanied in some cases by feelings of sickness or anxiety. No significant somatic effects were measured. The EEG, however, revealed a rhythmic pattern which corresponded to each light impression, registering between 50 and 20 milliseconds after the stimulus. In the case of mentally "abnormal" patients, the psychological effects sometimes involved hallucinations and emotional reactions, while the somatic effects produced were characteristic of a state of anxiety.[8] As expected, the stimulus was found to be unendurable by certain epileptic subjects.[9] Gastaut and Roger drew the following conclusions from their experiment:

1. that intermittent luminous stimulation is, by itself, capable of producing very important psychological, somatic and EEG effects;

2. that these effects are largely due to the irradiation of impulses which circulate in the visual path toward the cerebral area;

3. that this irradiation depends upon:
    a. the state of excitability of the subject....
    b. the interval separating the light stimuli, which has its greatest effect between 40 and 100 milliseconds, with an optimum of 70 milliseconds (corresponding to 15 cycles per second).[10]

EEG studies became the focus of most of the psycho-physiological testing employed by filmology during the next several years. In fact, in 1954, issue 16 of the *Revue* was devoted entirely to three major articles treating the results of EEG tests: "Modification of the EEG during Cinematic Projection," "Retention of the 'Filmic Fact' on the Bio-electric Rhythms of the Brain," and "Note on Electroencephalography During the Projection of Films to Maladjusted Children."[11] Mario Roques's introduction to the issue offered both an explanation and an apology to readers:

Undoubtedly, not all our readers are familiar with the method and technique of electroencephalography and its related processes of observation, and we are certainly not qualified to initiate them. But we can, without taking on the task of examining the methods employed and controlling the conditions of the experiments, direct our attention, at least for the moment, to the announced results and the justifications offered us.[12]

Perhaps the most esoteric number of the *Revue* ever to appear, issue 16 indicates the problems raised by the increasing specialization of the various fields of filmology. It was this divergence of interests, and the increasing specialization required in pursuing them separately which marked the definitive end of the eclectic, formative period of filmology.

Interestingly, Cohen-Séat is credited as co-author of all three articles which appeared in issue 16. During 1954, he published a series of studies, in collaboration with Jacques Faure of the Faculté de Médecine of Bordeaux, on electroencephalography and the projection of films, not only for the *Revue*, but also in the *Revue Neurologique* and the *Annales Médico-Psychologiques*.[13] In a report presented by Cohen-Séat and Faure at the Second International Congress of Filmology in February 1955, they summarized the major results obtained from their numerous experiments. The activity of the superior nervous system, they reported, changes constantly during filmic projection.

This superior nervous activity tries to adapt the entire organism to the filmic reality. *The psycho-physiological state of the viewer facilitates or impedes the reception of messages.* When the filmic material becomes awkward or embarrassing, the viewer brings *defense mechanisms* into play and begins to filter the message. . . . But the influence of the filmic fact also depends on *the nature and parameters of the elements presented.* Quick variations in the brightness of the image, the quick, jerky quality of its movement, quick variations in intensity and the rapidity of a character's speech *constitute elements which are aggressive to the nervous system.* The activities of play, a solemn tone of voice and moderately paced speech *constitute pacifying elements.* Our research also distinguished phenomena of *posture-motor currents.* These, which at some times reinforce affective and somatic tension, and at others augment affective relaxation, appear in any case to lend the viewer a *compensatory means of somatic defense* (a system of postural security). In brief, it seems that the repercussion of the projection on the viewer depends upon the quality of his superior nervous activity.[14]

This statement of results represents the substance of filmological progress in the psycho-physiological field during the first decade of the movement.

As director of the Institut de Filmologie during the late 1940s and throughout the 1950s, Cohen-Séat remained a key figure in determining the course such research would take in France. Virtually all of the psycho-physiological research published during this period concerns the monitoring of viewer responses via the EEG. Apparently, during this same period, however, Cohen-Séat also conducted experiments on the effects of subliminal imagery in film, in preparation of his *thèse des lettres* on the subject. In the course of his research in 1950, he discovered what he believed to be a powerful causal link between subliminal images inserted in a film for so brief a period that they were not consciously perceived, and the subsequent behavior of the viewer. Taking his discovery to the government, he was asked by French President Vincent Auriol to keep his research a secret in the interest of national security. Cohen-Séat complied and his thesis was never completed.[15]

Psychological Testing and Filmology

The application of the methods of psychological testing by filmology produced more accessible and immediately practical results than those of psycho-physiological research. Psychological testing was employed as a means of measuring the responses of the film audience, and its goal was the generation of empirical data which might be applied in a properly scientific manner. Nevertheless, methodologies varied radically among the actual studies undertaken, with subjects often selected for convenience, and researchers compiling data in questionnaires, in personal interviews, and in some cases, by photographing subjects or recording the sounds they made during the projection of a film.[16]

The chief concern demonstrated by researchers in this field was the evaluation of the viewer's comprehension of a film. The most important researchers on this subject were René and Bianka Zazzo, who conducted an important series of tests involving the relationship between film comprehension and the viewer's mental level. The empirical evaluation of the subject's "mental level" had enjoyed an important place in French psychology since the late nineteenth century, when the chief of the Sorbonne's laboratory of experimental psychology Alfred Binet was commissioned by the government to develop intelligence tests to aid in the evaluation of mentally deficient students in the public school system. The test which evolved from Binet's extensive studies involving Parisian school children provided the basis for subsequent tests administered to determine the "mental age" of subjects according to established norms.[17] These norms provided the methodological basis for the studies proposed by René Zazzo, a former student of Henri Wallon and teacher at the Ecole des Hautes Etudes, in his first article for the *Revue* in 1949.

> ... whether it is a question of adults or children, if we wish to study the intellectual or affective reactions to film, it is first necessary, *from the filmological point of view*, to begin with individuals whose mental characteristics are already known.[18]

By establishing the viewer as the known quantity in the equation, it becomes possible to make the film the object of analysis. This, Zazzo strongly asserts, is the mission of filmology.

The essential point for researchers coming from such diverse fields is to realize that film is not a new *means* in service of an old discipline, but a new object. Short of that, so-called filmological discussions constitute nothing but an incomprehensible collective monologue.[19]

In outlining a course of research, Zazzo poses the question of comprehension in terms of children. Employing Jean Piaget's concept of "de-centering," he writes,

The ability to establish logical relations between things . . . supposes the possibility of varying the points of view from which things are considered. The very young child is incapable of changing his point of view, of "de-centering" himself. His subjectivity is his sole perspective, and he is therefore unaware of it.[20]

Comprehending a film requires the ability to de-center oneself in space and time, according to techniques which occur quickly and with great complexity. Such techniques as the shot/reverse-shot and the narrative ellipsis of time are elements of a "new language, a new discourse which is defined by its manner of dominating, utilizing and transforming the boundaries of space and time."[21] The question therefore becomes: at what stage of mental development is a person capable of comprehending a film? In addition, which are the elements grasped most easily? In illustration, Zazzo cites the observation of a teaching colleague who had noted the difficulty experienced by children under the age of nine in interpreting the filmic technique of the superimposition.[22]

More than the comprehension of filmic syntax is involved, Zazzo notes. Two individuals of the same mental level, capable of the same logical operations, may still differ according to mental fluidity," which is less a matter of "intellectual personality" than it is of the "voluntary personality" of feeling or "affectivity." In this way, Zazzo accounts for preferential differences among viewers, which he suggests may bear some relationship to the rhythms of certain types of films.[23]

The preliminary results of the tests conducted by René Zazzo and his wife Bianka appeared in the following issue of the *Revue.* The goal of these tests was to establish a hierarchical relationship between the level of comprehension of a filmic sequence and the mental ages of specific viewers. The test group was made up of 42 subjects between the ages of 6 and 25, whose mental ages had been established as ranging between 4 years, 7 months and 14 years. All of the subjects were patients of the Psychological Branch of the Henri-Rousselle Hospital, which meant that full psychological and medical dossiers were already available on each of them.[24] The subjects were shown a short sequence of film depicting a confrontation between two groups of people. This was followed by personal interviews with each subject which began by asking them to talk about what they had seen, then proceeded with a number of fixed questions and concluded with variable questions intended to fill in any information the interviewer considered necessary.[25] The subjects' answers were then evaluated with a simple plus or minus in six categories corresponding to six specific aspects of comprehension which were established empirically, without regard for the specific sequence.

A. comprehension (even if imperfect) of the *movement of the action* and its overall significance. (This will be negative for subjects who limit themselves to listing or describing scenes without indicating a logical line.)

B. capacity to reconstruct space as tied together by the movement of the action. This is a matter of interpreting *alternating sequences as simultaneous events.*

C. capacity to follow and to recall the *chronological sequence* of events presented throughout the sequence....

D. understanding of roles. (We seek only to verify if the distinction between the two groups in the story is clearly made, and if the role of the leaders is understood.)

E. *interpretation of shot/reverse-shot,* one of the essential points of our research since it indicates the subject's capacity for de-centering himself.

F. capacity for a spontaneous recounting of the story which demonstrates a logical unity in the action.[26]

The *Revue* published the results of this test in substantial detail, with excerpts from the subjects' responses and a chart ranking them by mental age and indicating their capacities in each of the categories A through F. Thirty-seven of the 42 subjects followed the movement of the action (A) acceptably; and the same number were able to interpret the alternating scenes as simultaneous actions (B). In the most difficult category, only 15 of the subjects could distinguish between the roles in the sequence (D), which is accounted for by the hypothesis that their attention was held more by the action than by the characters. As for the key category of the shot/reverse-shot (E), only 16 of the 42 could explain the meaning of the technique, which the researchers determined was less a matter of comprehension than of memory. Overall, the level of comprehension corresponded rather closely to the mental age of the subjects.[27]

In a second test involving quite similar methods, the Zazzos attempted to determine at what mental age the same subjects understood the significance of a *dissolve* in a brief sequence of film. The comprehension of this technique corresponded even more closely with mental age than did the results of the first test, with the mental age of eight years, three months as the dividing point between those who understood and those who did not.[28]

Evaluating their results, the Zazzos note the obvious difference between the overall comprehension of a film and the comprehension of an isolated detail (which their study entailed). They also acknowledge that comprehension is not exclusively a function of mental age, but of a "cultural level" as well.[29] Nevertheless, they offer several conclusion:

This first experiment allows us to state that the meaning of a sequence . . . was grasped, on the whole, far more quickly than we had supposed; that the dynamism of film leads to a dynamism in the recounting of the story at an age when children are still at the stage of listing or static description when it is a matter of images or even of lived experience; that the comprehension of condensation by means of the ellipses of time comes much later.[30]

In issue 9 of the *Revue,* two issues later, Bianka Zazzo reported the results of a similar test administered to a group of "normal" subjects: 53 girls from a Parisian school between the ages of 6 and 12. The single significant change in the method of testing involved asking the subjects to arrange a number of still photographs from the film in their proper sequential order. Forty-four of the 53 proved capable of the task, with a competency level beginning at about the age of 7. Only 27 of the subjects succeeded in recounting the film verbally, while 26 did not, indicating "a *disparity of three years* between the demonstration of comprehension by non-verbal means (the arrangement of the photos) and verbal demonstration."[31] With the additional evidence provided by this experiment, Bianka Zazzo was willing to state her conclusion that the comprehension of action in a film begins at the surprisingly early age of seven years. She accounts for this in the following way:

To follow and understand the progression of action, the child is not forced to *talk about and interpret it,* to go from the images to their meaning; it is enough for him to *watch* movements which are perfectly intelligible, since they are concrete, and which succeed one another in a passage of time which is that of reality.[32]

It is intriguing that Bianka Zazzo's observations on this point provide a certain empirical support to the phenomenological view of film which argues that the viewer immediately apprehends the meaning in the image, in opposition to the linguistic notion that film produces meaning in a manner analogous to language. Further, to the extent that she demonstrates the child's capacity to understand a film prior to the capability to verbalize about it, her findings support the notion of the universality of filmic language, which plays such an important role in Cohen-Séat's *Essai* and in the conception of the humanistic mission of filmology. What she fails to consider, however, is the subjects' previous experience of films as a variable which might affect their capacity to comprehend certain filmic techniques. Still, her findings would assert an influence in the field of pedagogy, since they suggested that film might offer a means of conveying information to young children or those with learing difficulties who might not be reached otherwise.

The sociological problematic of filmology provides one of the most significant links between the diverse studies involving psychological testing. In their article "Regarding a Filmological Inquiry Concerning Maladjusted Children and Adolescents," for example, Dr. G. Heuyer, professor of child psychiatry at the Faculté de Médecine in Paris, Dr. Serge Lebovici and Dr. Georges Amado combine the methods of the sociological survey and the psychological case study to make a social point about the cinema. Observing that it is through "the study of the way in which filmic impressions affect the personality, and what these impressions are, that one can determine how the cinema influences children, and how and under what conditions this influence may be good or bad," these researches examine the responses of three maladjusted adolescents, two boys and one girl, regarding their filmgoing habits and preferences, and compare their responses to their case histories.[33] Reaching only tentative conclusions, the doctors warn against the tendency to generalize.

> It seems important to us to insist on prudence in approaching the cinema and personality disorders, especially in the case of questions about cinema and delinquency. Only a thorough study of each case can, in our opinion, determine the precise influence of the cinema on the behavior of a child or adolescent.[34]

Clearly recognizing the limitations of a general application of such studies, Heuyer, Lebovici and Amado affirm their intentions to continue research in the same directions in hopes of attaining more positive results.

Two issues later, Heuyer and Lebovici published the results of another psychological study involving maladjusted children, sponsored by the Institut de Filmologie and carried out at the Clinique de Psychiatrie Infantile during the early part of 1951. The study involved 22 children between the ages of 7 and 17, hospitalized for personality disorders. These children were shown six programs of films, including comedies, cartoons, adventure and crime movies, and an animal film. Pursuing the method of individualized evaluation and treatment, the researchers observed the behavior of each child during the projection and then interviewed each of the subjects individually in order to evaluate (1) the child's general comprehension of the film as compared to his/her mental level, (2) his/her reaction to the comedies, (3) his/her reaction to the cartoons, and (4) the relation between his/her affective state and reactions to the film.[35]

Among their conclusions, Heuyer and Lebovici determined that only the children over the mental age of 12 could synthesize their impressions into an accurate recounting of the films viewed; and that those below the mental age of 9 were unable to provide anything more coherent than a recall of certain images. More specifically, the researchers observed that those children diagnosed as "paranoiacs" did not enjoy the comedies, that an appreciation of satire was not apparent in any of the children beneath the mental age of 12, and that, curiously, "the particular humor of Charlie Chaplin is infinitely less appealing to children than it is to adults."[36] Further, only 4 out of the 20 children observed expressed any liking for the cartoons.[37]

The results of this study are certainly less generally applicable and derived with less methodological rigor than those obtained in the similar studies conducted by René and Bianka Zazzo. The importance of Heuyer and Lebovici's study, however, is that it takes into account an individual subjectivity which could not be figured into the Zazzos' conclusions. For whatever reasons, the results regarding the correlations of mental age and filmic comprehension differ widely between the two studies, demonstrating the difficulties inherent in filmology's attempts to draw "precise results" from tests relying on a variety of uncoordinated empirical methodologies.

Another significant difference between these two studies lies in their stated objectives. In the concluding article concerning her experiment, Bianka Zazzo reiterates the problematic asserted by her husband several issues earlier.

> In the *filmological perspective*, from which this study arises, film is not the instrument, the means, as it may be in the psychological laboratories where it serves in the recording of observations, or as is also the case in its pedagogical application; here, it is the very *object* of research.[38]

In the same issue of the *Revue*, Heuyer and Lebovici assert an opposing theoretical perspective for their study when they observe that

> the film utilized as a projective test is obviously an excellent instrument for character study.... The reactions to films constitute a precious material for the study of character, whether it be in denoting general character tendencies or in revealing a relationship between a given filmic situation and a personal conflict.[39]

This preference for the use of film as an instrument in psychological testing is even more pronounced in the filmological research coming from Italy during this period. In a 1950 article in the *Revue,* the most influential of the Italian filmologists, Enrico Fulchignoni, asserts that film provides one of the best means for refining the "projective test" in psychoanalysis, avoiding many of the methodological flaws in current research on the psychoanalytic phenomenon of projection, which he defines as "a mechanism which consists of attributing our own structures, character traits and tendencies to a person we are involved in judging."[40] Attacking the "philosophico-literary" tendency of psychoanalysis to theorize without empirical evidence, he asserts,

> It is extremely dangerous to renounce such concepts as *level of consciousness, inhibition,* etc., which are the fruits of a half century of clinical and laboratory experiments, and which cannot be suppressed except through gross terminological approximations chosen by those who, separating themselves from biology, physiology and experimental psychology, attribute a fictive significance to consciousness, because they deny it any biological reality.[41]

Current projective tests, according to Fulchignoni, demand that the subject make judgments on a variety of conscious levels, including "abstraction, symbolization and actual recognition," which raises important theoretical questions since projection is itself an unconscious phenomenon. The cinema, he claims, provides a means of circumventing this problem.[42]

Returning to the observations of nineteenth-century French psychologist Pierre Janet regarding states of consciousness, Fulchignoni distinguishes between the "realist" state, where "we are most preoccupied by the material content of our actions and their exterior results"; the "spectacular" state, in which "a large portion of our secondary actions disappear" in a situation like that of the theatre, where we share the responses of the audience but are not required to act ourselves; and finally, the "hypnotic" state, which he asserts is closest to that of the spectator in the cinema, and the most useful in terms of seeking unconscious impulses.[43] Therefore, the cinema provides an ideal situation for projective testing, since

> During the projection of a film—that is, amidst circumstances to which the individual is not already adapted according to an anterior psychological organization—the subject who perceives scenes which seem veracious and to which he would like to react, finds himself in the most favorable state for the exterior projection of some of his deepest tendencies.[44]

To demonstrate his point, Fulchignoni provides data from a filmic test intended to determine the projective tendencies of a group of 30 normal subjects, ages 8 to 11, and 40 abnormal subjects, ages 8 to 15.[45] Showing them a short film on the life of canaries, which anthropomorphically defines the familial roles of the birds in a story of the young canaries learning to fly, Fulchignoni posed a variety of open-ended questions to each of the viewers in order to determine their preferences for the "characters" and their actions in the story.[46] Analyzed according to existing psychoanalytic precepts, the responses revealed the children's preference for or fixation on one parent or the other, as well as certain Oedipal tensions and sibling jealousies.[47] In this way, Fulchignoni asserts the capacity of the filmic test to reveal unconscious projective tendencies, which is made even more exact both by the film's "autonomous narrative movement, which develops spontaneously without the subject's intervention," and by the anthropomorphism of the film's subject, which eliminates any suspicion in the subject of "autobiographical coincidence," allowing "processes of identification to take place in a completely natural way at an unconscious level."[48]

In its comparison of the viewer's state to hypnosis and its application of film as a tool of psychoanalysis, Fulchignoni's article recalls the more theoretical observations of Jean Deprun.[49] Despite the diverging empirical and "philosophical" tendencies which might separate Fulchignoni and Deprun, the work of the former nevertheless provides one of the few examples of filmology's capacity to correlate theory and practice. Yet, Fulchignoni's assertion of film as a psychological tool runs directly counter to the Zazzos' definition of the filmological problematic, and therefore might be condemned as falling outside the proper field of study. This basic theoretical conflict between the use of psychology in the study of film and the use of film in the study of psychology would remain unresolved throughout the history of filmology.

In an article on the study of film and memory which also appeared in issue 9, Paul Fraisse and G. de Montmollin are careful to situate their study within three separate areas of concern: psychological, pedagogical and filmological. Noting the relatively recent application of filmic tests to psychology, they suggest the contributions their study could make to this enterprise. If film is to become a pedagogical tool, they argue, it is of the utmost importance to know what and how much the viewer remembers. Finally, in the pursuit of "pure" filmology, the retention of the filmic fact in the viewer's memory adds important data to the discussion of film's effects on its audience.[50]

The memory test conducted by Fraisse and de Montmollin involved a group of 100 university level students who viewed a scene from the film *Le Camion blanc* and from newsreels of the previous year, and then were asked to write down everything they could remember. From this study, the researchers concluded that

> nothing remains in our minds from a film except its general meaning and atmosphere; our memory is not a reproduction but a recreation of the story: secondary details are abandoned, incongruous details are normalized, displacements are effected to place events in a more logical order, deformations intervene according to the interests and feelings of the subjects.[51]

Breaking down responses according to the correspondence of described images to actual shots, descriptions which condensed several shots, and descriptions which did not correspond to specific shots at all, Fraisse and de Montmollin prepared a series of graphs which cross the number of responses in each of these three categories with the individual shots in the films, and then with the shots arranged according to their length. Observing that, in general, the longer the shot, the more often it was recalled, they also noted that the precision with which these shots were described was not significantly greater than with the shorter shots. Instead the precision of a shot's description seems to be more closely associated with its "local and specific character," which is to say, its content and context.[52] "The best remembered shots," Fraisse and de Montmollin observe, "are those which are both explicit and which are the most essential to the drama."[53] After noting the kinds of condensations which occurred in the memories of their subjects (especially, the condensation of several shots as a unified space, the filling in of temporal gaps, and the melding of different points of view), the researchers observe,

During the running of a film, the viewer does not remain passive, but selects from what he sees and hears that which is necessary to his comprehension; at the same time, he carries out a hierarchization of story elements; and this does not include his affective tendencies and interests, which contribute equally to transforming the objective given into the subjective perceived.[54]

Fraisse and de Montmollin's study of film and memory was the only significant treatment of this subject by filmology; and though its conclusions are hardly incontestable in a methodological sense, they provide one of the best descriptions to emerge from the movement on the process of the viewer's "reading" of a film. Explicit in their observations is an active role for the spectator, in contrast to the negative social stereotype of viewer passivity. Not only does the viewer watch the film; s/he also organizes, interprets, fills in and omits, creating meaning *with* the film.

Despite the divergence of methods and goals in the psychological studies of filmology, the juxtaposition of psychological testing and film provided some of the movement's most original results, in both a practical and a theoretical sense. Studies such as those by the Zazzos on filmic comprehension, by Fulchignoni on the unconscious processes of projection, and by Fraisse and de Montmollin on film and memory provided support for certain types of theoretical generalizations about the viewer's experience. In addition, they also contributed the information which might be of use to those who wished to apply film toward specific ends, to create specific effects. For filmology, those ends were almost exclusively pedagogical.

Pedagogical Applications of Film

When Cohen-Séat's *Essai* sounded the call to arms for scholars and intellectuals in 1946, it proclaimed that the cinema had begun to change the world and that, with the guidance of society's best minds, it might ultimately change it for the better. The rhetoric of a social mission had been with filmology from the beginning, but direct social applications of filmological research proved difficult in practice. Cohen-Séat's hopes for a universal brotherhood spawned by the common language of cinema seemed far beyond the capacities of the academic movement which filmology quickly became. It had proved impossible for filmologists to agree even on the interpretation of results from their common research, much less to propose a program of social control or social action. The application of film to psychological testing had resulted in some provocative methods and conclusions, but these were rather limited. Only in the use of films for education did filmology find a unified goal and the potential for a practical application of its research.

From the first issue of the *Revue*, the educational potential of film formed a recurrent theme for filmology. Articles ranged from the most theoretical observations on the subject to cases of direct application. In issue 1, Dr. Jean Dalsace observes the potential of films to encourage public hygiene, including the teaching of sex education to the young and the techniques of motherhood to pregnant women. He also notes the practical obstacles preventing such a program: the lack of sufficient projection facilities, the problems of distributing educational films, and most important, the lack of any really good films on these subjects.[55] From a sociological standpoint, Dr. Juliette Boutonier, director of the Psycho-Pedagogical Center of the Academy of Paris, observes the obstacles to teaching presented by the cinematic situation itself. Although strictly avoiding any correlation of film and delinquency, she nevertheless critiques the social role of movie theatres as meeting places for the young outside parental supervision, reiterating the old theme of the passivity of the filmgoer before the movie screen.[56] The problems involved in using films to educate the public were seen as both theoretical and practical; and it was in these areas that filmology sought to assert its strongest social influence.

Certainly, filmology did not pose the question of the pedagogical use of film for the first time. The educational potential of the medium had been an important concern both in Europe and America since the 1920s. In fact, as early as 1921, the Musée Pédagogique began to maintain a small film library for educational purposes.[57] In the United States, a journal by the name of *Educational Screen* appeared in January 1922; and over the next decade it would absorb the journals *Motion Picture Age* (in January 1923), *Visual Education* (in January 1925), and *Visual Instruction News* (in April 1932). America seemed to lead the world in the application of film to education. This was due partly to government support of such programs, and partly to an intense Progressive concern about the social uses of a medium which the United States had begun to dominate. Between 1927 and 1929, Eastman Kodak conducted learning experiments in cooperation with the National Education Association, resulting in the conclusion that students learned faster if their studies were accompanied by visual instruction through films.[58] Practical use of films in education had to await the development of the 16mm format in the late 1920s; and the development of sound film during the same period added further complications, outdating certain films and requiring more sophisticated facilities.[59]

In France, such people as Germaine Dulac and Jean Benoit-Lévy had adopted the cause of the educational film by the beginning of the 1930s; and their efforts were aided by the growing concern of the League of Nations for developing the sociological potential of the medium. Writing in the League's *International Review of Educational Cinematography* on an international conference on educational films held in Rome in 1931, Germaine Dulac seems to anticipate Cohen-Séat: "The Cinema is a teacher, it is also and above all an art, a new form of expression, but unfortunately in cinematic art, the instrument has preceded the thought."[60] Given proper attention, Dulac argues, the cinema could become education's most important tool.

> The Cinema, more especially since the introduction of sound and speech, can teach everything to children, holding their attention by presenting the true image and visual aspect of the object under discussion. Such is the precision of the Cinema that it does away with errors of imagination so often present in ordinary teaching methods.[61]

Citing a report by Benoit-Lévy, she observes the growing concern for educational cinema in France, while noting the superiority of its pedagogical applications in Germany, Italy and the United States.[62] Writing in 1951 in the *Revue,* M. Lebrun, director of the Musée Pédagogique, dates the real beginnings of pedagogical film in 1934, at the Congress of Educational Cinematography held in Rome, where the 16mm format was established as a standard in the field.[63] More than a decade after this Congress, however, André Lang's 1948 *Le tableau blanc* would still take the French government to task for its failure to provide facilities and funds for the educational use of the cinema.[64]

At about the same time, in the second issue of the *Revue,* Marc Soriano would pose the question of educational film in a far less optimistic, far more theoretical manner. As far as he was concerned, the most basic questions about film and education remained unanswered.

> It must always be remembered that the cinema has such an effect on the feelings of the viewer only because its effects on the senses are not mediated (by the intelligence) but immediate. In watching the cinema, the process is: sensation - emotion - idea; and not as in reading a book, where the idea is perceived in terms of signs - then, the representation of a sensual reality - emotion. Thus the instrument is effective, but dangerous—almost as dangerous as reality in the emotive power aroused in the subject.[65]

Thus for Soriano, the question remains whether films are capable of serving educational ends, due to the secondary role of the intellect in the cinematic experience of the viewer.

> ...we must...think of the problem of education by the cinema as a whole, and of films made in such a way as to sustain interest without upsetting the personality in formation. This will be an immense task, and one requiring a coordination of efforts and a great deal of money—none of which are available at this moment.[66]

Unlike Lang, for whom the cinema is clearly a powerful instrument in need of proper application, Soriano perceives film as a virtually unknown quantity, requiring careful research before any discussion of its application can take place.

Several issues later, Henri Wallon posed the question of the cinema's pedagogical uses in more philosophical, political terms:

> Should it project on the child what is considered truth by the greater or lesser group of which he is a part? That is the traditional and authoritarian conception, which has no lack of supporters. Or must it call forth the original aptitudes of each, sustaining and developing them? The problem cannot be absolutely resolved.[67]

For Wallon, then, the question of film's effect on students also involves issues of ideology, of *what* the student is to be taught by this powerful new tool. Assuming a universal, humanistic goal for culture, André Lang's impassioned plea for the state to utilize the cinema's potential never touches on so delicate a question; nor, for that matter, does Cohen-Séat's *Essai*. In fact, among the filmologists, only Wallon and Morin seem concerned with the ideological and political implications of the movement's social mission.

Soriano's tentative questions about the pedagogical capabilities of film fell more fully within the ideology of filmology itself; and despite the economic and sociological obstacles of the postwar period in France, research in the effects of film on youth took a high priority in filmological research. In addition, the Institut de Filmologie focused the attention of teachers, psychologists and physiologists on this specific question to the extent that M. Lebrun of the Musée Pédagogique could cite as results, only three years after Soriano's article, a significant improvement in teaching techniques and in the making of films for teaching. According to Lebrun in 1951, the teaching film had become a reality in France which "is used, or will be used more and more, for the young between the ages of five or six and the university level." Quoting Rousseau to the effect that "the child is not a small adult," Lebrun emphasizes the importance of tailoring educational films to the age group for which they are intended. He praises the advances made by filmology in studying other types of films (especially documentaries and informational films) and in observing the reactions of children to them.[68] These contributions to the advancement of the pedagogical film arose from the combination of filmology's concern about the effects of film on children and its emphasis on the methods of experimental psychology.

One of the most basic questions addressed by filmology in regard to teaching films was posed by Henry Wallon in his article "The Child and the Film." If films are to educate young children, he argues, it is important to know at what age this technique becomes effective: "Is the kindergarten-age child (3-6 years) sensitive to film and, if so, to what films?"[69] Clearly, the studies of filmic comprehension undertaken by René and Bianka Zazzo represented filmology's most sincere attempt to answer such questions; but it was fully three years after Wallon's article that Bianka Zazzo posed the question in the same way, asking "at what level is the *threshold of comprehension* situated, below which any cinematic presentation risks becoming nothing but a chaos of images?"[70] Most of her article is devoted to a discussion of responses to a questionnaire distributed to elementary school teachers in advance of their annual conference in 1952, where the major topic was "Cinema in the Elementary School." Teachers who had used films with young classes generally noted a favorable emotional response from the children, while questioning whether the films actually made any intellectual impression.[71] Overall, the questionnaire responses reflected a preference for using films as a recreational activity with younger children. Curiously, one response noted, "They love Charlie Chaplin, and applaud him as soon as he appears on the screen"[72]—an empirical observation diametrically opposed to the reports of Heuyer and Lebovici regarding slightly older children.[73]

The most direct application of empirical study to the teaching film undertaken by filmology involved the testing of a film produced specifically for kindergarten-age children with students of the target age group. Made by Mme. S. Herbinière-Lebert, Inspectrice-Générale of Elementary Schools, *Mains blanches* [*Clean Hands*] was a seven-minute, 16mm film intended to impress upon pre-schoolers the necessity of personal hygiene, as well as to provide a test case for studying the effectiveness of such films with this age group. As Mme. Herbinière-Lebert describes the project,

> For a first film and the first experiments we freely chose to make an educational film stripped of all the attractions of entertainment which might falsify our interpretations and results, and because we were still unsure if film could be used at the kindergarten level toward educational ends.[74]

Gearing her techniques to these specific ends, she constructed the film to be as easily understood as possible, employing the following guidelines: (1) little dialogue, leaning toward silent demonstration, (2) scenes prolonged to enhance comprehension, (3) avoidance of angles and points of view which might be distracting, (4) avoidance of such process techniques as superimpositions, slow motion, etc., (5) the prudent use of dissolves, and (6) clear speech, with the voices of women and children instead of men.[75]

The completed film was used in two different studies, one psychological and one pedagogical. The former was undertaken by Hélène Gratiot-Alphandéry at the Institut de Filmologie, and involved the screening of *Mains blanches*, along with a silent documentary entitled *A Day at the Zoo*, to kindergarten-age children. Researchers in different parts of the screening room observed (1) the constitution of the audience, i.e., the way in which the children grouped themselves, (2) their attitudes during the screening (movement, posture, fatigue), and (3) their verbal responses (cries, exclamations). These observations were then carefully noted on the script for each film. Afterwards, the children were interviewed individually about the subjects of the films. Gratiot-Alphandéry notes

the impossibility at this level of artificially isolating the origins of affective responses or the actual levels of comprehension, asserting once again the necessity of limiting oneself to recording progress without the need to establish a hierarchy of causes.

Despite the difficulties in gleaning precise results from the test, the observers were still able to note that children of this age group did possess certain perceptive skills, and that their attention seemed most often drawn by action on the screen.[76]

The pedagogical study, carried out by Mlle. Léandri, Inspectrice of Grade Schools in Paris, and M. Ravé of the Teachers' League, involved the presentation of *Mains blanches* to kindergarten-age children under a variety of circumstances: (1) without any preparation or commentary, (2) preceded by an explanation of the film's theme, (3) with commentary during the film to emphasize the major points, (4) with a second screening of the film, (a) immediately, or (b) several hours or days later, and (5) once with sound and a second time without, with the children invited to recall the dialogue.[77] Following observations of the children and individual interviews with them, the researchers noted the importance of the short length in maintaining attention as well as the fact that certain parts of *Mains blanches* still seemed too fast to allow pre-school-age comprehension. Their final conclusion was that, for pre-school children, the educational film seems to have some value beginning at the age of four or five, on the condition that the subject of the film is explained to them beforehand.[78]

Commenting on the results of the studies involving her film, Herbinière-Lebert writes,

... this is only a first attempt, which must be followed by many others. Its only merit is that it has taken place. It should serve to reveal what suits children and to permit the making of better films for them. If this occurs, we have attained the modest goal we set for ourselves.[79]

Such modest goals were those which filmology could most rationally set in terms of practice. In 1951, Lebrun looked forward to further pedagogical advances from filmology:

This collaboration, to which many of those in the classes and laboratories bring a real and rapidly growing interest, now seeks better to adapt films to the age of the chidren for which they are destined, and thus to achieve an *amelioration of pedagogical tools*. Adding new means to old will lead us toward a new understanding of the child. When the spirit of synthesis takes over the establishment of an effective and necessary cohesion between such diverse activities, it will necessarily end in a tangible enlargement of filmological research.[80]

Since addressing the question of the film as a pedagogical tool had necessarily required the collaboration of educators, sociologists and psychologists, it was in this area that the eclecticism of filmology worked to its best advantage. For this reason, filmology could and would point to its research on the teaching film as one of its most significant social contributions; and if the movement could not claim sole responsibility for the success of the educational film, it could certainly claim to have focused concerns in such a way as to aid the progress of film as a pedagogical tool in France.

Some Conclusions: The Legacies of Filmology

The first decade of filmology was an extremely active one. Within its first two years, the movement had been able to institutionalize film study in France, create an international network of scholars interested in film and produce a substantial body of theoretical and experimental work. In the years which followed, filmology gave some appearance of a dynamic and dialectical development: dynamic in the sense that its studies multiplied and its positions seemed in constant flux, shifting under the weight of new ideas and data; dialectical to the extent that the various methods and disciplines within the movement seemed to influence one another, with certain approaches gaining ground while others fell by the wayside. This appearance, however, was somewhat deceptive; for filmology's attempt to produce a scientific discourse on film moved less toward the synthesis it proclaimed as its goal than toward a hierarchy of hermetic discourses attached to various university disciplines which acknowledged one another largely on the level of rhetoric.

Much of the problem lay in filmology's definition (or non-definition) of science. Clearly, the rhetoric of a "science of film" had expeditiously served Cohen-Séat's project of interesting and activating the academic establishment; but it had also situated the problematic of filmology squarely within an ideology of positivism. Science, therefore, represented something more than an epistemology, something more than a method for filmology. It provided a teleology directed toward the goal of explaining, exhausting and finally controlling the object of film—a teleology quite in keeping with the ideology of postwar humanism and its sense of social mission. Thus the organization of university disciplines under the aegis of filmology had less to do with a common methodology than with a common positivism, which saw science in seriousness and rigor.

As a result, filmology functioned at first as a free forum where all ideas related to a methodical study of film were welcome and sought out. But in the years of evaluation and selection which followed, it was the concept of science, and more specifically of empiricism, which decided which ideas were to dominate and which were to be pushed to the fringes of the movement. It is perhaps not surprising then that, by the time of the Second International Congress of Filmology in 1955, the empirical studies mounted in the fields of sociology and experimental psychology formed the core of the movement, while aesthetics, phenomenology, history and psychoanalysis seemed more and more irrevelant. Although the autonomy of the various academic disciplines and the influence of such figures as Souriau guaranteed a place at the Congress for the gamut of subjects raised in the early days of the movement, filmology had clearly established its central area of concern as an empirically oriented psychology and sociology of the film audience.

From the perspective of film theory, however, the achievements of filmology cannot be assessed simply in terms of the increasing empiricism which arose from the gradual exclusion of certain concerns, or by the ultimate fate of the movement's organizational framework. Its attempt to produce a comprehensive, rigorous systematization of film study, expressed most strongly in the early years of the movement, involves a problematic which extends beyond the period of filmology itself. It might be difficult (and it is certainly beyond the scope of this study) to trace a precise historical lineage from the institutionalization of film study in France to subsequent programs of film study in universities around the world. It should nevertheless be clear by this point that the movement marks the beginning of what Christian Metz describes as the second era of reflection on film: the "plural" and "syncretic" cataloguing of concerns. We can, however, quite clearly trace the influence of filmology on subsequent French film theory, and especially on the semiology of the cinema undertaken by Metz and others beginning in the 1960s; for it is in that way that filmology has most directly contributed a basis for contemporary film theory.

The scientific orientation of filmology seems to have pointed in two quite different directions. In one direction lay empiricism and experimental methods, providing the means by which the filmologists could collect and evaluate data applicable toward very limited practical ends. The general acceptance of this approach is evident in the Congress of 1955 and in the assumptions underlying the subsequent debate between the sociological and psychological branches of the movement. In the other direction, the scientific positivism of filmology, quite in keeping with Cohen-Séat's dictum that "to understand is to systematize," pointed toward the contemporary concerns of structuralism. Despite the fact that the writings of Roland Barthes in the *Revue* in 1960 provide the only direct link between filmology and structuralism, the similarities between the methodologies are suggested by their common enterprise of defining the structures which function within human phenomena.

Because my study is a history of theory, its conclusions are both historical and philosophical. First, we must examine what happened to filmology as a movement and to what point it was able to refine its problematic. We can then examine the way in which that problematic, in concert with the contemporary concerns of structuralism, set a course for the subsequent development of a semiology of the cinema and helped define the ideological parameters of film study to this day.

The Second International Congress of Filmology and After

The Second International Congress of Filmology took place almost eight years after the first. Bringing together some 350 delegates from 29 countries in the Grand Amphithéâtre of the Sorbonne during the week of February 19-23, 1955, the Congress provided substantial evidence of filmology's success as an international movement.[1] What had proven far more difficult for filmology was the adoption of a totalizing framework to correspond to its notions of positive science, or the establishment of clear goals and priorities, in relation to its still lively rhetoric of social mission.

The Congress was initiated by the Centre Français des Recherches Filmologiques in hopes of assessing the progress of the movement and of determining means by which filmological research might find practical applications. To this end an important part of the Congress' goal was not only to assemble filmological scholars, but also to bring together those who used films and those who made them, in order to establish "an inventory of problems posed by practical activity."[2] To this end, the Congress was divided into two sections. The first was devoted to filmological research in the social sciences, with an emphasis on psychology, psycho-physiology and sociology. The goals of this section were:

—to achieve a synthesis of the studies already accomplished and to determine the points at which they intersect

—to determine the extent to which the scientific techniques proper to these fields may be usefully applied to filmological research

—to define working hypotheses to form the basis of a plan of cooperation in new research.[3]

Each of these goals expresses a desire for a further unification of the filmological project as an organized and synthetic undertaking. The second section was devoted to practical considerations and brought together three different groups: those who used the cinema in their work (educators, the press, scientific researchers, therapists), those who made films (technicians, directors, producers), and those representing the public powers (government, university, special interests).[4]

After almost a decade of research and flux, the practical concerns expressed at the Congress remained virtually unchanged, reiterating the now-common tone of urgency. As Henri Laugier, who headed the second section of the Congress, put it,

> Science is often accused of putting in humanity's hands forces which are ultimately uncontrollable, and which risk making humanity their victim: radio, cinema and television are among these forces; the story of the sorcerer's apprentice, the victim of unleashed powers, has already been evoked in this respect. The comparison is unjust; in fact, the sorcerer's apprentice unleashed forces whose nature and laws were unknown.... On the contrary, the monumental forces created by science, be they the splitting of the atom, or broadcasting, or cinematography, exist only insofar as they have been invented by man in full knowledge of their nature and laws.... This Congress should therefore aid the public powers in conserving and mastering the control levers of this great force whose free development should be preserved, but which can be turned toward good or evil, depending upon what man decides.[5]

Laugier's comments reflect the rhetoric of practical concern which informed the Second Congress and indicate the primarily social goal behind its impulse to synthesize its research and methodologies. The narrowing of concerns in an attempt to accomplish this end is quite clear in the three major points of departure for research established by the Congress: (1) the film itself (as psycho-physiological stimulus, as social document, as aesthetic object); (2) the effects of film on the viewer; and (3) its effects on groups and society. Clearly, psychology and sociology had taken precedence, with the former considerations of the filmic fact, from the aesthetic to the psycho-physiological, relegated to a single category.[6] Despite the best of intentions and the attempts to reorganize its framework, the Second Congress was unable to coordinate its efforts effectively. As Zbigniew Gawrak notes, it "failed to accomplish a methodological discussion or even to present an outline from which general conclusions could be drawn."[7]

In the years following the Congress, the impetus behind filmology came more and more from Italy, centering on the experimental research of L. Chiarini and Umberto Barbaro.[8] Throughout the 1950s, the thrust of Italian filmology had been rigorously empirical in a desire to avoid "the facile aestheticism upon which almost all judgments on the cinema rest."[9] Noting this tendency, Gawrak observes,

> In Italy, the cinema as a social fact was the object of multiple reflections; of primary interest was the educational aspect, to the extent that the cinema sustained the critique of real experience.[10]

Given this orientation of Italian filmology toward the social sciences and education, it is hardly surprising, in light of the similar concerns expressed at the Second Congress, that the new phase of the movement was to be centered in Italy.

The years between the Second Congress in 1955 and the shift to Italy in 1961 were characterized by the continuation of debates over methods and goals. Perhaps the most characteristic of these is the exchange which took place between psychology professor E. Valentini and professor of education L. Volpicelli, both of Rome. In an article which appeared in issue 25 of the *Revue* (1956), Valentini argues that the point of departure for filmology has been, and should remain, psychology, with attention focused on the relationship between film and the viewer.[11] Answering objections raised by both Barbaro and Volpicelli regarding the narrowness of psychology's laboratory experimentation with film, Valentini responds,

> In primitive behaviorism, Watson could propose psychology as a science modelled after physics or chemistry, but in the modern conception of psychology, how can one believe in the position of reducing the examination of behavior in the face of whatever stimulation—and in particular, of a reaction such as the filmic reaction—to a simplistic relationship, not of cause and effect, which always provides the condition for scientific verification, whether experimental or not, but to a simplistic reduction of important effects to insignificant causes.[12]

Modern psychology, Valentini asserts, is fully equipped to deal with the subject of film—and not just within the laboratory. Furthermore, he continues, sociological theorists such as Volpicelli also employ emprical studies to document their work, and their rejection of psychology for doing something quite similar indicates a misunderstanding of modern developments in the field.

In the same issue of *Revue*, Volpicelli argues the opposing view in favor of a socio-historical basis for filmology. Noting that, "even in America," *scientism* has come under question, he asks whether the results of controlled experiments can ever be assimilated with field research, quoting Dallas W. Smythe to the effect that the findings of "history, of sociology and of political and economic science may be rejected as inept for founding a *science.*"[13] Simple correlations between film and behavior, for example, posit a simple cause and effect relationship without accounting for the multiplicity of factors affecting behavior. The problem of a psychologically oriented filmology, then, results from its posing of the filmological question in terms of film and viewer. From the beginning, Volpicelli argues, filmology has proposed a triangular relationship between the cinema, the viewer and society, the last term referring to the historically determined context within which both film and viewer exist.[14] Therefore, he concludes, filmology should break with the methods of the laboratory and recreate itself as a socio-historical endeavor.

As Gawrak points out, there seems to be no reason that psychological and socio-historical research should be incompatible.

The first emphasizes the typology of psychic processes, to which the cinema viewer must submit; the other examines the socio-historical conditions of his reactions. The two methods of research seem to be complementary, and the fact that this simple truth was not clearly confirmed, that so important a discussion between Valentini and Volpicelli was neither extended nor drew the commentary it deserved, was a symptom that filmology, at the end of its first decade, was entering the phase of a rather serious internal crisis. It appeared that the controversies over methods emerged from the more profound roots of the very goals of the research.[15]

The goals of filmology, grounded in the social mission of the cinema set out by Cohen-Séat in the immediate postwar years, had never been fully expressed or discussed. In practical terms, filmology had made certain advances in the use of film in psychology and education, but these remained somewhat minor areas in comparison with the rhetoric of the social project undertaken by the movement.

Gawrak distinguishes three groups of filmologists according to their orientation toward goals: the maximalists, the minimalists, and those who supported a sort of compromise. The maximalists, according to Gawrak, were those who "saw filmology as an organized and normative body of knowledge, permitting them not only to describe and explain cinematic phenomena, but to evaluate them according to a social program."[16] Within this group he includes Laugier, to the extent that he addressed the Second Congress regarding filmology's role in aiding public policy; Jean-Jacques Riniéri, who sought a science of film patterned after Souriau's science of aesthetics; and Edgar Morin.[17] The minimalists included the "anonymous mass of researchers" who ascribed to no particular global view of filmology or its mission. A minimalist position that film provokes "mental passivity" in the viewer without suggesting the variety of means by which such an effect can be and often is avoided, is itself "mentally passive," Gawrak asserts.[18] The position of compromise, he observes, is best represented by Cohen-Séat himself who

affirmed from the beginning that only after filmology was transformed into an orderly body of knowledge could one find the answer to what extent it would be capable of influencing policy or cinematic production.[19]

If filmology never became the synthetic theory or unified science which the maximalists wished, neither did it remain a disorganized collection of studies and data linked only by subject. In terms of its stated goals, its successes were restricted to the gathering of limited data in a fairly disorganized group of very specific tests. Yet in an important sense, the historical success of filmology lay in its very eclecticism and its attempts to organize and interrelate a wide variety of concerns, disciplines and methodologies. The scientific positivism which enabled the grouping of such diverse fields of study based only on their common rigor led eventually to a more traditional definition of science in empirical/experimental terms. Curiously, by the mid-1950s, when filmology demonstrated its strongest empirical biases, empiricism had itself come under intellectual fire for its reductive and simplistic view of phenomena; and these attacks came from the very camps of phenomenology and structuralism, which filmology had begun to abandon.

During an earlier period of its development, filmology might have avoided such criticism, since so important a part of its project involved the grouping of intellectual concerns in a plural approach intended to account for the complexities of the cinema. The theoretical problematic proposed by Cohen-Séat had begun to take on reality from the moment that the established disciplines, united by context and intent, though separate in their perspectives, turned the rigor normally devoted to their specialized fields toward examining filmic and cinematic phenomena. It is in this way that both an ideology and a related body of data—as syncretic and plural as it might be—arose to establish the problematic for a new era of reflection on the cinema.

Filmology and the Semiology of the Cinema

When Cohen-Séat writes in his *Essai* that film is a "logic awaiting its laws," he suggests a project of filmological analysis which is not only grounded in a positivist conception of science, but which is also quite close to the approach taken by structural linguistics and structural anthropology to their respective fields. As Robert Scholes has observed, "At the heart of the idea of structuralism is the idea of system: a complete, self regulating entity that adapts to new conditions by transforming its features while retaining its systematic structure."[20] Like structuralism, filmology involved the researcher in an attempt to discover the system, the "laws" underlying a human phenomenon.

The beginning of structuralism is usually considered to be the structural linguistics of Ferdinand de Saussure, who initiated the modern study of language by positing an arbitrary, non-determined relationship between signification and meaning, which allowed him to analyze language as a system.[21] Certain commentators, however, trace the roots of structuralism to Karl Marx and Sigmund Freud, both of whom attempted to explain social behavior by means of certain systematized determinations.[22] Saussure's attention to the system of language, Freud's concern with the processes of the human mind and Marx's definition of economic factors determining social relationships all represent the search for a "logic" underlying human phenomena—a project arising from the scientific positivism of the nineteenth century. Cohen-Séat's attempts to initiate a science which would define the "logic" of film and the cinema can therefore be seen as an outgrowth of a similar scientific impulse, and one which ultimately links filmology to a structuralist orientation.

Scholes defines structuralism as a response to the need for a "coherent system" in the face of the increasing atomism of specialization. As an epistemology, he continues, structuralism seeks "nothing less than the unification of all the sciences into a new system of belief."[23] Filmology, which developed at approximately the same time and place as Claude Lévi-Strauss's attempts to outline a structural anthropology, shares a similar, though certainly more limited goal. What Cohen-Séat called for in 1946 was a unification of the sciences in pursuit of specific phenomena. Structuralism emerged in a variety of social sciences, linked not by their object of study, but by the pursuit of a more rigorous method of analysis. Both structuralism and filmology share the goal of uniting the social sciences in a rigorous, methodical pursuit. Limited by its attention to filmic and cinematic phenomena, filmology never approached the global enterprise or influence of structuralism. Yet, as structuralism came to exert its influence more and more strongly on the sciences in France, it is hardly surprising that it came to encompass something of the problematic of filmology.

When in the mid-1960s Christian Metz embarked on an analysis of the cinema based on semiology, the science of signs proposed but not elaborated by Saussure, the concerns of filmology and structuralism were finally linked in a definitive manner. On one hand, it was the rigorous method of structural linguistics and anthropology, as well as Roland Barthes's elaboration of semiology, which led Metz to apply the structuralist method to film. On the other hand, many of the studies undertaken by filmology were based on a similarly rigorous analysis of phenomena and served as Metz's direct antecedents in the field. No one is more willing to admit that ancestry than Metz himself, whose first articles on the cinema copiously footnote the studies from the *Revue.*

In one of his earliest articles on film, "On the Impression of Reality in the Cinema," which appeared in *Cahiers du Cinéma* in 1965, Metz writes,

> Cinema is a vast subject, and there are more ways than one to enter it. Taken as a whole, it is first of all a fact, and as such it raises problems of aesthetics, of sociology and of semiotics as well as the psychologies of perception and intellection.[24]

In this passage, Metz presents the question of film in terms nearly identical to those employed by Cohen-Séat in his *Essai* two decades earlier. Pursuing the question of the cinema's "impression of reality," which was treated by Michotte van den Berck in issue 3/4 of the *Revue*, Metz takes on the project of synthesizing the observations made by a wide variety of filmologists. He begins by comparing Edgar Morin's observations in *Le cinéma ou l'homme imaginaire* regarding the belief imparted to the cinematic image by an audience, with those made by Roland Barthes in his 1964 article "The Rhetoric of the Image,"[25] in which he discusses the impression of reality in the still photograph. Morin notes that all photography carries with it a sense of the presence of the object photographed. For Barthes, the still photo does not convey the sense of the presence "being there," but the trace of a presence "having been there." Metz adopts a position close to that of Morin, contrasting the cinema with the qualities of the photograph described by Barthes, and asserting that the cinematic impression of the presence is: "There it is."[26]

To explain the effectiveness of the cinema's illusion of reality, Metz returns to Michotte van den Berck's observations, noting that objects only *appear* to be on the screen while the motion there is a *reality*. Since movement is never material, but always *visual*, Metz observes, "to reproduce its appearance is to duplicate its reality."[27] Turning to Henri Wallon and his comparisons of the cinema and theatre in "The Perceptive Act," Metz elaborates the distinction with the aid of Souriau's definition of the diegetic level of reality. The cinema creates a diegetic universe, enclosed and separate, Metz declares; while the theatre remains a part of the world in which the audience exists.[28] It is this *unreality* of the filmic means, according to Metz, which allows the filmic diegesis to assume a reality all its own. His conclusion, that "the secret of film is that it is able to leave a high degree of reality *in its images*, which are, nevertheless, still perceived as images,"[29] represents a substantial synthesis of observations by the filmologists.

It is clear that filmology functions for Metz as an important source of theoretical data. What is more significant is that its methodical approaches present certain models which are useful to Metz in constructing his semiology of the cinema. He begins *Language and Cinema*, his exhaustive and definitive 1971 application of structural linguistics to the cinema, by returning to Cohen-Séat's distinction between filmic and cinematic facts, which allows Metz to focus his attention on the filmic fact as "a more manageable, specifiable, signifying discourse."[30] With this distinction in hand, Metz can note that it is the filmic fact which constitutes the linguistic object under observation. Yet Metz also expands on Cohen-Séat to include his own concern with film as "signifying discourse."

> ...film, because it constitutes (contrary to the cinema) a delimitable space—an object devoted from beginning to end to signification, a closed discourse—can only be envisaged 'as a language system' in its entirety.[31]

Noting that the filmological distinction between filmic and cinematic is analogous to the semiological distinction of message and medium of expression, Metz observes that the system of signification operating within a film, though it may be common to a greater number of films and therefore a cinematic phenomenon, is still classified by Cohen-Séat as a part of the filmic fact, since it is manifest in the film itself.[32] Metz classifies the signifying system of film as a cinematic fact, because it functions as a part of the cinema as institution; yet he distinguishes his own definition of cinematic from that of Cohen-Séat: "the cinematic which is of interest to semiotics is the *cinematic-filmic*. The cinematic of Cohen-Séat is nothing other than the cinematic-non-filmic."[33] Despite the necessity Metz feels to elaborate Cohen-Séat's filmic/cinematic distinction, the care with which he develops it indicates his acceptance of its basic soundness as a foundation for a semiology of the cinema.

Just as significant for Metz's semiology is the rigorous division of the filmic field by Souriau, whose distinctions between the seven levels of filmic reality enable Metz to focus further on the areas of his concern. For Metz, the part of the filmic fact representing the object of his linguistic analysis is what Souriau defined as filmophanic or screenic reality.[34] However, when Metz discusses the question of filmic discourse in his 1966 articles "Notes Toward a Phenomenology of Narrative"[35] and "Some Points in the Semiotics of the Cinema,"[36] it is Souriau's "diegetic," the film's representation of a universe, which focuses Metz's concerns. For Metz, then, Souriau's distinctions provide a division of the filmic fact which is very basic to the structural analysis of the cinema.

Souriau's links to structuralism are clearer and more direct than those of any of the other filmologists. Most notably his *Les deux cent milles situations dramatiques* is a daring attempt to define and to systematize a universal structure of narrative events and characters in drama from ancient Greece to modern France. His method is quite similar, in fact, to that of another important proto-structuralist, Vladimir Propp, who catalogued the structural elements of the Russian folk tale.[37] A.J. Greimas has not only noted this similarity between the work of Souriau and Propp, but has elaborated upon a direct comparison of the elements identified by each in order to outline his own structural analysis of narrative.[38] Thus Souriau represents a direct link between the scientific project of aesthetics, which informed his filmological studies, and the structuralist enterprise which informs Metz's semiology of the cinema.

The clearest link between semiology and filmology, however, is a common concern with "film language," a term already used widely but imprecisely at the time filmology began. From the First Congress, where Mario Roques proposed the study of "the language of cinema, to establish its history and discern its semantics,"[39] through the debates in the *Revue* over whether or not the filmic image could be considered a signifier, filmology attempted to outline the ways by which film conveys meaning. It was a structural enterprise, not only in its search for a "linguistics" of film, but also because it placed an emphasis on the means by which the viewer understands film—in Merleau-Ponty's terms, on the perception of "structure, grouping or configuration."[40]

To this extent, the empirical studies of filmology provide an important contribution; especially significant are the experiments of Bianka and René Zazzo on the comprehension of film and the tests of Fraisse and de Montmollin regarding film and memory, which produced data pertinent to the viewer's selection, organization and interpretation of a filmic scene. From another perspective, Francastel's discussion of the organization of filmic representation according to a specific, culturally determined system (a conception quite in keeping with Maddison's anthropological observations on film and the African tribesmen) provides an important theoretical basis for the structural study of filmic signification.

Quite clearly, Metz explores the questions of film and language with more precision and coherence than filmology applied to the subject during its first decade; yet Metz is working in an intellectual context where structural linguistics has already begun to exert a very strong methodological influence. Further, Metz's early attempts at a semiology of the cinema are contemporary to Barthes's 1964 *Elements of Semiology*,[41] which carefully systematizes the study of signs defined by Saussure. Although Barthes is only marginally concerned with film, his work from the mid-1950s onward details an analytic method for the study of signification which provides an important model for Metz's approach to the cinema. Appropriately, however, Barthes represents a still more direct link between filmology and the semiology of the cinema because of an article on filmic signification which he published in 1960 in the pages of *Revue*.

In "The Problem of Signification in the Cinema," Barthes provides the first outline for an application of Saussure's linguistics to the study of film. Noting that certain elements of the filmic image have a "purely intellective content" and are therefore "true *messages*,"[42] Barthes procedes to analyze these "messages" according to Saussure's division of the "sign" into "signifier" and "signified," where the signifier is the material support of the sign which activates an idea, that idea being the signified. Barthes observes that the relationship between the signifier and signified in film is "analogical," that is, the signifier of an object (the filmic image) bears a perceptual similarity to that object. Therefore, the filmic sign is quite different from the linguistic sign, where the link between a word and its meaning is, as Saussure observed, both arbitrary and unmotivated. The link between the filmic signifier and signified is neither, since it is motivated by resemblance.[43] Four years later, in his article "The Cinema: Language or Language System?" Metz would pursue these precise points in far more detail.[44]

Barthes does not attempt to encompass all elements of the film in his semiology. "Certainly," he writes, "the film cannot be defined as a pure semiological field, for it cannot be reduced to a grammar of signs."[45] Nevertheless, certain elements of the film must be intelligible (at least in narrative films) in order to establish the requisite communication between filmmaker and audience.[46] These are the elements to which Barthes addresses himself.

Regarding the filmic signifier, Barthes observes that it is "heterogenous," "polyvalent" and "combinative." By the term "heterogenous" he refers to the multiple types of signifiers employed in a film, which, in addition to dialogue, include costume, set decoration, music and gestures, among others. His observation that these elements are used to create meaning recalls the remarks of Anne Souriau on costume and decor, François Guillot de Rode on sound, and Jean Germain on music, all of which appeared in *L'univers filmique*. Barthes simply relates these elements to a more strictly linguistic model. The "polyvalent" quality of the filmic signifier is two-sided:

> a signifier can express several signifieds (which linguistics calls polysemy); or a signified can be expressed through several signifiers (which is called synonymy).[47]

Polysemy, Barthes notes, is rare in the cinema, which is "essentially founded on a pretense of a significant relationship to nature." Polysemy, which posits a variety of meanings for a single representation, "becomes intolerable very quickly for an art which is constitutionally *analogical*."[48] Synonomy is far more frequent, for it refers to the variety of ways in which the film conveys a simple signified, or idea. The repetition of a signified by means of several signifiers leads to redundancy, where "the director accumulates signifiers as though he had no confidence in the intelligence of the audience."[49]

Finally, the "combinative" aspect of the filmic signifier refers to the syntax of the filmic message, its necessity "to unify signifiers, that is, to enumerate them bit by bit, without repeating them and still without losing sight of the signified it is expressing."[50] In this respect, signifiers such as costume and decor are conveyed in a stable, continuous manner, while gestures, for example, occur instantaneously and sporadically. Here Barthes simply indicates a whole area for study which Metz would explore in a series of articles on filmic narrative and filmic syntax; most notably in his "Problems of Denotation in the Fiction Film," "Syntagmatic Study of Jacques Rozier's film *Adieu Philippine,*"[51] and "Some Notes on the Semiotics of the Cinema," where he cites Anne Souriau's article "Succession and Simultaneity in Film" in his description of alternating syntax in the film.[52]

If Barthes represents the final link between filomology and Metz's semiology of the cinema, it is because, in semiology's "science of signs," Barthes discovered a means of organizing the observations on film and language which emerged from filmology's "science of film." On one hand, it is Barthes's semiological analyses of popular culture and of literature, especially his exhaustive dissection of Balzac's "Sarrasine" in *S/Z*,[53] which provide a model for the textual analyses of film undertaken in France during the 1970s. Yet, on the other hand, prior to filmology, film study lacked any coherent basis for such analyses. Film signification is both more complex and more diversified than verbal/written language; and there was simply no way to explore the cinema's function as communication, as discourse, as text, until its components were rigorously divided and examined. If Anne Souriau's discussion of filmic syntax and the alternation of shots in a film anticipates Metz's more systematic definition of syntagmatic structure in the narrative film, it may also be seen as a prefiguration of the textual analyses of films by Raymond Bellour and Thierry Kuntzel, who extend such linguistic concerns to an examination of the psychoanalytic structures at work in filmic syntax.[54]

In his 1980 obituary for Etienne Souriau, Metz acknowledges the debt owed filmology by current film theory:

> Basically, filmology was in certain regards a rather direct prefiguration of the semiology of the cinema. In both cases, it is a matter of approaching the cinema from the outside, of placing it within the discourse of the human sciences, and not that of cineastes, cinephiles or critics.[55]

It is precisely the "scientific distance" of filmology from its object of study—the distance for which it drew so much criticism from the community of cinephiles—which remains at the core of the problematic proposed by Cohen-Séat, rigorously pursued by Souriau, Morin and a host of others, and finally inherited by the semiology of the cinema.

Throughout this survey of filmology I have noted the ways in which the specific work which emerged from the movement applies to, suggests and even prefigures the approaches of subsequent film study. It remains simply to suggest that the ideology implicit in the filmological problematic continues to assert its influence as well. First, as we have seen, the problematic of filmology was characterized by a sense of social mission arising from the perception of a crisis: the uncontrolled, potentially dangerous, potentially utopian power of the cinema. This type of sociological concern remains an important part of the rhetoric of film studies and of its self-justification to this day; and not only in the empirical studies of film and television which adhere to an ideology of science. Clearly the rhetoric has changed; but it is significant that social concern has remained an important factor linking the variety of political critiques of film mounted since the time of the filmologists: from the explicitly Marxist and anti-humanist *Cahiers du Cinéma/Cinéthique* debates of the post-1968 period in France to the more recent, frequently psychoanalytic British and American studies of the representation of women in cinema.

Second, filmology perceived the lack of control of the cinema to be a result of the fact that Reason had played no part in its development. Only a positive science, empirical and directed toward humane goals, it was argued, could place the power of the cinema at the disposal of humankind. In this respect, as we have seen, rigorousness was substituted for a vague notion of science in pursuit of methods which might reveal the cinema's laws and logic. Both this pluralism and this commitment to scholarly exactitude characterize the study of film as we have inherited it. The detailed analyses which have emerged in the wake of film semiology and the continuing desire to submit the cinema to the critiques offered by psychoanalysis, Marxism and critical theory in general demonstrate the importance of "scientific" discourse in legitimating what is still considered in some quarters to be an upstart discipline. And, if empiricism itself has undergone a critique and been cast aside from the mainstream of film studies, it has largely been replaced by the rigors of structural analysis.

Third, the shape which filmology's "science of film" finally assumed corresponded directly to the compartmentalization of the university. In this respect, of course, academic film studies have changed very little, with university departments studying film in relation to more established fields, or, in the case of departments devoted specifically to film, with clear divisions between film production and film studies.

While only suggesting the historical links between filmology and contemporary film studies, these examples further demonstrate that the way in which filmology posed its questions about the cinema bears striking similarities to the way in which the medium is still approached. As a pluralist orientation of various disciplines toward the object of film, unified by a positivist belief in science and a certain sociological rhetoric, filmology may finally be seen as the first coherent statement of a problematic for the comprehensive study of film and as something of a model for subsequent film study in the Western university.

Despite philosophical critiques of positivism, it can hardly be denied that a certain teleological sense still informs the theory of film. If, in the era of filmology, we may cite the example of Cohen-Séat, who sees the cinema as the realization of the dreams of Diderot, Michelet and Nietzsche, we may equally note that, in the philosophical and psychoanalytic discussions of the filmic apparatus during the 1970s, Jean-Louis Baudry proclaims the cinema as the realization of Plato's "myth of the cave,"[56] while Thierry Kuntzel sees it as a kind of ultimate refinement of Freud's "mystic writing pad."[57] And if we may return for a last time to Metz's discussion of three eras of reflection on film to note that filmology belongs (with the semiology of the cinema) in the pluralistic second era, we need go no further than his projection of a third era, in which film theory is to be synthetic and systematized, to demonstrate that the semiology of the cinema is grounded in the same scientific positivist hopes which played so important a part in the problematic of filmology.

Notes

Chapter 1

1. Christian Metz, *Language and Cinema*, trans. Donna Umiker-Sebeok (The Hague: Mouton, 1974), pp. 21-22.

2. Gilbert Cohen-Séat's term *filmologie* will be anglicized throughout this study as "filmology."

3. Gilbert Cohen-Séat, *Essai sur les principes d'une philosophie du cinéma* (Paris: Presses Universitaires de France, 1946), p. 11. The translation of *fait cinématographique* as "cinematic fact" follows Umiker-Sebeok in Metz, *Language and Cinema*.

4. Louis Althusser, *For Marx*, trans. Ben Brewster (London: NLB, 1977), p. 32.

5. Cohen-Séat, p. 47.

6. Ibid., p. 19.

7. Ibid., pp. 30-31.

8. Thomas S. Kuhn, *The Structure of Scientific Revolutions* (Chicago: University of Chicago Press, 1970), pp. 16-17.

9. Cohen-Séat, p. 44.

10. Metz, p. 19.

Chapter 2

1. Alexander Werth, *France 1940-1955* (New York: Henry Holt & Co., 1956), pp. 236-38.

2. Ibid., pp. 250-51.

3. Ibid., pp. 239-42.

4. Ibid., pp. 271-74.

5. Ibid., p. 281.

6. Ibid., pp. 311-16.

7. Paul Leglisse, *Histoire de la politique du cinéma français, Tome II: Le cinéma entre deux Républiques (1940-1946)* (Paris: Filméditions, 1977), p. 5.

8. André Lang, *Le tableau blanc* (Paris: Horizons de France, 1948), p. 233.

9. Ibid., p. 200.

10. Marcel L'Herbier, *Intelligence du cinématographe* (Paris: Corréa, 1946).

11. David Curtis, *Experimental Cinema* (New York: Universe Books, 1971), pp. 9-10.

12. Lang, pp. 232-33.

13. Curtis, p. 9.

14. Lang, pp. 233-34.

15. Curtis, p. 10.

16. Georges Sadoul, *French Film* (London: Falcon Press, 1953); reprinted (New York: Arno Press, 1972), p. 34.

17. Lauren Rabinovitz, "Independent Journeyman: Man Ray, Dada and Surrealist Film-Maker," *Southwest Review,* LXIV, 4 (Autumn 1979), pp. 355-76.

18. Marcel L'Herbier, "L'Avenir du cinématographe," *Le Journal* (15 Mai 1928).

19. Noël Burch, *Marcel L'Herbier* (Paris: Editions Seghers, 1973), pp. 28-29.

20. Ibid., p. 30.

21. André Bazin, "Redécouvrons le cinéma," *L'Echo des Etudiants* (26 Juin 1943); reprinted in Bazin, *Le cinéma de l'occupation et de la résistance* (Paris: Union Générale d'Editions, 1975), p. 36.

22. Lang, pp. 231-33.

23. Ibid., p. 234.

24. Leglisse, pp. 5-13.

25. Ibid., p. 29.

26. Ibid., pp. 38-39.

27. Ibid., p. 61.

28. Lang, pp. 186-87.

29. Leglisse, pp. 41-42.

30. Ibid., p. 36.

31. François Truffaut, Introduction to Bazin, *Cinéma de l'occupation,* pp. 25-26.

32. Bazin, "*Les Visiteurs du soir* de Marcel Carné; *Les Anges du péché* de Robert Bresson," *Revue Jeux et Poésie* (Fin 1943); reprinted in Bazin, *Cinéma de l'occupation,* p. 57.

33. Leglisse, pp. 66-67.

34. Ibid., pp. 72-73.

35. Lang, pp. 204-5.

36. Bazin, "Bilan de la saison 43-44" (8 Juillet 1944); reprinted in Bazin, *Cinéma de l'occupation,* pp. 113-14.

37. Leglisse, p. 73.

38. Lang, p. 203.

39. Leglisse, pp. 109-11.

40. Quoted in Bazin, "L'avenir du cinéma français," *Parisien Libéré* (17 Septembre 1944); reprinted in Bazin, *Cinéma de l'occupation*, pp. 129-30.

41. Jean Painlevé, *Le Film Français*, no. 5 (5 Janvier 1945).

42. Bazin, "L'écran parisien," *Parisien Libéré* (9 Septembre 1944); reprinted in Bazin, *Cinéma de l'occupation*, p. 126.

43. François Truffaut in note, Bazin, *Cinéma de l'occupation*, p. 128.

44. Pétain quoted in Alexander Werth, *France 1940-1955* (New York: Henry Holt & Co., 1956), p. 15.

45. Leglisse, p. 14.

46. Maurice Bardèche and Robert Brasillach, *Histoire du cinéma, II: Le cinéma parlant* (Paris: André Martel, 1954), pp. 277-78.

47. See Werth, *France 1940-1955*, p. 240. Werth refers to Bardèche as a "die-hard pro-Nazi" (p. 373) and to Brasillach as an "all-out Fascist" (p. 17). For a fuller discussion of Brasillach's activities and the phenomenon of "collaborationism," see Pascal Ory, *Les collaborateurs, 1940-1945* (Paris: Editions du Seuil, 1976).

48. Bazin, "Bilan de la saison 43-44"; reprinted in Bazin, *Cinéma de l'occupation*, p. 113.

49. François Truffaut, Introduction to Bazin, *Cinéma de l'occupation*, p. 29.

50. Sadoul, p. 109.

51. Leglisse, pp. 142-43.

52. Sadoul, pp. 109-10.

53. The agreement was the result of negotiations taking place in Washington and signed by former French Président du Conseil Léon Blum and U.S. Secretary of State Byrnes.

54. Sadoul, pp. 109-10; Leglisse, pp. 168-69.

55. Leglisse, pp. 170-71.

56. Roger Leenhardt, "Bilan autour d'une crise," *Les Temps Modernes*, no. 1 (1 Octobre 1945), p. 183. For an overview and catalogue of the releases of films in the immediate postwar period in France, see "La saison cinématographique 1945/1947," *Revue du Cinéma*, numéro spécial, XXVII, n.d.

57. Louis Daquin quoted in Leglisse, pp. 165-66.

58. Bazin, "Réflexions pour une veillée d'armes," *Poésie 44* (Juillet à Octobre 1944); reprinted in Bazin, *Cinéma de l'occupation*, p. 119.

59. Lang, p. 202.

60. Georges Charensol, *Renaissance du cinéma français* (Paris: Sagittaire, 1946).

61. Fernand Grenier quoted in Leglisse, p. 172.

62. Bazin, "Le festival de Cannes 1946," *Courrier de l'Etudiant* (30 Octobre-13 Novembre 1946); reprinted in Bazin, *Cinéma de l'occupation*, pp. 167-69.

63. Georges Huismann in Denis Marion, ed., *Le cinéma par ceux qui le font* (Paris: Fayard, 1946).

64. Lang, *Le tableau blanc*, op. cit.

65. Ibid., pp. 176-77.

66. Lang, p. 210.

67. Ibid., pp. 210-11.

68. Ibid., pp. 211-12.

69. Ibid., p. 211.

70. Ibid., pp. 212-13.

71. Ibid., p. 213.

72. Ibid.

73. François Truffaut, note in Bazin, *Cinéma de l'occupation*, p. 189.

74. Lang, p. 234.

75. Ibid., p. 233.

76. Ibid., pp. 234-35.

77. Leglisse, p. 183.

78. Jean Grémillon in *Ecran Français*, no. 59 (14 Août 1946).

79. Bazin, "Créer un public" (18 Mars 1944); reprinted in Bazin, *Cinéma de l'occupation*, p. 86.

80. Leglisse, pp. 178-79.

81. Bazin, "En attendant Hollywood," *Courrier de l'Etudiant* (1 Février 1945); reprinted in Bazin, *Cinéma de l'occupation*, p. 133.

82. Maurice Merleau-Ponty, "The Film and the New Psychology," in *Sense and Non-Sense*, trans. Hubert L. Dreyfus and Patricia Allen Dreyfus (Evanston, IL: Northwestern University Press, 1964).

83. French literary critic Paul Souday, best known for his work on André Gide and Marcel Proust.

84. Bazin, "Pour une critique cinématographique," (11 Décembre 1943); reprinted in Bazin, *Cinéma de l'occupation*, pp. 70-71.

85. René Barjavel, *Cinéma total* (Paris: Denoël, 1944).

86. Leglisse, pp. 186-87.

87. Lang, p. 200.

88. Leglisse, pp. 175-76.

89. G. Michel Coissac, *Le cinématographe et l'enseignement* (Paris: Larousse et Cinéopse, 1926).

90. M. Prudhommeau, *Le cinéma éducatif et l'avenir* (Paris: Union Française Universitaire, 1944).

91. Jean Benoit-Lévy, *Les grandes missions du cinéma* (Montreal: Lucien Parizeau & Co., 1944).

92. Werth, pp. 295-96.

93. Léon Moussinac, *Cinéma expression sociale* (1923); *Naissance du cinéma* (1924); *Le cinéma soviétique* (1929); *Panoramique du cinéma* (1929).

94. Jean Epstein, *Cinéma bonjour* (1921); *Le cinématographe vu de l'Etna* (1926).

95. G. Michel Coissac, *Histoire du cinématographe de ses origines à nos jours* (Paris: Cinéopse et Gauthier Villars, 1925).

96. Georges Charensol, *Quarante ans de cinéma* (1895-1935) (Paris: Sagittaire, 1935).

97. Bardèche and Brasillach, *Histoire du cinéma* (Paris: Editions Denoël, 1935).

98. Georges Sadoul, *Histoire générale du cinéma, Tome I: L'invention du cinéma* (1832-1897) (Paris: Editions Denoël, 1946).

99. Alexandre Arnoux, *Du muet au parlant* (Paris: La Nouvelle Édition, 1946).

100. Sadoul, *Histoire générale du cinéma, Tome II: Les pionniers du cinéma* (1897-1909) (Paris: Editions Denoël, 1947).

101. R. Jeanne and Charles Ford, *Histoire encylopédique du cinéma, Tome I: Tout le cinéma français* (1896-1929) (Paris: R. Laffont, 1947).

102. L'Herbier, *Intelligence du cinématographe,* op. cit.

103. Epstein, *L'intelligence d'une machine* (Paris: J. Melot, 1946).

104. Moussinac, *L'âge ingrat du cinéma* (Paris: Sagittaire, 1946).

105. Marcel Lapierre, *Anthologie du cinéma* (Paris: La Nouvelle Edition, 1946).

106. Denis Marion, *Le cinéma par ceux qui le font,* op. cit.

107. H. Piraux, *Lexique technique anglais-français du cinéma* (Paris: La Nouvelle Edition, 1946).

108. A. Berthomieu, *Essai de grammaire cinématographique* (Paris: La Nouvelle Edition, 1946).

109. *Who's Who in France 1955-56* (Paris: Editions Jacques Lafitte, 1955), p. 388.

110. Albert Laffay, "L'évocation du monde au cinéma," *Les Temps Modernes,* no. 5 (Février 1946), pp. 925-38; "Bruits et langage au cinéma," no. 14 (Novembre 1946), pp. 371-75; "Le récit, le monde et le film," nos. 20-27 (Mai-Juin 1947).

111. André Malraux, *Esquisse d'une psychologie du cinéma* (Paris: Gallimard, 1946), limited edition of 1200. Reprinted in Malraux, *Scènes choisis* (Paris: Gallimard, 1946).

112. See Axel Madsen, *Malraux: A Biography* (New York: William Morrow, 1976); and Denis Marion, *André Malraux* (Paris: Editions Seghers, 1970).

113. Roignant Gilles, Introduction to "Malraux: Esquisse d'une psychologie du cinéma," *Cinématographe,* no. 24 (Fevrier 1977), p. 31.

114. Bazin, "A propos de *L'Espoir,* ou le style au cinéma," *Esprit* (1945); reprinted in Bazin, *Cinéma de l'occupation,* p. 175.

115. Sergei Eisenstein, "Le principe nouveau cinéma russe," *Revue du Cinéma,* no. 9 (1 Avril 1930), pp. 16-27.

116. Eisenstein, *The Film Sense* (London: Dobson, 1948); and *Film Form* (London: Dobson; New York: Harcourt, Brace & Co., 1949).

117. Rudolf Arnheim, *Film als Kunst* (Berlin: Rohwolt, 1932).

118. Béla Balázs, *Der Sichtbare Mensch, oder die Kultur des Films* (Wien: Deutsch-österreichische Verlag, 1924); and *Der Geist des Films* (Halle: Wilhelm Knapp, 1930).

119.   Bazin, "Ontologie de l'image photographique," in G. Diehl, ed., *Les problèmes de la peinture* (Paris: Confluences, 1945).

120.   Bazin, "Le mythe du cinéma total," *Critique,* no. 6 (1946).

121.   Sadoul, "Les apprentis sorciers (d'Edison à Méliès)," *Revue du Cinéma,* nouvelle série, no. 1 (Octobre 1946), pp. 34-44.

122.   Pierre Schaeffer, "L'élément non-visuel au cinéma (I-Analyse de la bande du son; II-Conception de la musique; III-Psychologie du rapport vision-audition)," *Revue du Cinéma,* nouvelle série, nos. 1, 2, 3 (Octobre, Novembre, Decembre 1946).

123.   Jean Georges Auriol, "Les origines de la mise en scène," *Revue du Cinéma,* nouvelle série, no. 1 (Octobre 1946), pp. 7-23.

124.   *Revue du Cinéma,* nouvelle série, no. 19/20 (Automne 1949).

125.   Jacques Doniol-Valcroze, "L'histoire de *Cahiers,*" *Cahiers du Cinéma,* no. 100 (Octobre 1959), pp. 63-64.

Chapter 3

1.   *Who's Who in France,* 1955-56 (Paris: Editions Jacques Lafitte, 1955), p. 388; and *Who's Who in France,* 1965-66, 7th edition, p. 798.

2.   Jean-Jacques Riniéri, "Présentation de la Filmologie," *Revue Internationale de Filmologie,* 1 (Juillet-Août 1947), p. 88.

3.   Gilbert Cohen-Séat, *Essai sur les principes d'une philosophie du cinéma* (Paris: Presses Universitaires de France, 1946), p. 19.

4.   Ibid.

5.   Ibid.

6.   For a concise overview of French Positivism and the place of each of these authors within its various branches, see Isaac Benrubi, *Contemporary Thought of France,* trans. Ernest B. Dicker (New York: Alfred A. Knopf, 1926).

7.   Emile Durkheim, *Socialism and St. Simon,* trans. Charlotte Sandler (Yellow Spring, OH: Antioch Press, 1958), pp. 104-5.

8.   Cohen-Séat, pp. 30-31.

9.   Ibid., p. 31.

10.   Ibid.

11.   Ibid.

12.   Ibid., p. 20.

13.   Emile Durkheim, *The Division of Labor in Society,* trans. George Simpson (New York: Free Press, 1964), pp. 79-80.

14.   Domenick LaCapra, *Emile Durkheim: Sociologist and Philosopher* (Ithaca and London: Cornell University Press, 1972), p. 91.

15.   Cohen-Séat, p. 20.

16.   Ibid., p. 21.

17.   Ibid.

18.   Ibid., p. 30.

19.   Ibid., pp. 21-22.

20.   Ibid., p. 22.

21.   Ibid., p. 23.

22.   Ibid., p. 24.

23.   Ibid., p. 34.

24.   Ibid.

25.   Ibid., p. 24.

26.   Ibid., p. 39.

27.   Ibid., p. 48. Cohen-Séat plays with the word *distraire*, which means both "to distract" and "to amuse."

28.   Ibid., p. 49.

29.   Ibid.

30.   Ibid.

31.   Ibid., p. 50.

32.   Ibid., p. 35.

33.   Ibid., p. 33.

34.   Ibid., p. 25.

35.   Ibid.

36.   Ibid., p. 26.

37.   Ibid.

38.   Ibid., p. 24.

39.   Ibid., pp. 26-27.

40.   Ibid., p. 27.

41.   Ibid., p. 23.

42.   Ibid., pp. 22-23.

43.   Ibid., p. 23.

44.   Ibid., p. 27.

45.   Ibid.

46.   Ibid., pp. 27-28.

47.   Ibid., p. 28.

48.   Ibid.

49.   Ibid., p. 29.

50. Ibid., p. 27.

51. Ibid., pp. 29-30.

52. Ibid., p. 30.

53. Ibid., p. 31.

54. Ibid., p. 50.

55. Ibid., p. 31.

56. Ibid., p. 34.

57. Ibid., p. 30.

58. Ibid., p. 37.

59. Ibid., p. 38.

60. Ibid.

61. Ibid., p. 45.

62. Ibid., pp. 45-56.

63. Ibid., p. 39.

64. Ibid., p. 37.

65. Ibid., p. 39.

66. Ibid., pp. 50-51.

67. Ibid.

68. Auguste Comte, *Cours de philosophie positive,* II, Lecture 28 (Paris: Bachelier, 1835), p. 311.

69. Cohen-Séat, p. 41.

70. Ibid., p. 40.

71. Ibid., p. 41.

72. Ibid.

73. Ibid.

74. Ibid., p. 44.

75. Ibid.

76. Ibid.

77. Ibid.

78. Ibid., p. 56.

79. Ibid., p. 24.

80. Emile Durkheim, *The Rules of Sociological Method,* trans. Sarah H. Solovay and John H. Meuller (Glencoe, IL: Free Press of Glencoe, 1950), p. 13.

81. Harry Alpert, *Emile Durkheim and His Sociology* (New York: Russell & Russell, Inc., 1961), p. 80.

82. Cohen-Séat, p. 57.

83. Ibid.

84. Ibid.

85. Ibid.

86. Cohen-Séat, *Essai,* 2nd ed. (1958), p. 54.

87. Cohen-Séat, 1st ed., p. 57.

88. Ibid., pp. 61-62.

89. Ibid., p. 56.

90. Christian Metz, *Language and Cinema,* trans. Donna Jean Umiker-Sebeok (The Hague & Paris: Mouton, 1974), p. 12.

91. Ibid., p. 13.

92. Ibid., p. 22.

93. Cohen-Séat, 1st ed., p. 63.

94. Ibid.

95. Ibid.

96. Ibid., p. 64.

97. Ibid.

98. Ibid.

Chapter 4

1. "Le premier Congrès International de Filmologie," *Revue Internationale de Filmologie,* 3/4 (Octobre 1948), p. 363. (Henceforth, references to this journal will be abbreviated *"RIF."*)

2. *RIF,* 1 (Juillet-Août 1947), frontispiece.

3. "Documents de l'Association pour la Recherche Filmologique," *RIF,* 1, pp. 96-97.

4. Ibid., p. 97.

5. Ibid.

6. Ibid.

7. Ibid., p. 98.

8. Ibid.

9. Ibid., p. 99.

10. Marc Soriano, "Position de la filmologie," *Synthèses,* no. 2 (1947), p. 149.

11. "Université de Paris: Institut de Filmologie," *RIF,* 5 (n.d.), pp. 109-10.

12. "Premier Congrès," *RIF,* 3/4, p. 364.

13. Ibid., p. 363.

14. Ibid., p. 365. These categories were announced prior to the Congress, in *RIF,* 1, p. 90.

15. Ibid.

16.   Ibid.

17.   Ibid., p. 366.

18.   Ibid.

19.   Ibid., pp. 366-67.

20.   Ibid., p. 367.

21.   Ibid.

22.   Ibid., p. 368.

23.   Ibid., p. 369.

24.   Ibid.

25.   Ibid.

26.   Ibid.

27.   Ibid., p. 370.

28.   *RIF*, 3/4, frontispiece.

29.   "Après le Congrès International de Filmologie," *RIF*, 3/4, p. 373.

30.   R.P. Fray Mauricio de Begoña, *Elementos de Filmología: Teoría de Cine* (Madrid: Dirección General de Cinematográfica y Teatro, 1953), pp. 4-5.

31.   "Université de Paris," *RIF*, 5, p. 109.

32.   Ibid., pp. 109-10.

33.   Ibid., pp. 110-11.

34.   Ibid., p. 111.

35.   "Université de Paris—Faculté des Lettres—Institut de Filmologie," *RIF*, 9 (Janvier-Mars 1952), pp. 89-90.

36.   "Université de Paris," *RIF*, 5, p. 109.

37.   Jean-Pierre Delaville, "La filmologie; Qu'est-ce que c'est?" *Jeune Cinéma*, 1 (1959), p. 19.

38.   Jean Tribut, "La peinture et le film," *RIF*, 10 (Avril-Juin 1952), pp. 149-67.

39.   "Thèse de Mlle. Poncet," *Annales de l'Université de Paris*, 22e année, no. 1 (Janvier-Mars 1952), p. 116.

40.   Marie-Thérèse Poncet, *L'esthétique du dessin animé* (Paris: Librairie Nizet, 1952), p. 3.

41.   *Annales*, pp. 116-17.

42.   Ibid., p. 118. For a discussion of these methods, see chapter 5.

43.   Marie-Thérèse Poncet, *Dessin animé, art mondial* (Paris: Cercle du Livre, 1956).

44.   "Université de Paris," *RIF*, 9, pp. 89-90.

45.   "Institut de Filmologie—Année 1958-1959," *RIF*, 30/31 (n.d.), p. 163.

46.   Marc Soriano, "Etat d'une science nouvelle," *RIF*, 1, p. 10.

47.   Ibid.

48. Ibid., p. 11.

49. Ibid., p. 10.

50. Henri Wallon, "De quelques problèmes psycho-physiologiques que pose le cinéma," *RIF*, 1, pp. 15-18.

51. Raymond Bayer, "Le cinéma et les études humaines," *RIF*, 1, pp. 31-35.

52. Etienne Souriau, "Nature et limite des contributions positives de l'esthétique à la filmologie," *RIF*, 1, pp. 47-64.

53. Georges Sadoul, "Georges Méliès et la première élaboration du langage cinématographique," *RIF*, 1, pp. 23-30.

54. Henri Agel, "Equivalences cinématographiques de la composition et du langage littéraire," *RIF*, 1, pp. 67-70.

55. Dr. Jean Dalsace, "Cinéma, biologie et médecine," *RIF*, 1, pp. 82-83.

56. André des Fontaines, "Position industrielle," *RIF*, 1, pp. 79-81.

57. Mario Roques, "Filmologie," *RIF*, 1, p. 8.

58. Jean-Jacques Riniéri, "Présentation de la filmologie," *RIF*, 1, p. 87.

59. Maurice Caveing, "Dialectique du concept du cinéma," *RIF*, 1, p. 71.

60. Ibid.

61. Ibid.

62. Ibid., p. 76.

63. Ibid., p. 72.

64. Ibid., p. 73.

65. Gilbert Cohen-Séat, "Filmologie et cinéma," *RIF*, 3/4, p. 237.

66. Riniéri, p. 89.

67. Ibid.

68. "Documents," *RIF*, 1, p. 97.

69. J.D. "Espoirs pour une science nouvelle," *RIF*, 2 (Septembre-Octobre 1947), pp. 109-10. The initials "J.D." probably refer to Jean Deprun, who published two other articles in the first two issues of the *Revue*.

70. Georges Poyer, "Psychologie différentielle et filmologie," *RIF*, 2, pp. 111-16.

71. Marc Soriano, "Problèmes de méthode posés par le cinéma considéré comme expérimentation psychologique nouvelle," *RIF*, 2, pp. 117-25.

72. Marcel Cohen, "Ecriture et cinéma," *RIF*, 2, pp. 183-85.

73. Pierre-Maxime Schuhl, "Pour un cinéma abstrait," *RIF*, 2, pp. 183-85.

74. Juliette Boutonier, "Réflexions sur la valeur éducative du cinéma," *RIF*, 2, pp. 193-95.

75. Jean Deprun, "Cinéma et transfert," *RIF*, 2, pp. 205-7; Robert Desoille, "Le rêve éveillé et la filmologie," *RIF*, 2, pp. 197-203.

76. "Note de la Rédaction," *RIF*, 3/4, p. 235.

77. Ibid.

78. A. Michotte van den Berck, "Le caractère de 'réalité' des projections cinématographiques," *RIF*, 3/4, pp. 249-61.

79. R.C. Oldfield, "La perception visuelle des images du cinéma, de la télévision et du radar," *RIF*, 3/4, pp. 263-79.

80. "Note de la Rédaction," *RIF*, 3/4, p. 235.

81. "Propositions de recherches," *RIF*, 5, pp. 95-102.

82. "International Survey (Conference of Filmology, Knokke-le-Zoute)," *RIF*, 5, p. 13.

83. Ibid.

84. Siegfried Kracauer, "Les types nationaux vus par Hollywood," *RIF*, 6 (n.d.), pp. 115-34.

85. Bianka and Réne Zazzo, "Une expérience sur la compréhension du film," *RIF*, 6, pp. 159-70.

86. Etienne Souriau, "La structure de l'univers filmique et le vocabulaire de la filmologie," *RIF*, 7/8 (n.d.), 231-40.

87. David Katz, "Le portrait composite et la typologie," *RIF*, 7/8, pp. 207-14.

88. Henri Gestaut and Annette Roger, "Effets psychologiques, somatiques et électro-encéphalographiques du stimulus lumineux intermittent rhythmique: Applications possibles à la filmologie," *RIF*, 7/8, pp. 215-29.

89. Bianka Zazzo, "Analyse des difficultés d'une séquence cinématographique par la conduite du récit chez l'enfant," *RIF*, 9 (Janvier-Mars 1952), pp. 25-36.

90. P. Fraisse and G. de Montmollin, "Sur la mémoire des films," *RIF*, 9, pp. 37-69.

91. G. Heuyer, S. Lebovici and L. Bestagna, "Sur quelques réactions d'enfants inadaptés," *RIF*, 9, pp. 71-79.

92. Georges Friedmann and Edgar Morin, "Sociologie du cinéma," *RIF*, 10, pp. 95-112.

93. Etienne Souriau, "Filmologie et esthétique comparée," *RIF*, 10, pp. 113-41.

94. Gilbert Cohen-Séat, "Introduction," *RIF*, 11 (Juillet-Décembre 1952), p. 176.

95. Ibid.

96. Edgar Morin, "Recherches sur le public cinématographique," *RIF*, 12 (Janvier-Mars 1953), pp. 3-19.

97. Gertrude Keir, "Le rôle, la nécessité et la valeur d'une censure cinématographique," *RIF*, 14/15 (Juillet-Décembre 1953), pp. 179-97.

98. Edgar Morin, "Le problème des effets dangereux du cinéma," *RIF*, 14/15, pp. 217-31.

99. Etienne Souriau, ed. *L'univers filmique* (Paris: Flammarion, 1953).

100. *L'univers filmique* was dedicated to the memory of Jean-Jacques Riniéri, who died in an automobile accident prior to its publication.

101. Souriau himself would publish only one more article in the *Revue:* "L'univers filmique et l'art animalier," *RIF*, 25 (Janvier-Mars 1956), pp. 51-62.

102. *RIF*, 20/24 (1955), frontispiece. This Congress marks the only known association of André Bazin with filmology.

103. Ibid.

104. Zbigniew Gawrak, "La filmologie: Bilan dès la naissance jusqu'à 1958," *Ikon*, 65/66 (Avril-Septembre 1968), p. 114.

105. Ibid.

106. E.g., Marc Soriano, "Position de la filmologie" (1947); and Henri Wallon, "Qu'est-ce que c'est la filmologie?" *La Pensée*, 15, nouvelle série (Novembre-Décembre 1947), pp. 29-34.

107. Jean Vidal, "Filmologues distingués," *L'Ecran Français*, no. 119 (7 Octobre 1947), p. 11.

108. Ibid.

109. André Lang, *Le tableau blanc* (Paris: Horizons de France, 1948), p. 181.

110. Ibid.

111. Ibid., p. 182.

112. Florent Kirsch, "Introduction à une filmologie de la filmologie," *Cahiers du Cinéma*, 5 (Septembre 1951), pp. 33-34.

113. Ibid., pp. 34-35.

114. Ibid., p. 36.

115. Ibid., p. 35.

116. Ibid., p. 36.

117. Ibid.; Kirsch's term "film-in-itself" is an ironic reference to Sartre's "being-in-itself," intended to highlight the philosophical pretentions of the filmologists.

118. Ibid.

119. Ibid., p. 37.

120. Ibid.

121. Ibid., p. 38.

122. Ibid.

123. Xavier Tilliette, "Les filmologues au Congrès," *Positif*, II, 14-15 (Novembre 1955), p. 164.

124. Ibid., p. 165.

125. Ibid.

126. *Congrès International de Filmologie* (Paris: Sorbonne, 1955).

127. Amédée Ayfre, "Cinéphile et filmologue," *Cahiers du Cinéma*, 48 (Juin 1955), p. 57.

128. Ibid., p. 58.

129. André-S. Labarthe, "Connaissez-vous l'Institut de Filmologie?" *Radio Cinéma Télévision*, 403 (6 Octobre 1957), p. 48.

130. Delaville, p. 19.

Chapter 5

1. Gilbert Cohen-Séat, *Essai sur les principes d'une philosophie du cinéma* (Paris: Presses Universitaires de France, 1946), p. 57.

2. Marc Soriano, "Position de la filmologie," *Synthèses,* no. 2 (1947), pp. 149-50.

3. Christian Metz, *Language and Cinema,* trans. Donna Jean Umiker-Sebeok (The Hague, Paris: Mouton, 1974), p. 12.

4. Cohen-Séat, p. 115.

5. Ibid.

6. Soriano, p. 150.

7. Ibid.

8. Metz, p. 48.

9. "Etienne Souriau, 1892-1979," *L'art instaurateur: Revue d'Esthétique,* 1980, 3/4, pp. 13-14.

10. Etienne Souriau, *Les deux cent milles situations dramatiques* (Paris: Flammarion, 1950).

11. F. Sciacca, *La Filosofia Oggi,* 11, (1954), p. 95; quoted in Luce de Vitry-Maubrey, *La pensée cosmologique d'Etienne Souriau* (Paris: Klincksieck, 1974), p. 14.

12. Souriau, *La correspondance des arts* (Paris: Flammarion, 1947; second ed, 1969), p. 67: "At least nine characteristic arts, we have seen, form the nucleus at the center of this human realm, the nebula of art. Traditionally, they are as follows: architecture, sculpture, drawing, painting, dance, poetry, music, plus that complex group often referred to as the minor arts (also called the decorative arts, the industrial arts; and each of these terms has its drawbacks). And of course, we must add the newcomer, whose position is no longer contested—the cinematic art."

13. *Correspondance des arts,* p. 64.

14. Luce de Vitry-Maubrey, *La pensée cosmologique d'Etienne Souriau* (Paris: Klincksieck, 1974), p. 219.

15. *Correspondance des arts,* p. 45.

16. Ibid.

17. Benedetto Croce, *Aesthetic as Science of Expression and General Linguistic,* trans. Donald Ainslie (London: Macmillan, 1909).

18. Eugene F. Kaelin, *An Existentialist Aesthetic* (Madison: University of Wisconsin Press, 1962), p. 56.

19. Vitry-Maubrey, p. 219.

20. Daniel Charles, "Présence et instauration," *L'art instaurateur: Revue d'Esthétique,* 1980, 3/4, p. 76.

21. As defined in 1945 by Maurice Merleau-Ponty, one of France's most noted existential phenomenologists, whose work exerted a notable influence on filmology, "Phenomenology is the study of essences; and according to it, all problems amount to finding definitions of essences: the essence of perception or the essence of consciousness, for example. But phenomenology is also a philosophy which puts essences back into existence, and does not

expect to arrive at an understanding of man and the world from any starting point other than that of their 'facticity.' It is transcendental philosophy which places in abeyance the assertions arising out of the natural attitude, the better to understand them; but it is also a philosophy for which the world is always 'already there' before reflection begins—as an inalienable presence; and all its efforts are concentrated upon re-achieving a direct and primitive contact with the world, and endowing that contact with a philosophical status. It is the search for a philosophy which shall be a 'rigorous science,' but it also offers an account of space, time, and the world as we 'live' them. It tries to give a direct description of our experience as it is, without taking account of its psychological origin and the causal explanations which the scientist, the historian, or the sociologist may be able to provide." (*Phénoménologie de la perception,* Paris: Gallimard, 1945; trans. Colin Smith, *The Phenomenology of Perception,* London: Routledge and Kegan Paul, 1962.)

22. Joseph Chiari, *Twentieth Century French Thought: From Bergson to Lévi-Strauss* (New York: Gordian Press, 1975), p. 61.

23. Ibid.

24. Ibid.

25. *Correspondance des arts,* pp. 45-46.

26. Vitry-Maubrey, p. 13.

27. Ibid., pp. 13-14.

28. *Correspondance des arts,* p. 67.

29. Ibid., p. 48.

30. Ibid., pp. 48-49.

31. Ibid., p. 50.

32. Souriau, *L'avenir de l'esthétique* (Paris: Presses Universitaires de France, 1929); especially chapter 25.

33. *Correspondance des arts,* p. 52.

34. Mikel Dufrenne, preface to Vitry-Maubrey, p. 4.

35. Edmund Husserl, *Being and Thinking;* quoted in English in Chiari, pp. 63-64.

36. *Correspondance des arts,* p. 52.

37. Ibid., p. 53.

38. Vitry-Maubrey defines *plérôme* as the "vast, structured and complete ensemble which comprises the sum total of realities of a certain type: the *plérôme* of philosophies, the *plérôme* of art works. . . . " (p. 220).

39. Ibid.

40. Ibid., pp. 24-25.

41. Robert Scholes, *Structuralism in Literature* (New Haven and London: Yale University Press, 1974), p. 41.

42. *Correspondance des arts,* p. 33.

43. René Passeron, "Le concept d'instauration et le développement de la poïétique," *L'art instaurateur: Revue d'Esthétique,* 1980, 3/4, p. 178.

44. Souriau, "Nature et limite des contributions positives de l'esthétique à la filmologie," *RIF*, 1 (Juillet-Août 1947), p. 48.

45. Ibid., p. 49.

46. Ibid., p. 48.

47. Ibid.

48. Ibid., p. 51.

49. Ibid., pp. 51-52.

50. Ibid., p. 52.

51. Chiari, p. 41.

52. "Nature et limite," p. 54.

53. Ibid., p. 55.

54. Ibid.

55. Ibid., pp. 56-57.

56. Ibid., p. 63.

57. Ibid., p. 64.

58. Ibid., p. 58.

59. Souriau, "Filmologie et esthétique comparée," *RIF*, 10 (Avril-Juin 1952), p. 113.

60. *Correspondance des arts*, preface to second edition, p. 9.

61. "Filmologie et esthétique comparée," p. 141.

62. Ibid.

63. Souriau, "Rythme et unanimité (compte rendu d'une expérience)," in *L'univers filmique* (Paris: Flammarion, 1953), p. 203.

64. Ibid., pp. 204-5.

65. Ibid., p. 207.

66. Souriau, "La structure de l'univers filmique et le vocabulaire de la filmologie," *RIF*, 7/8 (n.d.), p. 231.

67. Ibid., p. 233.

68. Ibid.

69. Ibid., p. 234.

70. Ibid., p. 235.

71. Ibid., p. 236.

72. Ibid., p. 233.

73. Ibid.

74. Ibid.

75. Ibid., p. 238.

76. Ibid.

77. Ibid., p. 240.

78. Ibid., p. 238.

79. Ibid.

80. Ibid., p. 239.

81. Souriau, "Les grands caractères de l'univers filmique," in *L'univers filmique,* p. 15.

82. Ibid., p. 13. Here, Souriau's observations are quite close to those offered by Hugo Munsterberg in his 1916 *The Photoplay: A Psychological Study* regarding the correspondences between filmic techniques and such mental mechanisms as attention and memory. See Munsterberg, *The Film: A Psychological Study* (New York: Dover Publications, 1970), especially Part I. Although it is unlikely that Souriau was familiar with Munsterberg's work on film, which was still untranslated and had not yet been "rediscovered," their similarities point to the importance of phenomenological psychology in Souriau's conception of the filmic fact.

83. Ibid., p. 16.

84. Metz, "Sur un profil d'Etienne Souriau," *L'art instaurateur: Revue d'Esthétique,* 1980, 3/4, p. 151.

85. Ibid., pp. 143-44.

86. Roland Caillois, "Le tragique à la scène et à l'écran," *RIF,* 3/4 (Octobre 1948), pp. 325-27.

87. Roland Caillois, "Le cinéma, le meurtre, et la tragédie," *RIF,* 5 (n.d.), p. 89.

88. Ibid., p. 90.

89. Henri Agel, "Equivalences cinématographiques de la composition et du langage littéraire," *RIF,* 1, pp. 67-68.

90. Agel, "Sur l'utilisation de la syntaxe cinématographique dans l'explication des textes classiques," *RIF,* 3/4, p. 360.

91. Agel, "Sur le lyrisme du film," *RIF,* 5, p. 94.

92. Agel, *Le cinéma, a-t-il une âme?* (Paris: Editions du Cerf, 1952), p. 5.

93. Agel, *Le cinéma et le sacré* (Paris: Editions du Cerf, 1953).

94. Dudley Andrew, *The Major Film Theories* (London, Oxford, New York: Oxford University Press, 1976), p. 243.

95. Ibid., p. 244.

96. Agel, "Un mot sur la filmologie," *Le Technicien du Film,* 36 (15 Février 1958-15 Mars 1958), p. 8.

97. *Le cinéma, a-t-il une âme?,* p. 29.

98. André Bazin, "The Ontology of the Photographic Image," in *What is Cinema?,* trans. Hugh Gray (Berkeley, Los Angeles: University of California Press, 1967), pp. 9-16.

99. Agel, "Finalité poétique du cinéma," in *L'univers filmique,* p. 194.

100. See Rudolf Arnheim, *Film as Art* (Berkeley, Los Angeles: University of California Press, 1957); especially "Film and Reality," pp. 8-34.

101. "Finalité poétique," p. 194.

102. Ibid.

103. Pierre-Maxime Schuhl, "Pour un cinéma abstrait," *RIF*, 2 (Septembre-Octobre 1947), p. 183.

104. Jean Lameere, "Le cinéma et ses écueils," *RIF*, 2, p. 143.

105. Ibid., p. 144.

106. Ibid., p. 146.

107. Bazin, "The Myth of Total Cinema," in *What is Cinema?*, pp. 17-22.

108. François Ricci, "Le cinéma entre l'imagination et la réalité," *RIF*, 2, p. 161.

109. Ibid., p. 162.

110. Ibid.

111. Ibid.

112. Mario Roques, "Filmologie," *RIF*, 1, p. 7.

113. *Language and Cinema*, p. 13.

114. François Guillot de Rode, "Le dimension sonore," in *L'univers filmique*, pp. 119-35.

115. Jean Germain, "La musique et le film," in *L'univers filmique*, pp. 137-55.

116. Pierre Schaeffer, "L'élément non-visuel au cinéma (I-Analyse de la bande de son; II-Conception de la musique; III-Psychologie du rapport vision-audition)," *La Revue du Cinéma*, nouvelle série, nos. 1, 2 and 3 (Octobre, Novembre, Décembre 1946).

117. *La Revue du Cinéma*, nouvelle série, no. 19-20 (Automne 1949).

118. Anne Souriau, "Fonctions filmiques des costumes et des décors," in *L'univers filmique*, pp. 88-94.

119. Ibid., p. 97.

120. Ibid.

121. Ibid., p. 98.

122. Ibid., p. 99.

123. Anne Souriau, "Succession et simultanéité dans le film," in *L'univers filmique*, pp. 61-62.

124. Ibid., p. 66.

125. Ibid., pp. 67-70.

126. Ibid., p. 71.

127. Ibid., p. 72.

128. Metz, "Problems of Denotation in the Fiction Film"; "Outline of the Autonomous Segments in Jacques Rozier's Film *Adieu Philippine*"; and "Syntagmatic Study of Jacques Rozier's Film *Adieu Philippine*," in *Film Language*, trans. Michael Taylor (New York: Oxford University Press, 1974).

129. Georges Sadoul, "Georges Méliès et la première élaboration du langage cinématographique," *RIF*, 1, pp. 23-30.

130. Lucien Sève, "Cinéma et méthode," *RIF*, 2, p. 171.

131. Ibid., p. 172.

132. Ibid.

133. Ibid.

134. Maurice Mouillard, "Qu'est-ce que c'est l'expression cinématographique?" *RIF*, 2, p. 189.

135. Cohen-Séat, "Filmologie et cinéma," *RIF*, 3/4, p. 241.

136. Jacques Guicharnaud, "L'univers magique et l'image cinématographique," *RIF*, 1, p. 39.

137. "Filmologie et cinéma," p. 241.

138. Ibid.

139. Kaelin, pp. 359-60.

140. Mikel Dufrenne, *Phénoménologie de l'expérience esthétique* (Paris: Presses Universitaires de France, 1953), pp. 4-5; passage translated in Kaelin, p. 359.

141. Maurice Caveing, "Dialectique du concept du cinéma," *RIF*, 1, pp. 74-75.

142. Cohen-Séat, "Le discours filmique," *RIF*, 5, p. 37.

143. Ibid., p. 38.

144. Ibid.

145. Ibid., p. 40.

146. Ibid., p. 43.

147. Ibid., p. 45.

Chapter 6

1. Gilbert Cohen-Séat, *Essai sur les principes d'une philosophie du cinéma* (Paris: Presses Universitaires de France, 1946), p. 57.

2. Christian Metz, *Language and Cinema,* trans. Donna Jean Umiker-Sebeok (The Hague: Mouton, 1974), p. 12.

3. Ibid., p. 18.

4. Marc Soriano, "Position de la filmologie," *Synthèses,* no. 2 (1947), p. 150.

5. André des Fontaines, "Position industrielle," *RIF*, 1 (Juillet-Août 1947), p. 79.

6. R.C. Oldfield, "La perception visuelle des images du cinéma, de la télévision et du radar," *RIF*, 3/4 (October 1948), pp. 263-79.

7. René Zazzo, "Espace, mouvement et cinémascope," *RIF*, 18/19 (Juillet-Décembre 1954), pp. 209-19.

8. Raymond Bayer, "Le cinéma et les études humaines," *RIF*, 1, p. 33.

9. Ibid., p. 34.

10. Georges Friedmann and Edgar Morin, "Sociologie du cinéma," *RIF*, 10 (Avril-Juin 1952), pp. 95-112.

11. Siegfried Kracauer, "Cinéma et sociologie (sur l'exemple d'Allemagne préhitlerienne)," *RIF,* 3/4, pp. 311-18.

12. Siegfried Kracauer, *From Caligari to Hitler* (Princeton, N.J.: Princeton University Press, 1947).

13. Ibid., p. v.

14. Ibid., pp. 5-6.

15. Ibid., p. v.

16. Siegfried Kracauer, "Les types nationaux vus par Hollywood," *RIF,* 6 (n.d.), pp. 115-34.

17. Siegfried Kracauer, "National Types as Hollywood Presents Them," *Public Opinion Quarterly* XIII, no. 1 (Spring 1949), pp. 53-72.

18. Ibid., p. 72.

19. Mario Ponzo, "Le cinéma et les images collectives," *RIF,* 6, p. 147.

20. Ibid., p. 149.

21. Ibid., p. 147.

22. Ibid., p. 151.

23. Ibid., p. 150.

24. John Maddison, "Le cinéma et l'information des peuples primitifs," *RIF,* 3/4, p. 307.

25. Ibid., pp. 307-8.

26. Ibid., p. 310.

27. "Le premier Congrès Internationale de Filmologie," *RIF,* 3/4, p. 367.

28. "Cinéma pour Africains," *RIF,* 7/8 (n.d.), p. 277.

29. Ibid.

30. David Caute, *Communism and the French Intellectuals, 1914-1960* (New York: MacMillan Co., 1964), p. 266.

31. Marcel Cohen, "Ecriture et cinéma," *RIF,* 2 (Septembre-Octobre 1947), p. 179.

32. Ibid., pp. 179-80.

33. Etienne Jules Marey, a French physician and scientist who took sequential photographs with a "photographic gun" around 1882.

34. The Lumière brothers conducted what is widely accepted as the first public projection of films at the Grand Café in Paris in December 1895. In April 1896, Georges Méliès began projecting his own films at the Théâtre Robert Houdin.

35. Cohen, p. 181.

36. Ibid., p. 182.

37. Mark Poster, *Existential Marxism in Postwar France: From Sartre to Althusser* (Princeton, N.J.: Princeton University Press, 1975), p. 36.

38. Caute, p. 127.

39. Poster, pp. 249-50.

40. Ibid., p. 250.

41. Edgar Morin, *Autocritique* (Paris: Julliard, 1959), p. 46; trans. in Caute, pp. 154-55.

42. Caute, p. 182.

43. Poster, p. 216.

44. Morin, *Le cinéma ou l'homme imaginaire* (Paris: Editions de Minuit, 1956; new edition, 1977), pp. vii-viii.

45. Ibid., p. viii.

46. Poster, pp. 215-17.

47. Friedmann and Morin, p. 95.

48. Ibid.

49. Ibid.

50. Ibid.

51. Ibid.

52. Ibid., p. 96.

53. Ibid., p. 97.

54. Ibid., p. 98.

55. Ibid., pp. 99-100.

56. Ibid., p. 100.

57. Ibid.

58. Ibid., p. 101.

59. Ibid.

60. Ibid., p. 102.

61. Ibid.

62. Ibid., p. 103.

63. Ibid.

64. Lester Asheim, "From Book to Film: Simplification," *Hollywood Quarterly,* V, no. 3 (Spring 1951), pp. 289-304.

65. Friedmann and Morin, pp. 104-5.

66. Ibid., p. 105.

67. Ibid., p. 106.

68. Ibid., p. 107.

69. Ibid.

70. Ibid., p. 108.

71.   Ibid., p. 109.

72.   Ibid.

73.   Ibid., p. 110.

74.   Ibid., p. 111.

75.   Reports of audience studies in Britain appeared in the *Revue* as early as issue number 2: John Maddison and Flora Meaden, "Réactions sociales du cinéma en Angleterre," *RIF,* 2, pp. 211-16. Morin refers specifically to J.P. Mayer, *British Cinemas and Their Audiences* (London, 1948); Moss and Box, *The Cinema Audience;* Leo Handel, *Hollywood Looks at Its Audience* (Urbana: University of Illinois Press, 1950); and the work of Paul Lazarsfeld.

76.   Morin, "Recherches sur le public cinématographique," *RIF,* 12 (Janvier-Mars 1953), pp. 3-4.

77.   Ibid.

78.   Ibid., pp. 4-5.

79.   Ibid., p. 5.

80.   Ibid., p. 7.

81.   Ibid., pp. 8-9.

82.   Ibid., p. 9.

83.   Ibid., p. 10.

84.   Ibid.

85.   Ibid., p. 11.

86.   Ibid.; Morin cites Paul Lazarsfeld, "Audience Research in the Movie Field," *Annals of the American Academy of Political and Social Science,* 254 (November 1947), pp. 160-68.

87.   Ibid., pp. 11-12.

88.   Ibid., p. 12.

89.   Ibid., p. 13.

90.   Ibid., p. 14.

91.   Ibid., p. 15.

92.   Ibid., p. 16.

93.   Ibid., p. 17; Morin cites Edgar Dale, *Children's Attendance at Motion Pictures* (New York: Macmillan Co., 1935).

94.   Ibid.

95.   Ibid.

96.   Ibid., p. 18.

97.   Morin, *L'homme et la mort* (Paris: Buchet-Chastel, 1951; Editions du Seuil, 1970, 1976).

98.   *Le cinéma ou l'homme imaginaire,* p. ix.

99.   Ibid.

100.   Ibid.

101. Ibid.

102. Morin's phrase is a clever one: *génie* is equivalent to the English "genius," thus referring to the ingeniousness of photography; it is also translated as "spirit," corresponding to the transcendant quality attributed to the photo by the viewer; finally, the phrase is a play on *photogénie*, which refers to the quality of being photogenic, and thus encompasses that indefinable relationship between camera and object.

103. *Le cinéma ou l'homme imaginaire*, p. 25.

104. Ibid., p. 26.

105. André Bazin, "Ontologie de l'image photographique," in G. Diehl, *Les problèmes de la peinture* (Paris: Confluences, 1945), trans. Hugh Gray, in Bazin, *What is Cinema?* (Berkeley and Los Angeles: University of California Press, 1967), p. 14.

106. *Le cinéma ou l'homme imaginaire*, p. 40.

107. Ibid., p. 31.

108. Ibid., p. 32.

109. Ibid., p. 33.

110. Ibid., p. 42.

111. Ibid., p. 52.

112. Ibid., pp. 72-73.

113. Edgar Morin, *Les Stars* (Paris: Editions du Seuil, 1957); trans. Richard Howard, *The Stars* (New York: Grove Press, 1960), p. 165.

114. Edgar Morin, "Pour un nouveau cinéma vérité," *France-Observateur* (Janvier 1960).

115. Jean Rouch and Edgar Morin, *Chronique d'un été* (Paris: Inter-Spectacles, 1962), p. 8.

116. Ibid., pp. 8-9.

117. Ibid., p. 9.

118. Cohen-Séat, *Problèmes du cinéma et de l'information visuelle* (Paris: Presses Universitaires de France, 1961).

119. Poster, p. 211.

120. Pierre Fougeyrollas, *La philosophie en question* (Paris, 1960), p. 55.

121. Cohen-Séat and Pierre Fougeyrollas, *L'action sur l'homme: Cinéma et télévision* (Paris: Presses Universitaires de France, 1961), p. 9.

122. Poster, p. 229.

123. Morin, "Les problèmes des effets dangereux du cinéma," *RIF*, 14/15 (Juillet-Décembre 1953), p. 217.

124. Maddison and Meaden, *RIF*, 2, pp. 211-16.

125. W.D. Wall and E.M. Smith, "Les adolescents et le cinéma," *RIF*, 6, pp. 153-58.

126. Hélène Gratiot-Alphandéry, *L'école des parents et des éducateurs* (Année 1952-1953, no. 3).

127. Cohen-Séat, "Introduction," *RIF*, 14/15, p. 172.

128.   Ibid., p. 171.

129.   Ibid., p. 173.

130.   A. Mergen, "Cinéma et hygiène mentale," *RIF*, 14/15, p. 233.

131.   Ibid., p. 241.

132.   Morin, "Problèmes des effets dangereux," p. 226.

133.   Ibid., p. 227.

134.   Gertrude Keir, "Le rôle, la nécessité et la valeur d'une censure cinématographique," *RIF*, 14/15, p. 188.

135.   Morin, "Problèmes des effets dangereux," p. 227.

136.   Ibid., p. 231.

137.   Serge Lebovici, "Cinéma et criminalité," *RIF*, 14/15, p. 199.

138.   Ibid., p. 213.

139.   Ibid., pp. 213-14.

140.   Ibid., p. 214.

Chapter 7

1.   Mario Roques quoted in "Documents de l'Association pour la Recherche Filmologique," *RIF*, 1 (Juillet-Août 1947), p. 97.

2.   Henri Wallon, "Qu'est-ce que c'est la filmologie?" *La Pensée*, 15 (Décembre 1947), p. 30.

3.   Hélène Gratiot-Alphandéry, introduction to *Lecture d'Henri Wallon* (Paris: Editions Sociales, 1976), p. 12.

4.   Ernesto Valentini, "Perspectives psychologiques en filmologie," *RIF*, 25 (Janvier-Mars 1956), p. 5.

5.   Etienne Souriau, "Nature et limite des contributions positives de l'esthétique à la filmologie," *RIF*, 1, pp. 47-64.

6.   Wallon, "De quelques problèmes psycho-physiologiques que pose le cinéma," *RIF*, 1, p. 16.

7.   Ibid.

8.   Ibid., p. 17.

9.   Ibid.

10.   Maurice Merleau-Ponty, "The Film and the New Psychology," in *Sense and Non-Sense*, trans. H. and P. Dreyfus (Evanston: Northwestern, 1964), p. 50.

11.   Ibid., p. 51.

12.   Ibid., p. 54.

13.   Ibid.

14.   Ibid., pp. 58-59.

15.   Ibid., p. 59.

16. R.C. Oldfield, "La perception visuelle des images du cinéma, de la télévision et du radar," *RIF*, 3/4 (Octobre 1948), p. 265.

17. Ibid., p. 264.

18. Ibid., p. 265.

19. Ibid., p. 272.

20. Ibid., pp. 275-77.

21. Albert Michotte van den Berck, "Le caractère de 'réalité' des projections cinématographiques," *RIF*, 3/4, p. 249.

22. Ibid., p. 251.

23. Ibid., pp. 257-58.

24. Pierre Francastel, "Espace et illusion," *RIF*, 5 (n.d.), p. 65.

25. Ibid.

26. Ibid., p. 66.

27. Ibid., p. 68.

28. Francastel, *Peinture et société: Naissance et destruction d'un espace plastique de la Renaissance au Cubisme* (Paris, Lyon: Audin, 1951).

29. Francastel, "Espace et illusion," p. 68.

30. Ibid., p. 73.

31. Michotte [van den Berck], "A propos de l'article de M.P. Francastel 'Espace et illusion,'" *RIF*, 6 (n.d.), pp. 139-40.

32. Marc Soriano, "Lire, assister," *RIF*, 3/4, p. 303.

33. Ibid., p. 304.

34. Jean-Jacques Riniéri, "L'impression de réalité au cinéma: les phénomènes de croyance," in Etienne Souriau, ed., *L'univers filmique* (Paris: Flammarion, 1953), pp. 33-35.

35. Ibid., p. 35.

36. Ibid., pp. 44-45.

37. Henry Wallon, "L'acte perceptive et le cinéma," *RIF*, 13 (Avril-Juin 1953), p. 97. Reprinted in *Lecture d'Henri Wallon*.

38. Ibid., p. 100.

39. Ibid.

40. Serge Lebovici, "Psychanalyse et cinéma," *RIF*, 5, p. 49.

41. Ibid., pp. 50-51.

42. Ibid., p. 51.

43. See especially the articles by Thierry Kuntzel, "Le travail du film," *Communications*, 19 (1972); trans. L. Crawford, K. Lockhart, C. Tysdal, *Enclitic*, 2, no. 1 (Spring 1978); and "Le travail du film, 2," *Communications*, 23 (1975); trans. Nancy Huston, *Camera Obscura*, 5 (Spring 1980).

44.   Lebovici, p. 52.

45.   Ibid., p. 53.

46.   Ibid., p. 55.

47.   Hugo Munsterberg, *The Film: A Psychological Study* (New York: Dover, 1970).

48.   Lebovici, p. 55.

49.   Jean Deprun, "Cinéma et identification," *RIF,* 1, p. 37.

50.   Ibid.

51.   Ibid.

52.   This theme would not be developed in any significant way until the late 1970s when Raymond
       Bellour began to elaborate the relationship between hypnosis and cinema; see Janet
       Bergstrom, "Alternation, Segmentation, Hypnosis: Interview with Raymond Bellour,"
       Camera Obscura, 3/4 (Summer 1979), pp. 71-103.

53.   Deprun, p. 37.

54.   Jean Deprun, "Cinéma et transfert," *RIF,* 2 (September-Octobre 1947), p. 206.

55.   Ibid., p. 207.

56.   Robert Desoille, "Le rêve éveillé et la filmologie," *RIF,* 2, pp. 197-203.

57.   Agostino Gemelli, "Le film procédé d'analyse projective," *RIF,* 6, pp. 135-38.

Chapter 8

1.   Christian Metz, *Language and Cinema,* trans. Donna Jean Umiker-Sebeok (The Hague,
      Paris: Mouton, 1974), p. 14.

2.   Henri Wallon, "Introduction au symposium de filmologie (au XIIIe Congrès International de
      Psychologie, Stockholm, Juillet 1951)," *RIF,* 9 (Janvier-Mars 1952), pp. 21-22.

3.   M. Toulousse and R. Mourgue, "Des réactions respiratoires au cours des projections
      cinématographiques," *RIF,* 5 (n.d.), p. 77. In 1911, Toulousse co-authored the landmark
      manual of procedures for experimental psychology in France, *Technique de psychologie
      expérimentale.*

4.   Ibid., p. 78.

5.   Yves Galifret, "Expériences de filmologie en 1920," *RIF,* 5, pp. 75-76.

6.   Galifret and J. Segal, "Cinéma et la physiologie des sensations," *RIF,* 3/4 (Octobre 1948), pp.
      292-93.

7.   Henri Gestaut and Annette Roger, "Effets psychologiques, somatiques et électro-
      encéphalographiques du stimulus lumineux intermittent rythmique: Applications possibles à
      la filmologie," *RIF,* 7/8 (n.d.), p. 216.

8.   Ibid., pp. 216-23.

9.   Ibid., p. 229.

10.   Ibid.

11. Cohen-Séat, Gastaut and J. Bert, "Modification de l'E.E.G. pendant la projection cinématographique"; Gilbert Cohen-Séat and Jacques Faure, "Retentissement du 'Fait Filmique' sur des rythmes bioélectriques du cerveau"; G. Heuyer, Cohen-Séat, Serge Lebovici, Mme. Rebeillard and Mlle. Daveau, "Note sur l'électroencéphalographie pendant la projection cinématographique chez les enfants inadaptés," *RIF*, 16 (Janiver-Mars 1954).

12. Mario Roques, "Introduction," *RIF*, 16, p. 4.

13. Cohen-Séat and Jacques Faure, "Réponses aux stimulations sensorielles de l'activation realisée par la projection filmique," *Revue Neurologique*, XC, no. 4 (1954), pp. 307-11; "Film et encéphalie," *Annales Médico-Psychologiques*, II, no. 3 (Octobre 1954), p. 445.

14. Faure and Cohen-Séat, "Correlations à partir des effets de la projection filmique sur l'activité nerveuse supérieure," *Congrès International de Filmologie* (Paris, 19-23 Février 1955), n.p.

15. Apparently in exchange for Cohen-Séat's silence, the French government provided financial support for his Groupe de Recherches et d'Etudes Cinématographiques Appliquées until 1959, when Cohen-Séat was informed that his research no longer needed to be kept secret. In 1962, Cohen-Séat filed suit for damages from the government. J.L. "M. Cohen-Séat réclame 620,000 NF au Premier Ministre," *Le Monde* (26 Avril 1962); and A.P. Richard, "Une fructueuse découverte," *La Cinématographie Française* (26 Mai 1962).

16. The technique of recording the audial responses of subjects is discussed in Vincent Bloch, "Concours International du film récréatif pour enfants," *RIF*, 13 (Avril-Juin 1953), p. 167. The photographic recording of subject responses is discussed in Georges Tendron, "Nouvelles techniques d'enregistrement," *RIF*, 13, p. 167. For the results of a Danish experiment involving both techniques, see Ellen Siersted and H. Lund Hansen, "Réactions des petits enfants au cinéma: Résumé d'une série d'observations faites au Danemark," *RIF*, 7/8, pp. 241-43.

17. W.B. Pillsbury, *The History of Psychology* (New York: W.W. Norton & Co., 1929), p. 233.

18. Réne Zazzo, "Niveau mental et compréhension du cinéma," *RIF*, 5, p. 30.

19. Ibid.

20. Ibid., p. 31.

21. Ibid., p. 34.

22. Ibid.

23. Ibid., p. 35.

24. Bianka Zazzo and René Zazzo, "Une expérience sur la compréhension du film," *RIF*, 6 (n.d.), p. 163.

25. Ibid., pp. 161-62.

26. Ibid., p. 163.

27. Ibid., pp. 164-65.

28. Ibid., pp. 166-68.

29. Ibid., p. 159.

30. Ibid., p. 169.

31. Bianka Zazzo, "Analyse des difficultés d'une sequence cinématographique par la conduite du récit chez l'enfant," *RIF*, 9, pp. 30-31.

32. Ibid., p. 35.

33. G. Heuyer, Serge Lebovici and G. Amado, "A propos d'une enquête filmologique chez les enfants et adolescents inadaptés," *RIF*, 5, p. 58.

34. Ibid., p. 63.

35. Heuyer, Lebovici and L. Bertagna, "Sur quelques réactions d'enfants inadaptés," *RIF*, 9, pp. 71-73.

36. Ibid., pp. 74-76.

37. Ibid., p. 77.

38. Bianka Zazzo, p. 25.

39. Heuyer, Lebovici, Bertagna, p. 79.

40. Enrico Fulchignoni, "Examen d'un test filmique," *RIF*, 6, p. 173.

41. Ibid., p. 174.

42. Ibid., p. 175.

43. Ibid., pp. 175-76.

44. Ibid., p. 176.

45. Ibid., p. 178.

46. Ibid., p. 177.

47. Ibid., p. 181.

48. Ibid., pp. 182-83.

49. Jean Deprun, "Le cinéma et l'identification," *RIF*, 1 (Juillet-Août 1947), pp. 36-38; "Cinéma et transfert," *RIF*, 2 (Septembre-Octobre 1947), pp. 205-7.

50. Paul Fraisse and G. de Montmollin, "Sur la mémoire des films," *RIF*, 9, pp. 37-38.

51. Ibid., p. 53.

52. Ibid., p. 57.

53. Ibid., p. 69.

54. Ibid.

55. Jean Dalsace, "Cinéma, biologie et médecine," *RIF*, 1, p. 82.

56. Juliette Boutonier, "Réflexions sur la valeur éducative du cinéma," *RIF*, 2, pp. 193-95.

57. André Lang, *Le tableau blanc* (Paris: Horizons de France, 1948), p. 228.

58. Garth Jowett, *Film: The Democratic Art* (Boston, Toronto: Little, Brown and Co., 1976), p. 149.

59. Ibid.

60. Germaine Dulac, "The Meaning of Cinema," *International Review of Educational Cinematography (Interciné,* League of Nations International Educational Cinematographic Institute), No. 12 (December 1931), p. 1094.

61. Ibid., p. 1100.

62. Ibid., pp. 1101-2.

63. M. Lebrun, "Film d'enseignement et filmologie" (Conference faite à l'Institut de Filmologie—Février 1951), *RIF*, 7/8, p. 266.

64. Lang, pp. 124-55.

65. Marc Soriano, "Problèmes de méthode posés par le cinéma considéré comme expérimentation psychologique nouvelle," *RIF*, 2, pp. 124-25.

66. Ibid., p. 124.

67. Henri Wallon, "L'enfant et le film," *RIF*, 5, pp. 21-22.

68. Lebrun, p. 266.

69. Wallon, "L'enfant et le film," p. 24.

70. Bianka Zazzo, "Le cinéma à l'école maternelle," *RIF*, 9, p. 87.

71. Ibid., p. 85.

72. Ibid., p. 84.

73. See Note 36.

74. S. Herbinière-Lebert, "Pourquoi et comment nous avons fait *Mains blanches*; Premières expériences avec un film éducatif réalisé spécialement pour les moins de sept ans," *RIF*, 7/8, p. 249.

75. Ibid., p. 250.

76. Hélène Gratiot-Alphandéry, "L'enfant et le film," *RIF*, 6, pp. 171-72.

77. Herbinière-Lebert, p. 251.

78. Ibid., p. 254.

79. Ibid., p. 255.

80. Lebrun, p. 272.

Chapter 9

1. "Deuxième Congrès International de Filmologie," *RIF*, 20/24 (Année 1955), p. 3.

2. Ibid., p. 4.

3. Ibid., p. 5.

4. Ibid.

5. "Allocution du Professeur Henri Laugier," *RIF*, 20/24, p. 20.

6. W.D. Wall, "Compte rendu général," *RIF*, 20/24, p. 71.

7. Zbigniew Gawrak, "La filmologie: Bilan dès la naissance jusqu'à 1958," *Ikon*, 65/66 (April-September 1968), p. 113.

8. Ibid., p. 114.

9. Alberto Marzi and Renzo Canestrari, "Recherches sur les problèmes du cinéma—Italie," *RIF*, 11 (Juillet-Décembre 1952), pp. 179-92.

10. Gawrak, p. 114.

11. Ernesto Valentini, "Perspectives psychologiques en filmologie," *RIF*, 25 (Janvier-Mars 1956), p. 5.

12. Ibid., p. 15.

13. Luigi Volpicelli, "La filmologie en tant que recherche socio-historique," *RIF*, 25, p. 19.

14. Ibid., p. 22.

15. Gawrak, p. 116.

16. Ibid.

17. Ibid.

18. Ibid.

19. Ibid.

20. Robert Scholes, *Structuralism in Literature* (New Haven and London: Yale University Press, 1974), p. 10.

21. Ferdinand de Saussure, *Course in General Linguistics,* trans. Wade Biskin (New York: McGraw-Hill, 1966). (First French edition, 1916)

22. DeGeorge, Richard and Fernande, eds. *The Structuralists from Marx to Lévi-Strauss* (Garden City, NJ: Doubleday, 1972), see Introduction.

23. Scholes, p. 2.

24. Christian Metz, "On the Impression of Reality in the Cinema," in *Film Language,* trans. Michael Taylor (New York: Oxford University Press, 1974), p. 3. Taylor translates the French term *sémiologie* as "semiotics," which seems confusing, especially to the extent that the French *sémiotique* is sometimes employed with a slightly different meaning. *Sémiologie* is translated as "semiology" throughout this book, except in direct quotes and titles taken from Taylor's translation.

25. Roland Barthes, "Rhetoric of the Image," in *Image/Music/Text,* trans. Stephen Heath (New York: Hill and Wang, 1977), pp. 32-51.

26. "On the Impression of Reality in the Cinema," p. 6.

27. Ibid., p. 9.

28. Ibid., p. 11.

29. Ibid., pp. 13-14.

30. Metz, *Language and Cinema,* trans. Donna Umiker-Sebeok (The Hague: Mouton, 1974), p. 12.

31. Ibid., p. 17.

32. Ibid., p. 22.

33. Ibid., p. 48.

34. Ibid., p. 13.

35. Metz, "Notes Toward a Phenomenology of the Narrative," *Film Language,* pp. 16-28.

36.   Metz, "Some Points in the Semiotics of the Cinema," *Film Language*, pp. 92-107.

37.   Vladimir Propp, *Morphology of the Folk Tale* (Austin: University of Texas Press, 1970).

38.   Scholes, pp. 104-6.

39.   "Le premier Congrès de Filmologie," *RIF*, 3/4 (Octobre 1948), p. 368.

40.   Maurice Merleau-Ponty, "The Film and the New Psychology," in *Sense and Non-Sense*, trans. Hubert L. Dreyfus and Patricia Allen Dreyfus (Evanston: Northwestern University Press, 1964), p. 50.

41.   Barthes, *Elements of Semiology*, trans. Annette Lavers and Colin Smith (New York: Hill and Wang, 1968).

42.   Barthes, "Le problème de la signification du cinéma," *RIF*, 32/33 (Janvier-Juin 1960), p. 83.

43.   Ibid., p. 88.

44.   Metz, "The Cinema: Language or Language System?" *Film Language*, pp. 31-91.

45.   Barthes, "Problème de la signification," p. 83.

46.   Ibid., p. 84.

47.   Ibid., p. 85.

48.   Ibid., p. 86.

49.   Ibid.

50.   Ibid.

51.   Metz, "Problems of Denotation in the Fiction Film," and "Syntagmatic Study of Jacques Rozier's Film *Adieu Philippine*," in *Film Language*, pp. 177-82.

52.   Metz, "Some Points," p. 103.

53.   Roland Barthes, *S/Z*, trans. Richard Miller (New York: Hill and Wang, 1974).

54.   Among the most significant textual analyses of film written in France during the 1970s are Raymond Bellour's analysis of Hitchcock's *North by Northwest*, "Le blocage symbolique," *Communications*, 23 (1975), 235-350; Thierry Kuntzel's analysis of the opening sequence of Lang's *M*, "Le travail du film," *Communications*, 19 (1972), trans. L. Crawford, K. Lockhart; C. Tysdal, *Enclitic*, II, 1 (Spring 1978); and Kuntzel's analysis of *The Most Dangerous Game*, "Le travail du film, 2," *Communications* 23 (1975), trans. Nancy Huston, *Camera Obscura*, 5 (Spring 1980).

55.   Metz, "Profil d'Etienne Souriau," *L'art instaurateur: Revue d'Esthétique*, 1980, 3/4, p. 144.

56.   Jean-Louis Baudry. "The Apparatus," trans. Jean Andrews and Bertrand Augst, in Theresa Hak Kyung Cha, ed., *Apparatus* (New York: Tanam Press, 1980), pp. 41-62.

57.   Thierry Kuntzel, "A Note Upon the Filmic Apparatus," *Quarterly Review of Film Studies*, 1:3 (August 1976), pp. 266-71.

Bibliography

Agel, Henri, "Activité ou passivité du spectateur." In *L'univers filmique*, pp. 47-58. Edited by Etienne Souriau. Paris: Flammarion, 1953.

_____. *Le cinéma, a-t-il une âme?* Paris: Editions du Cerf, 1952.

_____. *Le cinéma et le sacré.* Paris: Editions du Cerf, 1953.

_____. "Equivalences cinématographiques de la composition et du langage littéraire." *RIF*, 1 (Juillet-Août 1947), 67-70.

_____. "Finalité poétique." In *L'univers filmique*, pp. 193-201. Edited by Etienne Souriau. Paris: Flammarion, 1953.

_____. "Sur le lyrisme du film," *RIF*, 5 (n.d.), pp. 92-94.

_____. "Sur l'utilisation de la syntaxe cinématographique dans l'explication des textes classiques." *RIF*, 3/4 (Octobre 1948), pp. 357-60.

"Allocution du Professeur Henri Laugier." *RIF*, 20/24 (Année 1955), pp. 19-20.

Alpert, Harry. *Emile Durkheim and His Sociology.* New York: Russell & Russell, 1961.

Althusser, Louis. *For Marx.* Translated by Ben Brewster. London: NLB, 1977.

Andrew, J. Dudley. *The Major Film Theories.* London, Oxford, New York: Oxford University Press, 1976.

"Après le Congrès International de Filmologie," *RIF*, 3/4 (Octobre 1948), p. 373.

Arnheim, Rudolf. *Film as Art.* Berkeley, Los Angeles: University of California Press, 1957.

Arnoux, Alexandre. *Du muet au parlant.* Paris: La nouvelle Edition, 1946.

Asheim, Lester. "From Book to Film: Simplification." *Hollywood Quarterly*, V, 3 (Spring 1951), pp. 289-304.

Auriol, Jean George. "Les origines de la mise en scène." *Revue du Cinéma*, nouvelle série, 1 (Octobre 1946), pp. 7-23.

Ayfre, Amédée. "Cinéphile et filmologue." *Cahiers du Cinéma*, 48 (Juin 1955), pp. 57-58.

Bardèche, Maurice, and Brassilach, Robert. *The History of Motion Pictures.* Translated and edited by Iris Barry. New York: W.W. Norton & Co., 1938.

_____. *Histoire du cinéma*, Vol. II: *Le cinéma parlant.* Paris: André Martel, 1954.

Barjeval, René. *Cinéma total.* Paris: Denoël, 1944.

Barthes, Roland. *Elements of Semiology.* Translated by Annette Lavers and Colin Smith. New York: Hill & Wang, 1968.

_____. "Le problème de la signification du cinéma." *RIF*, 32/33 (Janvier-Juin 1960), pp. 83-89.

_____. "Rhetoric of the Image." In *Image/Music Text*, pp. 32-51. Translated by Stephen Heath. New York: Hill & Wang, 1977.

_____. *S/Z.* Translated by Richard Miller. New York: Hill & Wang, 1974.

_____. "Les 'unités traumatiques' au cinéma." *RIF*, 34 (Juillet-Septembre 1960), pp. 13-21.

Baudry, Jean-Louis. "The Apparatus." Trans. Jean Andrews and Bertrand Augst. In Theresa Hak Kyung Cha, ed. *Apparatus.* New York: Tanam Press, 1980.

Bayer, Raymond. "Le cinéma et les études humaines." *RIF,* I (Juillet-Août 1947), pp. 31-35.

Bazin, André. *Le cinéma de l'occupation et de la résistance.* Edited and prefaced by François Truffaut. Paris: Union Générale d'Editions, 1975.

_____. *What is Cinema?* Translated and edited by Hugh Gray. Berkeley, Los Angeles, 1967.

Begoña, R.P. Mauricio de. *Elementos de Filmología: Teoría de Cine.* Madrid: Dirección General de Cinematográfica y Teatro, 1953.

Bellour, Raymond. "Le blocage symbolique." *Communcations,* 23 (1975), pp. 235-350.

Benoit-Lévy, Jean. *Les grandes missions du cinéma.* Montréal: Lucien Parizeau & Co., 1944.

Benrubi, Isaac. *Contemporary Thought of France.* Translated by Ernest B. Dicker. New York: Alfred A. Knopf, 1926.

Bergstrom, Janet. "Alternation, Segmentation, Hypnosis: Interview with Raymond Bellour." *Camera Obscura,* 3/4 (Summer 1979), pp. 71-103.

Berthomieu, A. *Essai de grammaire cinématographique.* Paris: La Nouvelle Edition, 1946.

Bloch, Vincent. "Concours International du film récréatif pour enfants," *RIF,* 13 (Avril-Juin 1954), p. 167.

Boutonier, Juliette. "Réflexions sur la valeur éducative du cinéma." *RIF,* 2 (Septembre-Octobre 1947), pp. 193-95.

Burch, Noël. *Marcel L'Herbier.* Paris: Editions Seghers, 1973.

Caillois, Roland. "Le tragique à la scène et à l'écran." *RIF,* 3/4 (Octobre 1948), pp. 325-29.

_____. "Le cinéma, le meurtre, et la tragédie," *RIF,* 5 (n.d.), pp. 87-91.

Caute, David. *Communism and the French Intellectuals, 1914-1960.* New York: Macmillan, 1964.

Caveing, Maurice. "Dialectique du concept du cinéma." *RIF,* I (Juillet-Août 1947), pp. 71-78; *RIF,* 3/4 (Octobre 1948), pp. 343-350.

Charensol, Georges. *Quarante ans de cinéma (1895-1935).* Paris: Sagittaire, 1935.

_____. *Renaissance du cinéma français.* Paris: Sagittaire, 1946.

Charles, Daniel. "Présence et instauration." *L'art instaurateur: Revue d'Esthétique,* 1980, 3/4, pp. 75-84.

Chiari, Joseph. *Twentieth Century French Thought: From Bergson to Lévi-Strauss.* New York: Gordian Press, 1975.

"Cinéma pour Africains." *RIF,* 7/8 (n.d.), pp. 277-82.

Cohen, Marcel. "Ecriture et cinéma." *RIF,* 2 (Septembre-Octobre 1947), pp. 179-82.

Cohen-Séat, Gilbert. "Le discours filmique." *RIF,* 5 (n.d.), pp. 37-48.

_____. *Essai sur les principes d'une philosophie du cinéma.* Paris: Presses Universitaires de France, 1946; 2nd edition, 1958.

_____. "Filmologie et cinéma." *RIF,* 3/4 (Octobre 1948), pp. 237-46.

_____. "Introduction." *RIF,* 11 (Juillet-Décembre 1952), p. 176.

_____. "Introduction." *RIF,* 14/15 (Juillet-Décembre 1953), pp. 171-77.

_____. *Problèmes du cinéma et de l'information visuelle.* Paris: Presses Universitaires de France, 1961.

Cohen-Séat, Gilbert and Faure, Jacques. "Correlations à partir des effets de la projection filmique sur l'activité nerveuse supérieure." In *Congrès International de Filmologie,* n.p. Paris: Sorbonne, 19-23 Février 1955.

Cohen-Séat, Gilbert and Faure, Jacques. "Film et encéphalie." *Annales Médico-Psychologiques,* II, 3 (Octobre 1954), p. 445.

Cohen-Séat, Gilbert and Faure, Jacques. "Réponses aux stimulations sensorielles de l'activation réalisée par la projection filmique." *Revue Neurologique,* XC, 7 (1954), pp. 307-11.

Cohen-Séat, Gilbert and Faure, Jacques. "Retentissement du 'Fait Filmique' sur les rhythmes bioélectriques du cerveau." *RIF,* 16 (Janvier-Mars 1954), pp. 27-50.

Cohen-Séat, Gilbert and Fougeyrollas, Pierre. *L'action sur l'homme: Cinéma et télévision.* Paris: Presses Universitaires de France, 1961.

Cohen-Séat, Gilbert; Gastaut, Henri; and Bert, J. "Modification de l'E.E.G. pendant la projection cinématographique." *RIF*, 16 (Janvier-Mars 1954), pp. 7-25.

Coissac, G. Michel. *Le cinématographe et l'enseignement.* Paris: Larousse et Cinéopse, 1926.

———. *Histoire du cinématographe de ses origines à nos jours.* Paris: Cinéopse et Gauthier Villars, 1925.

Comte, Auguste. *Cours de philosophie positive.* Vol. II, Lecture 28. Paris: Bachelier, 1835.

Congrès International de Filmologie. Paris: Sorbonne, 19-23 Février 1955.

Croce, Benedetto. *Aesthetic as Science of Expression and General Linguistic.* Translated by Donald Ainslie. London: Macmillan, 1909.

Curtis, David. *Experimental Cinema.* New York: Universe Books, 1971.

D., J. "Espoirs d'une science nouvelle." *RIF*, 2 (Septembre-Octobre 1947), pp. 109-10.

Dale, Edgar. *Children's Attendance at Motion Pictures.* New York: Macmillan, 1935.

Dalsace, Jean. "Cinéma, biologie et médecine." *RIF*, 1 (Juillet-Août 1947), pp. 82-83.

DeGeorge, Richard and DeGeorge, Fernande, eds. *The Structuralists from Marx to Lévi-Strauss.* Garden City, NJ: Doubleday, 1972.

Delaville, Jean-Pierre. "La filmologie, Qu-est-ce que c'est?" *Jeune Cinéma,* 1 (1959), p. 19.

Deprun, Jean. "Cinéma et identification." *RIF*, 1 (Juillet-Août 1947), pp. 36-38.

———. "Cinéma et transfert." *RIF*, 2 (Septembre-Octobre 1947), pp. 205-7.

des Fontaines, André. "Position industrielle." *RIF*, 1 (Juillet-Août 1947), pp. 79-81.

Desoille, Robert. "Le rêve éveillé et la filmologie." *RIF*, 2 (Septembre-Octobre 1947), pp. 197-203.

"Deuxième Congrès International de Filmologie," *RIF*, 20/24 (Année 1955), pp. 3-10.

"Documents de l'Association pour la Recherche Filmologique," *RIF*, 1 (Juillet-Août 1947), pp. 93-100.

Doniol-Valcroze, Jacques. "L'histoire de *Cahiers.*" *Cahiers de Cinéma*, 100 (Octobre 1959).

Dufrenne, Mikel. *Phénoménologie de l'expérience esthétique.* Paris: Presses Universitaires de France, 1953.

Dulac, Germaine. "The Meaning of Cinema." *International Review of Educational Cinematography,* 12 (December 1931).

Durkheim, Emile. *The Division of Labor in Society.* Trans. George Simpson. New York: Macmillan Co., 1933.

———. *The Rules of Sociological Method.* Translated by Sarah H. Solovay and John H. Mueller. Glencoe, IL: Free Press of Glencoe, 1950.

———. *Socialism and St. Simon.* Translated by Charlotte Sandler. Yellow Springs, OH: Antioch Press, 1958.

Eisenstein, Sergei. "Le principe nouveau cinéma russe." *Revue du Cinéma,* 9 (1 Avril 1930), pp. 16-27.

Epstein, Jean. *Cinéma bonjour.* Paris: La Sirène, 1921.

———. *Le cinématographe vu de l'Etna.* Paris: Ecrivains Réunis, 1926.

———. *L'intelligence d'une machine.* Paris: J. Melot, 1946.

"Etienne Souriau, 1892-1979." *L'art instaurateur: Revue d'Esthétique,* 1980, 3/4, pp. 13-14.

Fougeyrollas, Pierre. *La philosophie en question.* Paris: Presses Universitaires de France, 1960.

Fraisse, Paul and de Montmollin, G. "Sur la mémoire des films." *RIF*, 9 (Janvier-Mars 1952), pp. 37-69.

Francastel, Pierre. "Espace et illusion." *RIF*, 5 (n.d.), pp. 65-74.

———. *Peinture et société: Naissance et destruction d'un espace plastique de la Renaissance au Cubisme.* Paris, Lyon: Audin, 1951.

Friedmann, Georges and Morin, Edgar. "Sociologie du cinéma." *RIF*, 10 (Avril-Juin 1952), pp. 95-112.

Fulchignoni, Enrico. "Examen d'un test filmique." *RIF*, 6 (n.d.), pp. 174-84.

Galifret, Yves. "Expériences de filmologie en 1920." *RIF*, 5 (n.d.), pp. 75-76.

Galifret, Yves and Segal, J. "Cinéma et physiologie des sensations." *RIF*, 3/4 (Octobre 1948), pp. 289-93.

Gastaut, Henri and Roger, Annette. "Effets psychologiques, somatiques et électro-encéphalographiques du stimulus lumineux intermittent rythmique: Applications possibles à la filmologie." *RIF,* 7/8 (n.d.), pp. 213-29.

Gawrak, Zbigniew. "La filmologie: Bilan dès la naissance jusqu'à 1958." *Ikon,* 65/66 (August-September 1968), pp. 111-18.

Gemelli, Agostino. "Le film procédé d'analyse projective." *RIF,* 6 (n.d.), pp. 135-38.

Germain, Jean. "La musique et le film." In *L'univers filmique,* pp. 137-55. Edited by Etienne Souriau. Paris: Flammarion, 1953.

Giddens, Anthony. *Durkheim.* Hassocks, Sussex: Harvester Press, 1978.

Gilles, Roignant. "Malraux: Esquisse d'une psychologie du cinéma." *Cinématographe,* 24 (Février 1977).

Gratiot-Alphandéry, Hélène. "L'enfant et le film." *RIF,* 6 (n.d.), pp. 171-72.

Guicharnaud, Jacques. "L'univers magique et l'image cinématographique." *RIF,* 1 (Juillet-Août 1947).

Guillot de Rode, François. "Le dimension sonore." In *L'univers filmique,* pp. 119-35. Edited by Etienne Souriau. Paris: Flammarion, 1953.

Handel, Leo. *Hollywood Looks at Its Audience.* Urbana: University of Illinois Press, 1950.

Herbinière-Lebert, S. "Pourquoi et comment nous avons fait *Mains Blanches:* Premières expériences avec un film éducatif réalisé specialement pour les moins de sept ans." *RIF,* 7/8 (n.d.) pp. 247-55.

Heuyer, G.; Lebovici, Serge; and Amado, G. "A propos d'une enquête filmologique chez les enfants et adolescents inadaptés." *RIF,* 5 (n.d.), pp. 57-64.

Heuyer, G.; Lebovici, Serge; and Bertagna, L. "Sur quelques réactions d'enfants inadaptés." *RIF,* 9 (Janvier-Mars 1952), pp. 71-79.

Heuyer, G. et al. "Note sur l'électroencéphalographie pendant la projection cinématographique chez les enfants inadaptés." *RIF,* 16 (Janvier-Mars 1954), pp. 51-64.

"Institut de Filmologie—Année 1958-59." *RIF,* 30/31 (n.d.), pp. 163-64.

"International Survey (Conference of Filmology, Knokke-le-Zoute)." *RIF,* 5 (n.d.), pp. 12-20.

Jeanne, R. and Ford, Charles. *Histoire encyclopédique du cinéma.* Vol. I: *Tout le cinéma français (1896-1926).* Paris: R. Laffont, 1947.

Jowett, Garth. *Film: The Democratic Art.* Boston, Toronto: Little Brown & Co., 1976.

Kaelin, Eugene F. *An Existentialist Aesthetic.* Madison: University of Wisconsin Press, 1962.

Katz, David. "Le portrait composite et la typologie." *RIF,* 7/8 (n.d.), pp. 207-14.

Keir, Gertrude. "Le rôle, la nécessité et la valeur d'une censure cinématographique." *RIF,* 14/15 (Juillet-Décembre 1953), pp. 179-97.

Kirsch, Florent. "Introduction à une filmologie de la filmologie." *Cahiers du Cinéma,* 5 (Septembre 1951), pp. 33-38.

Kracauer, Siegfried. "Cinéma et sociologie (sur l'exemple d'Allemagne préhitlerienne)." *RIF,* 3/4 (Octobre 1948), pp. 311-18.

_____. *From Calgari to Hitler.* Princeton, NJ: Princeton University Press, 1947.

_____. "National Types as Hollywood Presents Them." *Public Opinion Quarterly,* XIII, 1 (Spring 1949), pp. 53-72; reprinted as "Les types nationaux vus par Hollywood." *RIF,* 6 (n.d.), pp. 115-34.

Kuhn, Thomas S. *The Structure of Scientific Revolutions.* Chicago: University of Chicago Press, 1970.

Kuntzel, Thierry. "A Note Upon the Filmic Apparatus." *Quarterly Review of Film Studies,* 1:3 (August 1976). pp. 266-71.

_____. "Le travail du film." *Communications,* 19 (1972). Translated by L. Crawford, K. Lockhart, C. Tysdal as "The Film Work." *Enclitic,* II, 1 (Spring 1978).

_____. "Le travail du film, 2." *Communications,* 23 (1975). Translated by Nancy Huston as "The Film Work, 2." *Camera Obscura,* 5 (Spring 1980).

Labarthe, André-S. "Connaissez-vous l'Institut de Filmologie?" *Radio-Cinéma-Télévision*, 403 (6 Octobre 1957), p. 44.

LaCapra, Domenick. *Emile Durkheim: Sociologist and Philosopher*. Ithaca, London: Cornell University Press, 1972.

Laffay, Albert. "Bruits et langage au cinéma." *Les Temps Modernes*, 14 (Novembre 1946), pp. 371-75.

_____. "L'évocation du monde au cinema." *Les Temps Modernes*, 5 (Février 1946), pp. 925-38.

_____. "Le récit, le monde et le film." *Les Temps Modernes*, 20/27 (Mai-Juin 1947).

Lameere, Jean. "Le cinéma et ses écueils." *RIF*, 2 (Septembre-Octobre 1947), pp. 143-48.

Lang, André. *Le tableau blanc*. Paris: Horizons de France, 1948.

Lapierre, Marcel. *Anthologie du cinéma*. Paris: La Nouvelle Edition, 1946.

Lazarsfeld, Paul. "Audience Research in the Movie Field." *Annals of the American Academy of Political and Social Science*, 254 (November 1947), pp. 160-68.

Lebovici, Serge. "Cinéma et criminalité." *RIF*, 14/15 (Juillet-Décembre 1953), pp. 199-215.

_____. "Psychanalyse et cinéma." *RIF*, 5 (n.d.), pp. 49-55.

Lebrun, M. "Film d'enseignement et filmologie." *RIF*, 7/8 (n.d.), pp. 265-72.

Leenhardt, Roger. "Bilan autour d'une crise." *Les Temps Modernes*, 1 (1 Octobre 1945), 183-88.

Leglisse, Paul. *Histoire de la politique du cinéma français*. Vol. II: *Le cinéma entre deux Républiques (1940-1946)*. Paris: Filméditions, 1970.

L'Herbier, Marcel. "L'avenir du cinématographe." *Le Journal* (15 Mai 1928).

_____. *Intelligence du cinématographe.*" Paris: Corréa, 1946.

Maddison, John. "Le cinéma et l'information mentale des peuples primitifs." *RIF*, 3/4 (Octobre 1948), pp. 305-10.

Maddison, John and Meaden, Flora. "Réactions sociales du cinéma en Angleterre." *RIF*, 2 (Septembre-Octobre 1947), pp. 211-16.

Madsen, Axel. *Malraux: A Biography*. New York: William Morrow, 1976.

Malraux, André. *Esquisse d'une psychologie du cinéma*. Paris: Gallimard, 1946. Reprinted in *Scènes choisis*. Paris: Gallimard, 1946.

Manser, Anthony. *Sartre: A Philosophic Study*. London: Athalone Press, 1966.

Marion, Denis, *André Malraux*. Cinéma d'aujourd'hui, no. 65. Paris: Editions Seghers, 1970.

_____, ed. *Le cinéma par ceux qui le font*. Paris: Fayard, 1946.

Marzi, Alberto and Canestrari, Renzo. "Recherches sur les problèmes du cinéma—Italie." *RIF*, 11 (Juillet-Décembre 1952), pp. 179-92.

Mergen, A. "Cinéma et hygiène mentale." *RIF*, 14/15 (Juillet-Décembre 1953), pp. 233-41.

Merleau-Ponty, Maurice. "The Film and the New Psychology." In *Sense and Non-Sense*. Translated by Hubert L. Dreyfus and Patricia Allen Dreyfus. Evanston: Northwestern University Press, 1964.

_____. *The Phenomenology of Perception*. Translated by Colin Smith. London: Routledge & Kegan Paul, 1963.

Metz, Christian. *Film Language*. Translated by Michael Taylor. New York: Oxford University Press, 1974.

_____. *Language and Cinema*. Translated by Donna Umiker-Sebeok. The Hague, Paris: Mouton, 1974.

_____. "Sur un profil d'Etienne Souriau." *L'art instaurateur: Revue d'Esthétique*, 1980, 3/4, pp. 143-58; translated in *On Film*, 12 (Spring 1984), pp. 5-8.

Michotte van den Berck, Albert. "A propos de l'article de M.P. Francastel 'Espace et illusion.'" *RIF*, 6 (n.d.), p. 139.

_____. "Le caractère de 'réalité' des projections cinématographiques." *RIF*, 3/4 (Octobre 1948), pp. 249-61.

Mitry, Jean. *Esthétique et psychologie du cinéma*. 2 vols. Paris: Editions Universitaires, 1963, 1965.

Morin, Edgar. *Autocritique*. Paris: Julliard, 1959.

_____. *Le cinéma ou l'homme imaginaire*. Paris: Editions de Minuit, 1956; 2nd ed., 1977.

_____. "Pour un nouveau cinéma vérité." *France-Observateur* (Juin 1960).

_____. "Recherches sur le public cinématographique." *RIF,* 12 (Janvier-Mars 1953), pp. 3-19.

_____. *Les Stars*. Paris: Editions du Seuil, 1957. Translated by Richard Howard as *The Stars*. New York: Grove Press, 1960.

Mouillard, Maurice. "Qu'est-ce que c'est l'expression cinématographique?" *RIF,* 2 (Septembre-Octobre 1947), pp. 187-91.

Moussinac, Léon. *L'âge ingrat du cinéma*. Paris: Sagittaire, 1946.

_____. *Le cinéma soviétique*. Paris: NRF, 1928.

Munsterberg, Hugo. *The Photoplay: A Psychological Study*. New York: D. Appleton, 1916. Reprint ed., New York: Dover, 1970.

"Note de la rédaction." *RIF,* 3/4 (Septembre-Octobre 1947), p. 235.

Oldfield, R.C. "La perception visuelle des images du cinéma, de la télévision et du radar." *RIF,* 3/4 (Septembre-Octobre 1947), pp. 263-79.

Ory, Pascal. *Les collaborateurs, 1940-1945*. Paris: Editions du Seuil, 1976.

Passeron, René. "Le concept d'instauration et le développement de la poïétique," *L'art instaurateur: Revue d'Esthétique,* 1980, 3/4, pp. 174-98.

Pillsbury, W.B. *The History of Psychology*. New York: W.W. Norton, 1929.

Piraux, H. *Lexique technique anglais-français de cinéma*. Paris: La Nouvelle Edition, 1946.

Poncet, Marie-Thérèse. *Dessin animé, art mondial*. Paris: Cercle du Livre, 1956.

_____. *L'esthétique du dessin animé*. Paris: Librairie Nizet, 1952.

Ponzo, Mario. "Le cinéma et les images collectives." *RIF,* 6 (n.d.), pp. 141-51.

Poster, Mark. *Existential Marxism in Postwar France: From Sartre to Althusser*. Princeton, NJ: Princeton University Press, 1975.

Poyer, Georges. "Psychologie différentielle et filmologie." *RIF,* 2 (Septembre-Octobre 1947), pp. 111-16.

"Le premier Congrès International de Filmologie." *RIF,* 3/4 (Octobre 1948), pp. 371-72.

"Propositions de recherches." *RIF,* 4 (n.d.), pp. 105-8.

Propp, Vladimir. *Morphology of the Folk Tale*. Austin: University of Texas Press, 1970.

Prudhommeau, M. *Le cinéma éducatif et l'avenir*. Paris: Union Française Universitaire, 1944.

Rabinovitz, Lauren. "Independent Journeyman: Man Ray, Dada and Surrealist Film-Maker." *Southwest Review,* LXIV, 4 (Autumn 1979), pp. 355-76.

Ricci, François. "Le cinéma entre l'imagination et la réalité." *RIF,* 2 (Septembre-Octobre 1947), pp. 161-63.

Riniéri, Jean-Jacques. "L'impression de la réalité au cinéma: Les phénomènes de croyance." In *L'univers filmique*. Edited by Etienne Souriau. Paris: Flammarion, 1953.

_____. "Présentation de la filmologie." *RIF,* 1 (Juillet-Août 1947), pp. 87-91.

Roques, Mario. "Filmologie." *RIF,* 1 (Juillet-Août 1947), pp. 5-8.

_____. "Introduction." *RIF,* 1 (Janvier-Mars 1954), pp. 3-6.

Rouch, Jean and Morin, Edgar. *Chronique d'un été*. Paris: Inter-Spectacles, 1962.

Sadoul, Georges. "Les apprentis sorciers (d'Edison à Méliès)." *Revue du Cinéma,* nouvelle série, 1 (Octobre 1946), pp. 34-44.

_____. *French Film*. London: Falcon Press, 1953. Reprint ed. New York: Arno Press, 1972.

_____. "Georges Méliès et la première élaboration du langage cinématographique." *RIF,* 1 (Juilliet-Août), pp. 23-30.

_____. *Histoire générale du cinéma*. Vol. I: *L'invention du cinéma (1832-1897);* Vol. II: *Les pionniers du cinéma (1897-1909)*. Paris: Editions Denoël, 1947.

"La saison cinématographique 1945/47." *La Revue du Cinéma*. Numéro spécial, xxvii, n.d.

Saussure, Ferdinand de. *Course in General Linguistics*. Translated by Wade Biskin. New York: McGraw-Hill, 1966.

Scholes, Robert. *Structuralism in Literature.* New Haven, London: Yale University Press, 1974.

Schuhl, Pierre-Maxime. "Pour un cinéma abstrait." *RIF,* 2 (Septembre-Octobre 1947), pp. 183-85.

Sève, Lucien. "Cinéma et méthode." *RIF,* 1 (Juillet-Août 1947), pp. 42-46; *RIF,* 2 (Septembre-Octobre 1947), pp. 171-74; *RIF,* 3/4 (Octobre 1948), pp. 351-55.

Siersted, Ellen and Lund Hansen, H. "Réactions des petits enfants au cinéma: Résumé d'une série d'observations faites au Danemark." *RIF,* 7/8 (n.d.), pp. 241-45.

Soriano, Marc. "Etat d'une science nouvelle." *RIF,* 1 (Juillet-Août 1947), pp. 9-12.

_____. "Lire, assister." *RIF,* 3/4 (Octobre 1948), pp. 299-304.

_____. "Position de la filmologie." *Synthèses,* 2 (1947), pp. 147-54.

_____. "Problèmes de méthode posés par le cinéma considéré comme expérimentation psychologique nouvelle." *RIF,* 2 (Septembre-Octobre 1947), pp. 117-25.

Souriau, Anne. "Fonctions filmiques des costumes et des décors." In *L'univers filmique.* Edited by Etienne Souriau. Paris: Flammarion, 1953.

_____. "Succession et simultanéité dans le film." In *L'univers filmique.* Edited by Etienne Souriau. Paris: Fammarion, 1953.

Souriau, Etienne. *L'avenir de l'esthétique.* Paris: Presses Universitaires de France, 1929.

_____. *La correspondance des arts.* Paris: Flammarion, 1947; 2nd ed., 1967.

_____. *Les deux cent mille situations dramatiques.* Paris: Flammarion, 1950.

_____. "Filmologie et esthétique comparée." *RIF,* 10 (Avril-Juin 1952), pp. 113-41.

_____. *L'instauration philosophique.* Paris: Presses Universitaires de France, 1939.

_____. "Nature et limite des contributions positives de l'esthétique à la filmologie." *RIF,* 1 (Juillet-Août 1947), pp. 47-64.

_____. "La structure de l'univers filmique et le vocabulaire de la filmologie." *RIF,* 7/8 (n.d.), pp. 231-40.

_____. "L'univers filmique et l'art animalier." *RIF,* 25 (Janvier-Mars 1956), pp. 51-62.

_____, ed. *L'univers filmique.* Paris: Flammarion, 1953.

Tendron, Georges. "Nouvelles techniques d'enregistrement." *RIF,* 13 (Avril-Juin 1953), p. 167.

"Thèse de Mlle. Poncet." *Annales de l'Université de Paris,* 22e année, 1 (Janvier-Mars 1952), p. 116.

Tilliette, Xavier. "Les filmologues au Congrès." *Positif,* II, 14/15 (Novembre 1955), pp. 164-65.

Toulousse, M. and Mourgue, R. "Des réactions respiratoires au cours des projections cinématographiques." *RIF,* 5 (n.d.), pp. 77-83.

Tribut, Jean. "La peinture et le film." *RIF,* 10 (Avril-Juin 1952), pp. 149-67.

"Université de Paris: Institut de Filmologie." *RIF,* 5 (n.d.), pp. 109-12.

"Université de Paris—Faculté des Lettres—Institut de Filmologie." *RIF,* 9 (Janvier-Mars 1952), pp. 89-90.

Valentini, Ernesto. "Perspectives psychologiques en filmologie." *RIF,* 25 (Janvier-Mars 1956), pp. 3-18.

Vidal, Jean. "Filmologues distingués." *L'Ecran Français,* 119 (7 Octobre 1947), p. 11.

Vitry-Maubrey, Luce de. *La pensée cosmologique d'Etienne Souriau.* Paris: Klincksieck, 1974.

Volpicelli, Luigi. "La filmologie en tant que recherche socio-historique." *RIF,* 25 (Janvier-Mars 1956), pp. 19-28.

Wall, W.D. and Smith, E.M. "Les adolescents et le cinéma." *RIF,* 6 (n.d.), pp. 153-58.

Wallon, Henri. "De quelques problèmes psycho-physiologiques que pose le cinéma." *RIF,* 1 (Juillet-Août 1947), pp. 15-18.

_____. "L'enfant et le film." *RIF,* 5 (n.d.), pp. 21-28.

_____. "Introduction au symposium de filmologie (au XIIIe Congrès International de Psychologie, Stockholm, Juillet 1951)." *RIF,* 9 (Janvier-Mars 1952), pp. 21-23.

_____. *Lecture d'Henri Wallon.* Paris: Editions Sociales, 1976.

_____. "Qu'est-ce que c'est la filmologie?" *La Pensée,* nouvelle série, 15 (Novembre-Décembre 1947), pp. 29-34.

Werth, Alexander. *France 1940-1955*. New York: Henry Holt & Co., 1956.

Zazzo, Bianka. "Analyse des difficultés d'une séquence cinématographique par la conduite du récit chez l'enfant." *RIF*, 9 (Janvier-Mars 1952), pp. 25-36.

———. "Le cinéma à l'école maternelle." *RIF*, 9 (Janvier-Mars 1952), pp. 81-88.

Zazzo, Bianka and Zazzo, René. "Une expérience sur la compréhension du film." *RIF*, 6 (n.d.), pp. 159-70.

Zazzo, René. "Espace, mouvement et cinémascope." *RIF*, 18/19 (Juillet-Décembre 1954), pp. 209-19.

———. "Niveau mental et compréhension du cinéma." *RIF*, 5 (n.d.), pp. 29-36.

Index